Whoa, daddy...music's my normal beat, but 〔...............〕headed monster whose names is Carter and John drops a heap o'inky pages on me and both of him sez write and I do cuz it's got words I can read and pictures I can glom and I thinks how hard can this be cuz I know from comix but hey this is not my father's comix nor is it my son's and right out the chute it's dark and scary and swirly and LOUD how can a page be loud but it is and so is the next one and the next and it shifts gears like a super stock bang-shift hydro comin' off the line 'cept that ain't nothin' human driving neither on the page nor the dos cabesa-ed shiny-eyed beast(s) what wrote and drawed it but still the ground opens and the dialogue ratchets on dizzying and whirling and jest when methinks I've got a handle on it it breaks and spreads again and I'm seein' with a new pair of eyes which at first is good but they keep takin' 'em out and puttin' in yet another pair but I never see better just different and the earth beneath me won't hold still and so I'm wonderin' who is these brutal bastids cuz everything is OFF sometimes just a bit other times a whole lot but I gots to get to the bottom of this cuz evil nay EVIL is definitely afoot and if'n ya don't chase it down it spreads and grows so I continues to chase but the mawkish, stinky pool sprawls off one page and onto the next and the closer we get to the end the worse things get and maybe some shit is best left unsolved or unexamined cuz even when it's funny it's as much strange as ha-ha and the humor bites like bleach in the eyes and no those ain't tears of joy daddy-o they're just some of my water that gots to leave my skull cuz I'm feeding it bad mojo from out the nightmarish tome in my hands which has moved all the furniture in my brain-pan and has started going through my sock drawer and finally it sinks in that it's really only a hellish sack o'murdering mysteries and the body count seems as high as my blood pressure which has been squeezed ever upward with each page turned but for every enigma I solve there's two more behind it and I'm thinkin' DAMN they got me too I'm sinkin' back away from my eyes and I call out Momma and a bobblehead dashboard Jesus is holdin' my hand and smilin sez it's okay boy yer with me now and I guess I'm okay with that cuz it's sure dark and dirty out there and nobody speaks except with fork-ed tongue what the hell is goin' on here I ask ya...

Jim Musser, July 2003

Candle Light Press Presents:

Man Is Vox!

Barracudae

John Thomas & Carter Allen

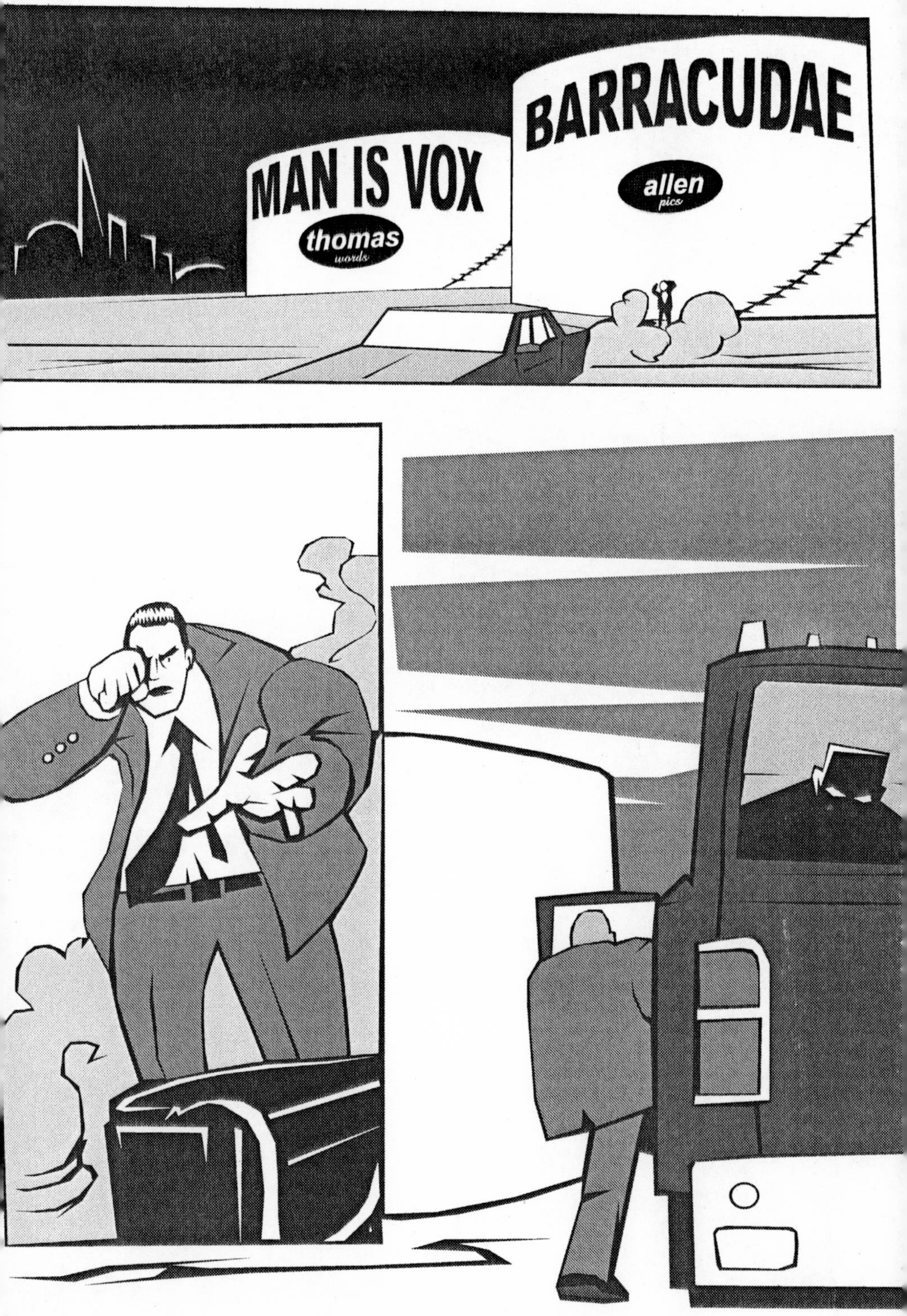
MAN IS VOX
thomas
words
BARRACUDAE
allen
pics

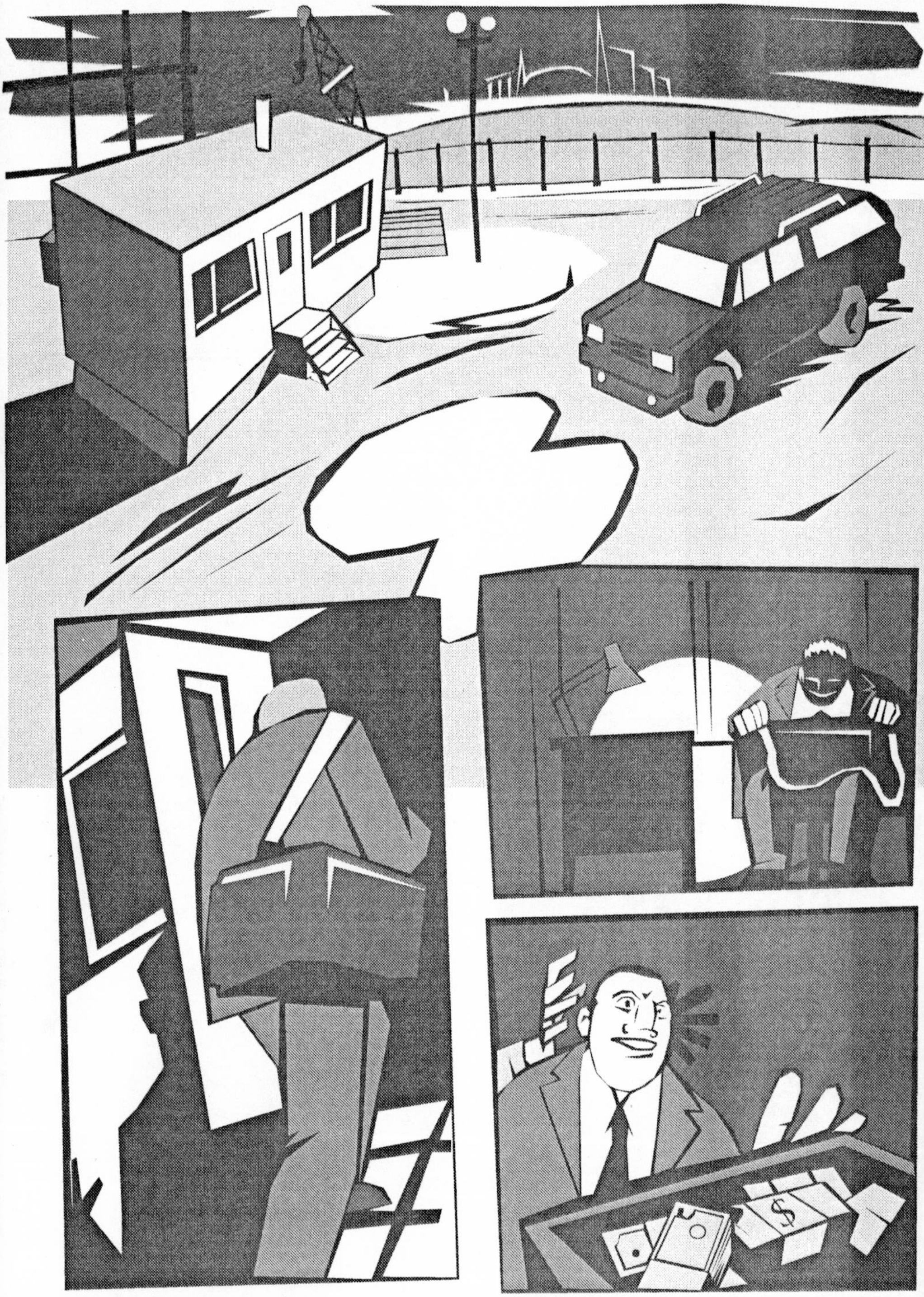

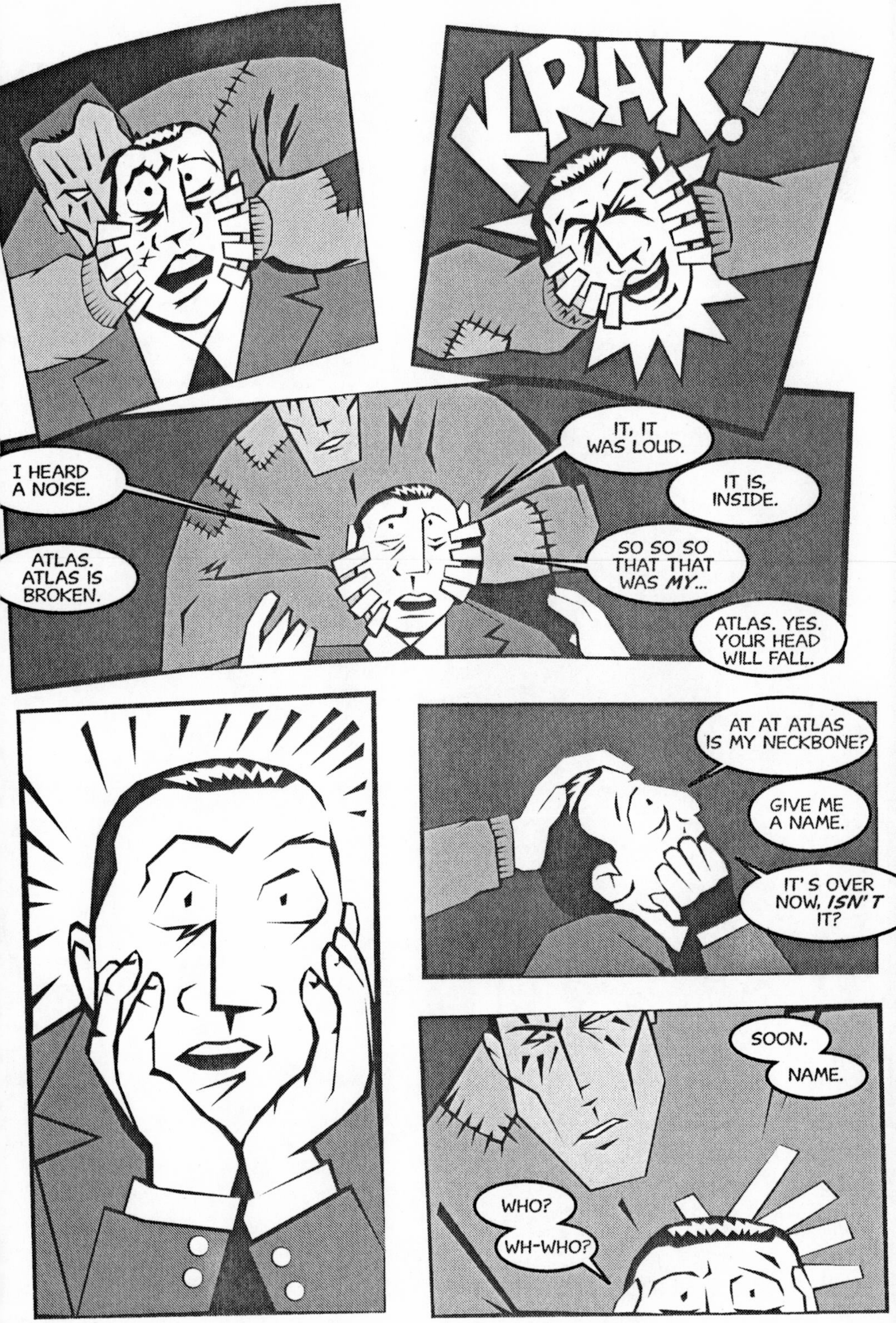
KRAK!
I HEARD A NOISE.
ATLAS. ATLAS IS BROKEN.
IT, IT WAS LOUD.
IT IS, INSIDE.
SO SO SO THAT THAT WAS *MY*...
ATLAS. YES. YOUR HEAD WILL FALL.
AT AT ATLAS IS MY NECKBONE?
GIVE ME A NAME.
IT'S OVER NOW, *ISN'T* IT?
SOON.
NAME.
WHO?
WH-WHO?

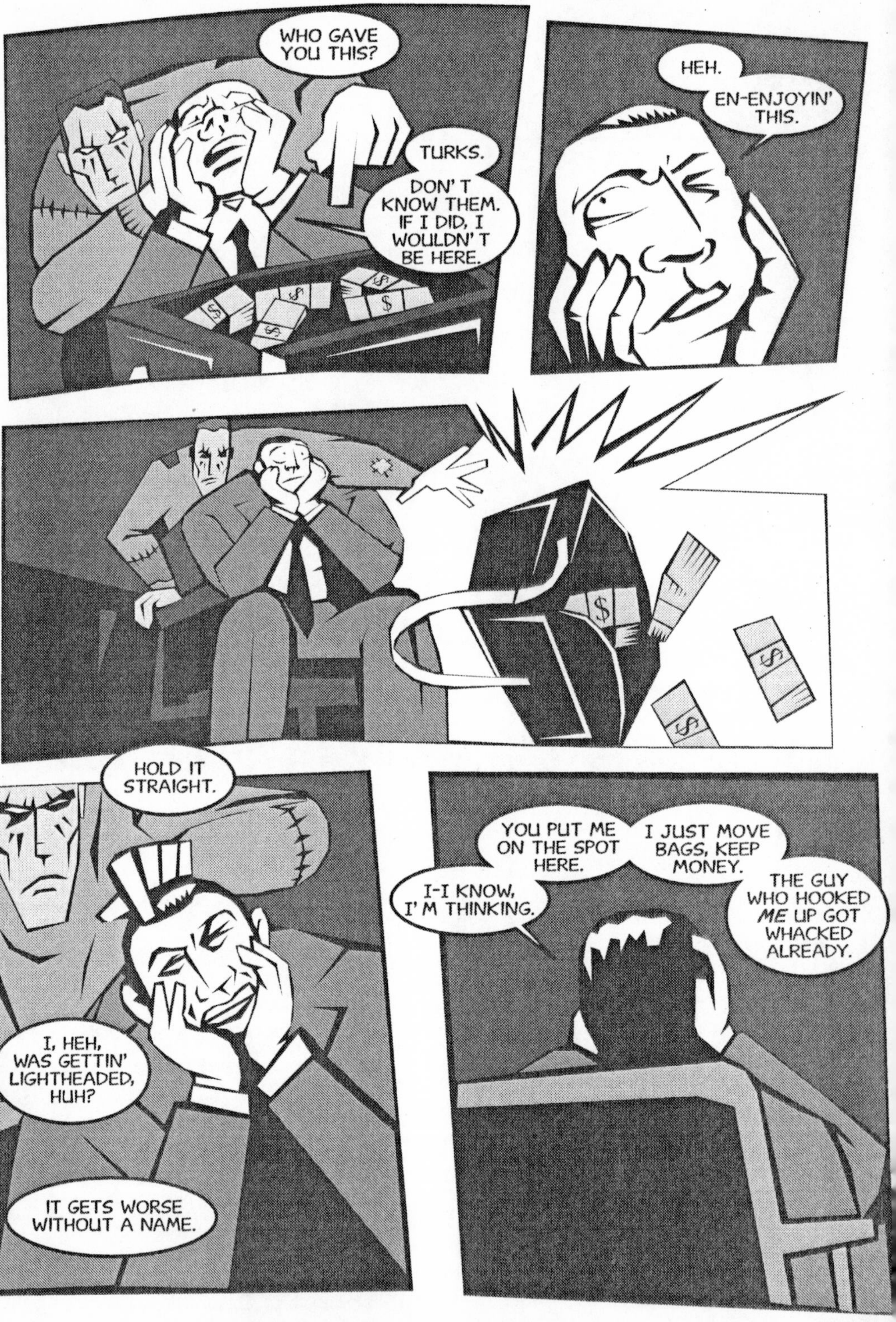
WHO GAVE YOU THIS?
TURKS.
DON'T KNOW THEM. IF I DID, I WOULDN'T BE HERE.
HEH.
EN-ENJOYIN' THIS.
HOLD IT STRAIGHT.
I, HEH, WAS GETTIN' LIGHTHEADED, HUH?
IT GETS WORSE WITHOUT A NAME.
YOU PUT ME ON THE SPOT HERE.
I-I KNOW, I'M THINKING.
I JUST MOVE BAGS, KEEP MONEY.
THE GUY WHO HOOKED *ME* UP GOT WHACKED ALREADY.

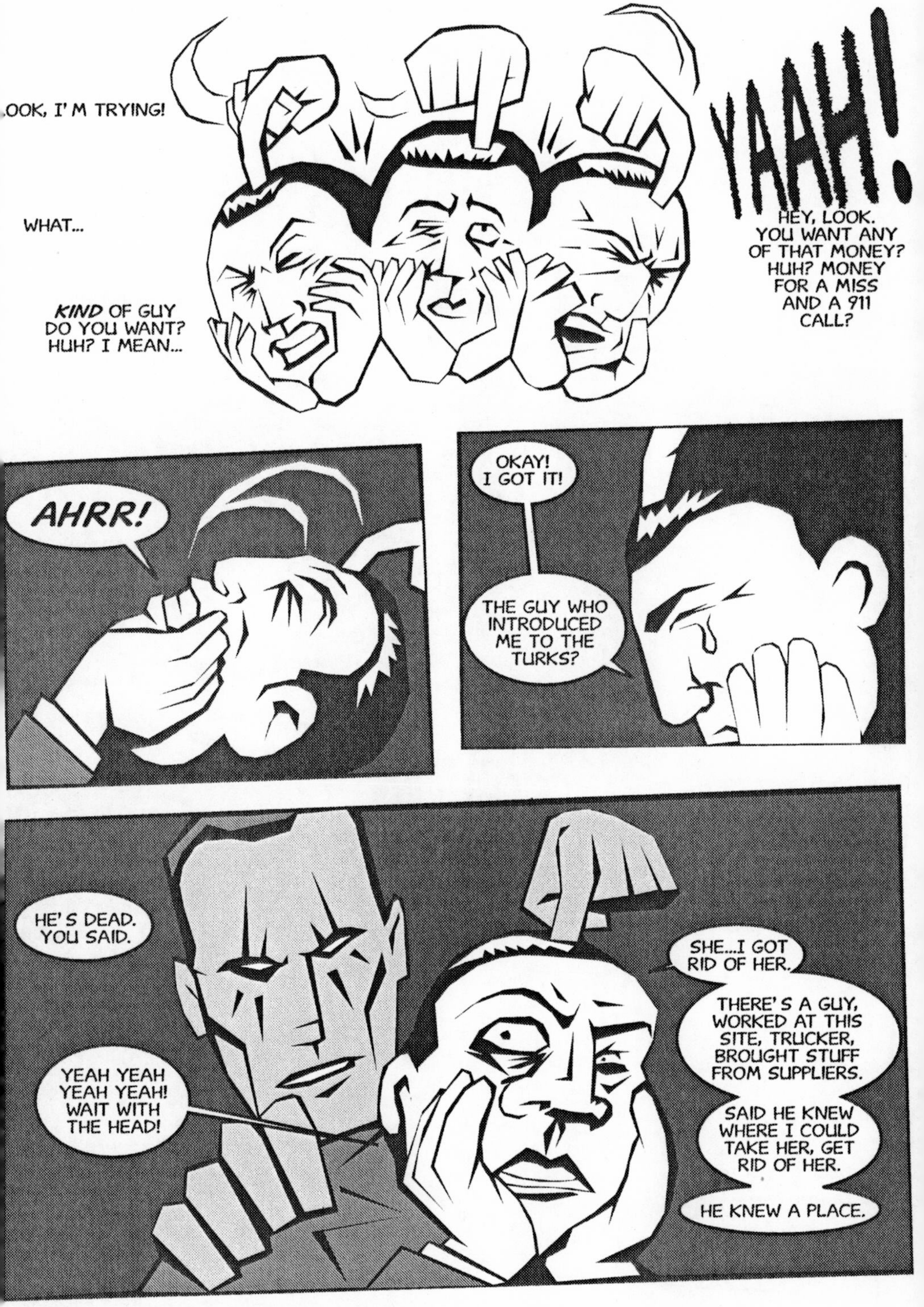

.OOK, I'M TRYING!
WHAT...
KIND OF GUY DO YOU WANT? HUH? I MEAN...
YAAH!
HEY, LOOK. YOU WANT ANY OF THAT MONEY? HUH? MONEY FOR A MISS AND A 911 CALL?
AHRR!
OKAY! I GOT IT!
THE GUY WHO INTRODUCED ME TO THE TURKS?
HE'S DEAD. YOU SAID.
YEAH YEAH YEAH YEAH! WAIT WITH THE HEAD!
SHE...I GOT RID OF HER.
THERE'S A GUY, WORKED AT THIS SITE, TRUCKER, BROUGHT STUFF FROM SUPPLIERS.
SAID HE KNEW WHERE I COULD TAKE HER, GET RID OF HER.
HE KNEW A PLACE.

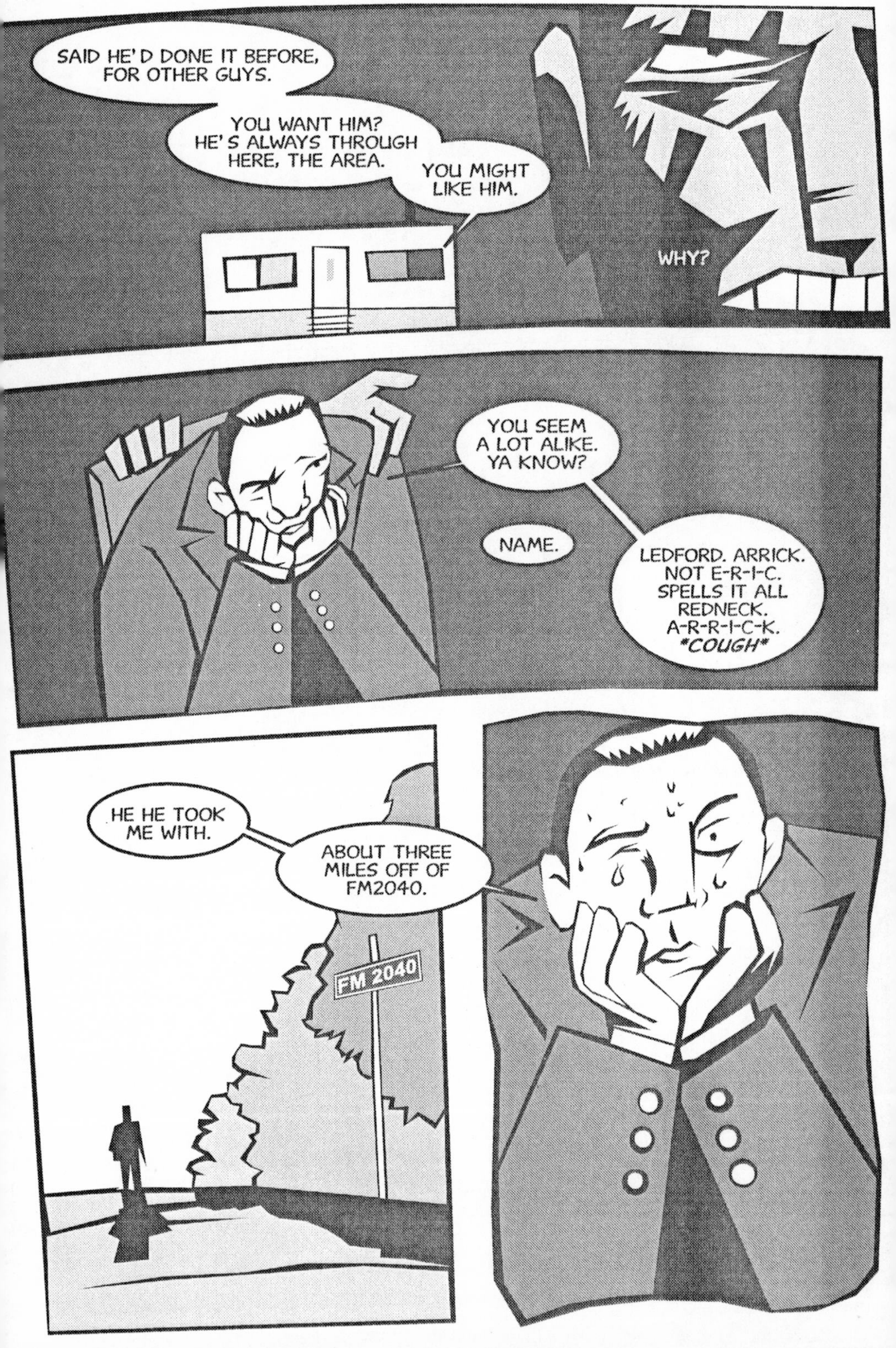
SAID HE'D DONE IT BEFORE, FOR OTHER GUYS.
YOU WANT HIM? HE'S ALWAYS THROUGH HERE, THE AREA.
YOU MIGHT LIKE HIM.
WHY?
YOU SEEM A LOT ALIKE. YA KNOW?
NAME.
LEDFORD. ARRICK. NOT E-R-I-C. SPELLS IT ALL REDNECK. A-R-R-I-C-K. *COUGH*
HE HE TOOK ME WITH.
ABOUT THREE MILES OFF OF FM2040.
FM 2040

THROUGH AN OLD BARBED-WIRE GATE, WITH A ROPE LATCH.

ABOUT A MINUTE INTO THE TREES.

YOU'LL SEE...

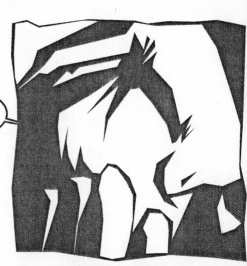

GONE.

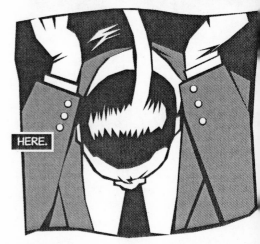

HERE.

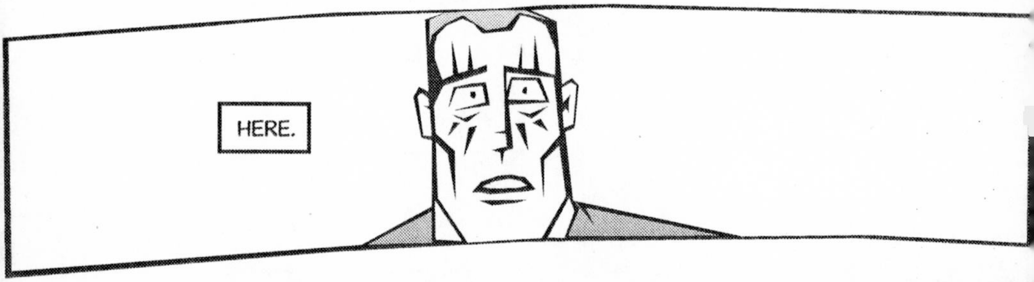
HERE.

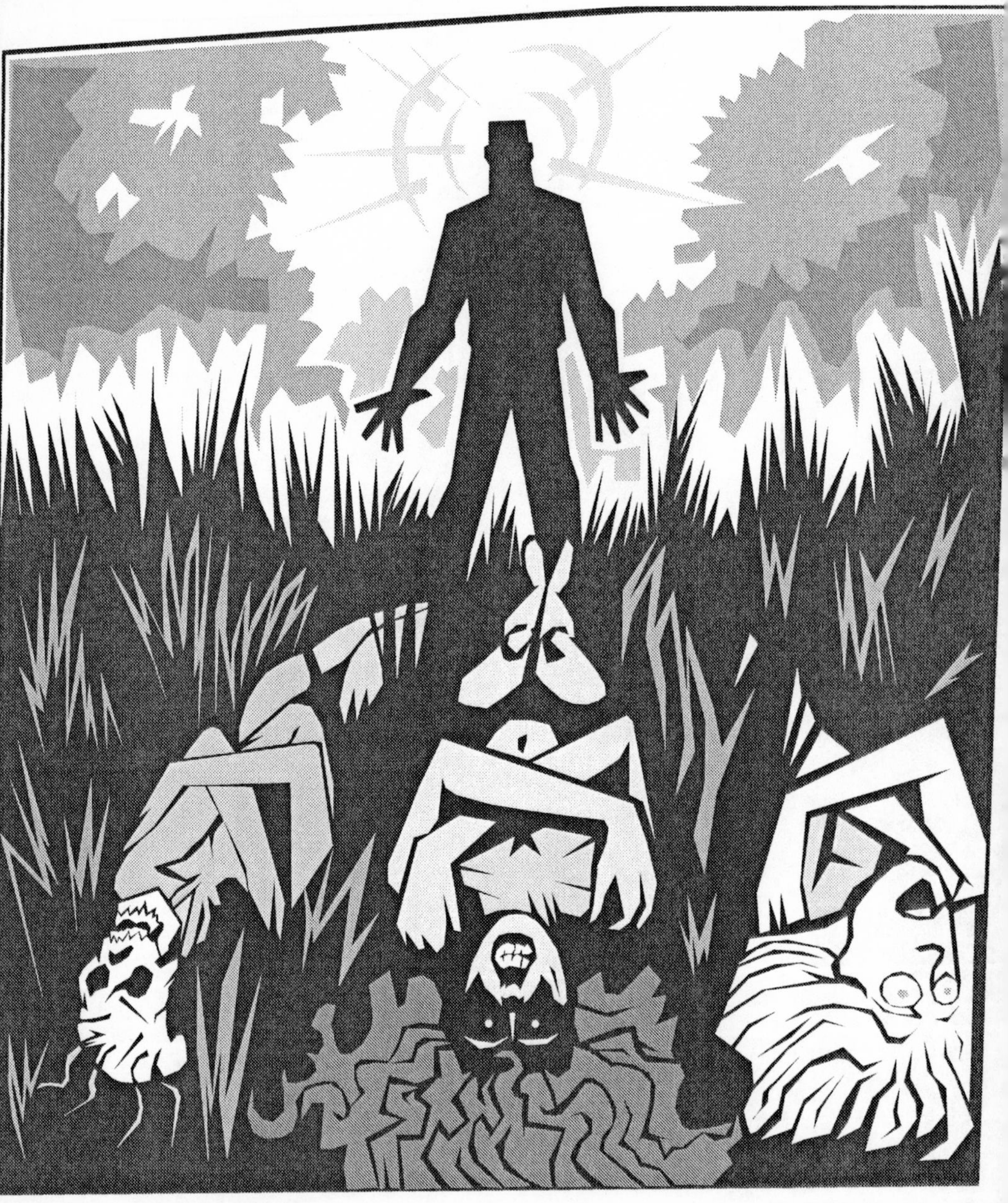

ARE THESE ALL HITS?

DON'T LOOK!

WHO ARE THEY?

DON'T LOOK! THEIR PARTS ARE SHOWING!

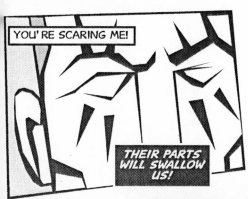

YOU'RE SCARING ME!

THEIR PARTS WILL SWALLOW US!

BUT...

GET AWAY! LOOK AWAY!

IS THAT BETTER?

WHY ARE WE STILL HERE?

THIS IS WHERE THE NAME TOOK US.

THE NAME. YES.

THIS APPEARS TO BE HIS DUMPING GROUND.

ALL TRASH GOES SOMEWHERE.

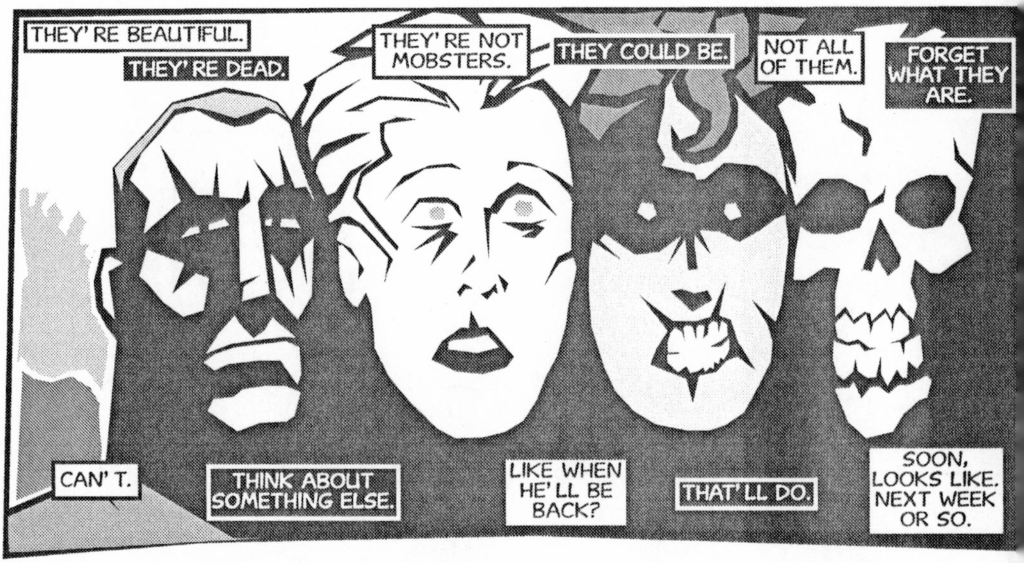
THEY'RE BEAUTIFUL.
THEY'RE DEAD.
THEY'RE NOT MOBSTERS.
THEY COULD BE.
NOT ALL OF THEM.
FORGET WHAT THEY ARE.
CAN'T.
THINK ABOUT SOMETHING ELSE.
LIKE WHEN HE'LL BE BACK?
THAT'LL DO.
SOON, LOOKS LIKE. NEXT WEEK OR SO.

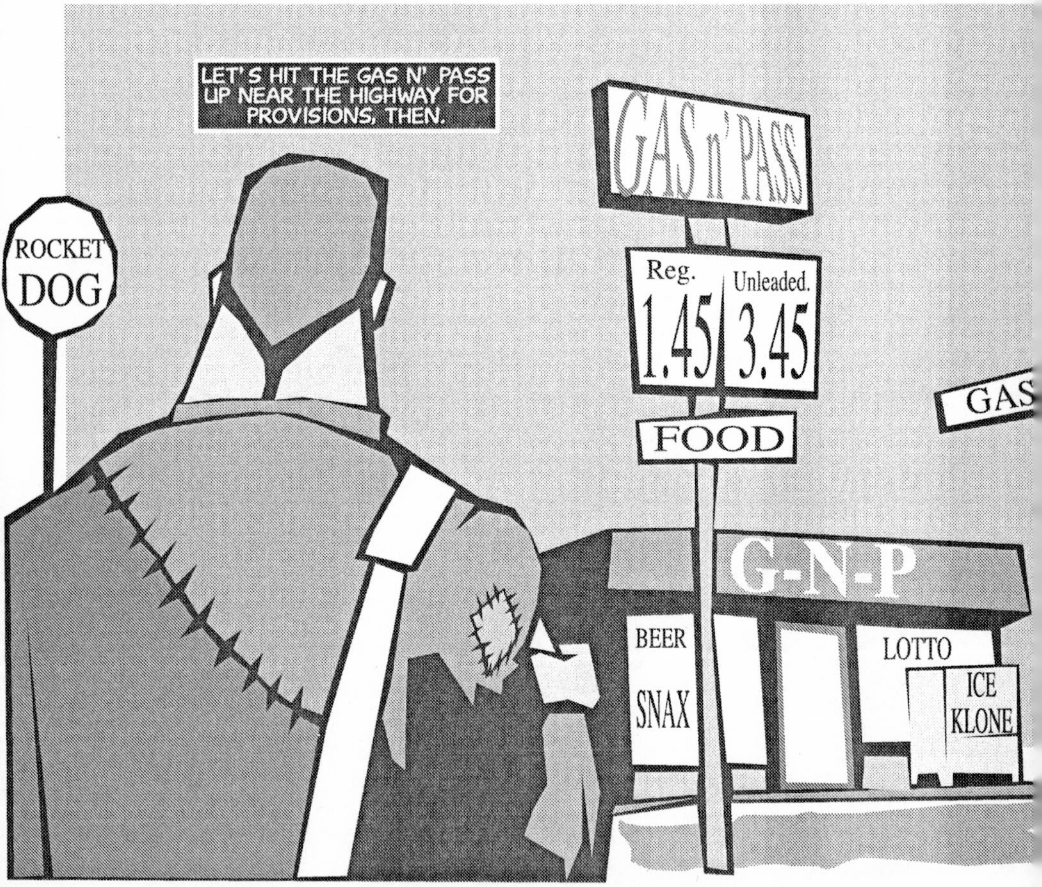
LET'S HIT THE GAS N' PASS UP NEAR THE HIGHWAY FOR PROVISIONS, THEN.
ROCKET DOG
GAS n' PASS
Reg.
1.45
Unleaded.
3.45
FOOD
GAS
G-N-P
BEER
SNAX
LOTTO
ICE KLONE

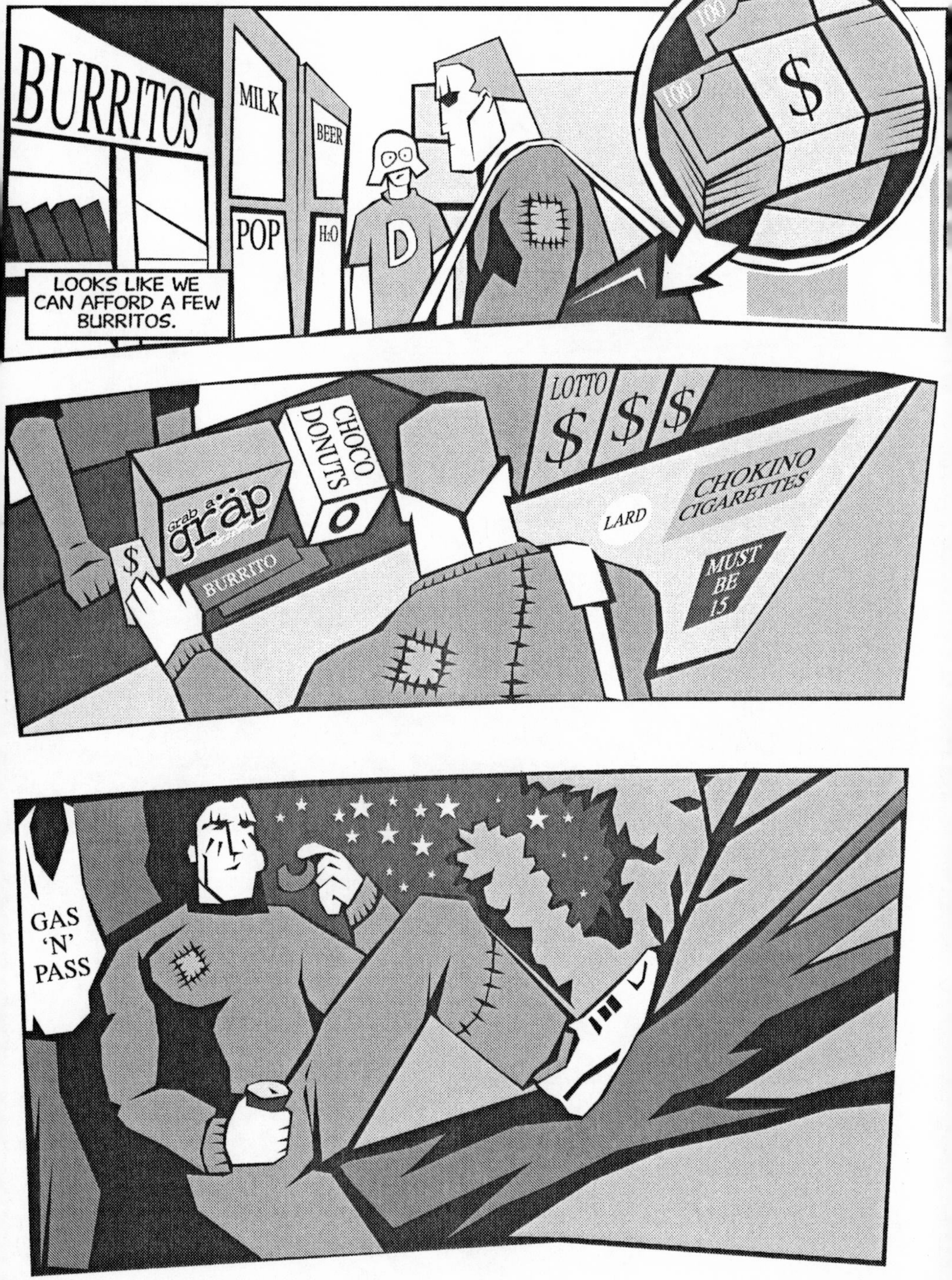
BURRITOS
MILK
BEER
POP
H2O
D
100
100
$
LOOKS LIKE WE CAN AFFORD A FEW BURRITOS.
LOTTO
$ $ $
CHOCO DONUTS
Grab a gräp
$
BURRITO
LARD
CHOKINO CIGARETTES
MUST BE 15
GAS 'N' PASS

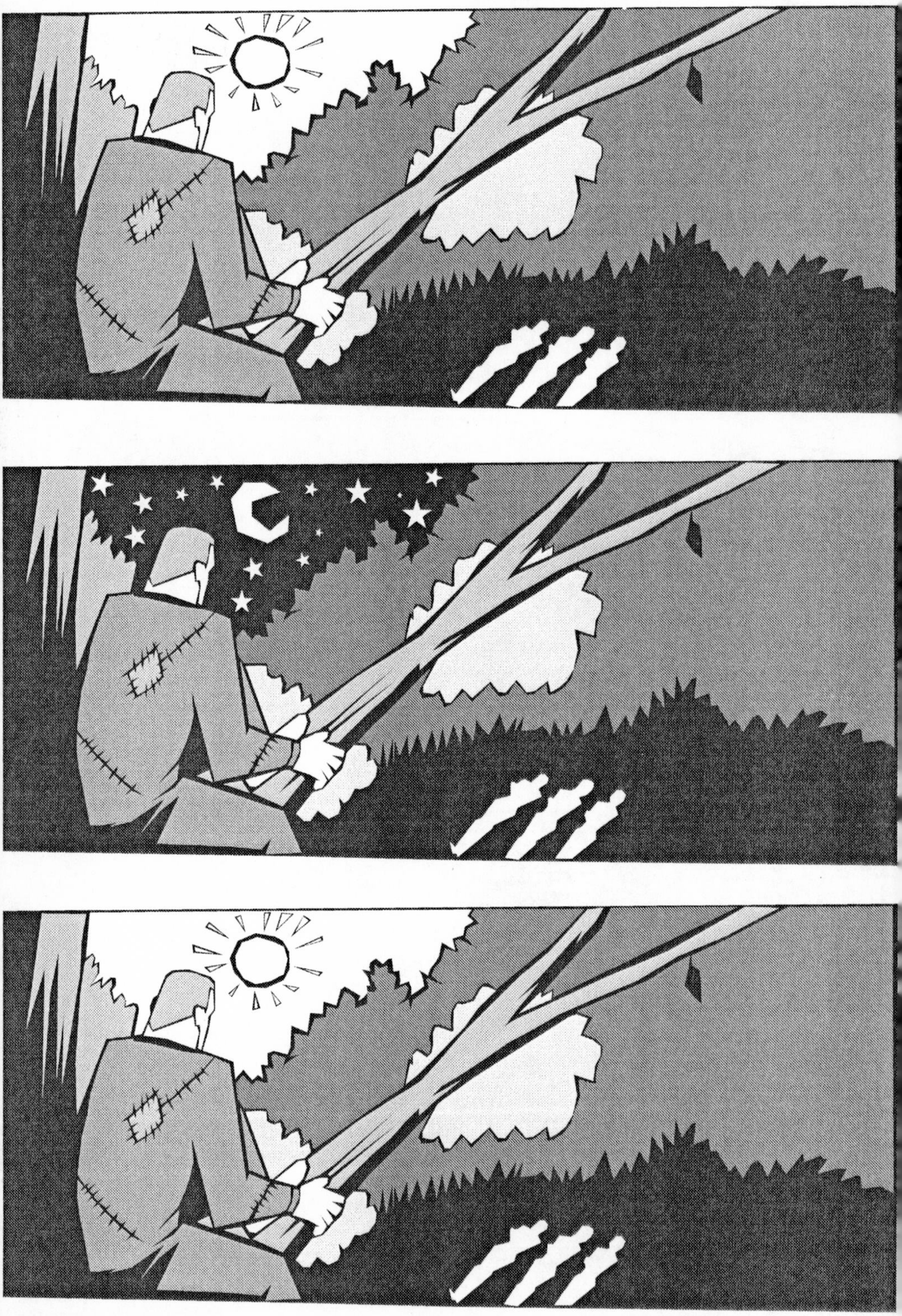

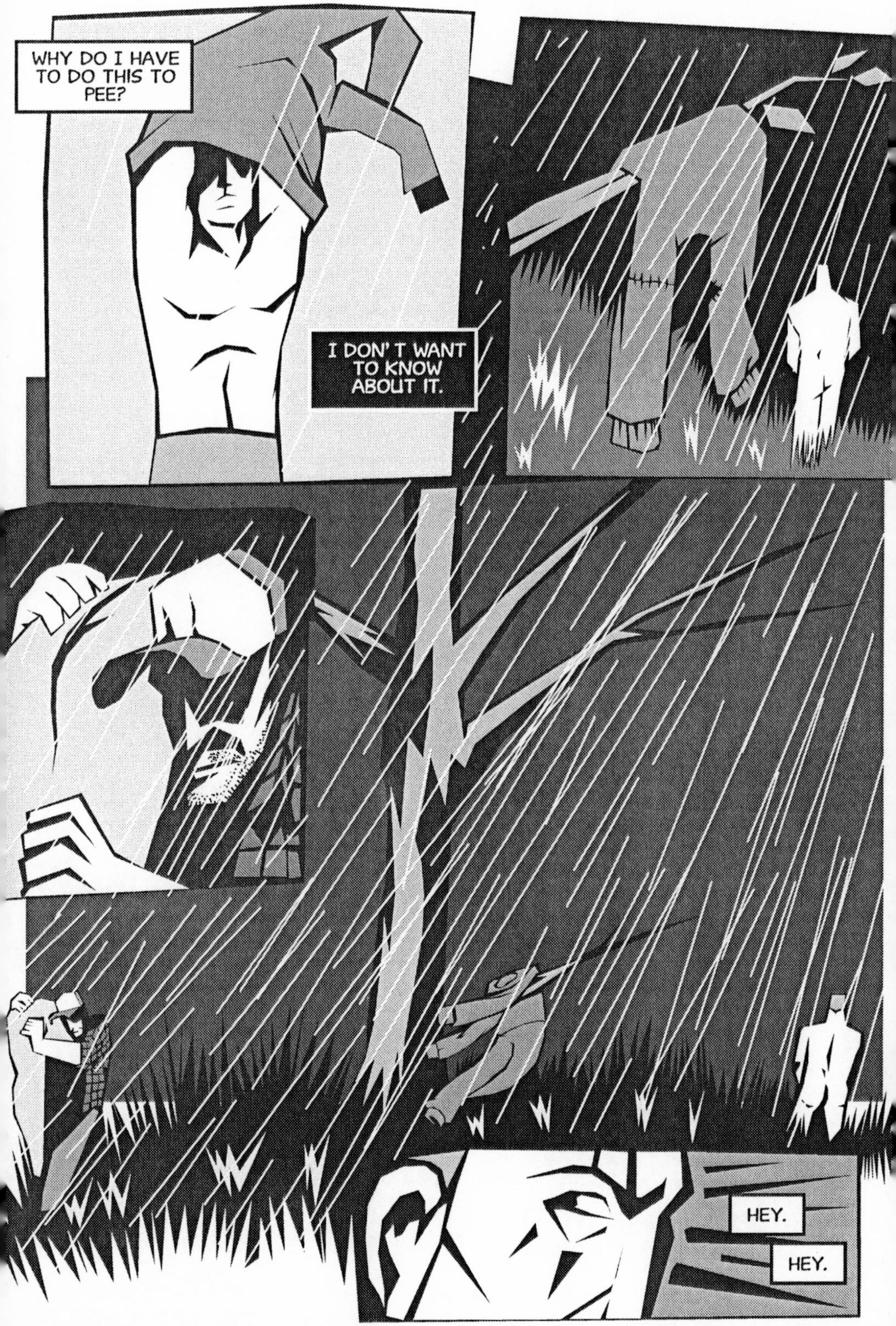
WHY DO I HAVE TO DO THIS TO PEE?
I DON'T WANT TO KNOW ABOUT IT.
HEY.
HEY.

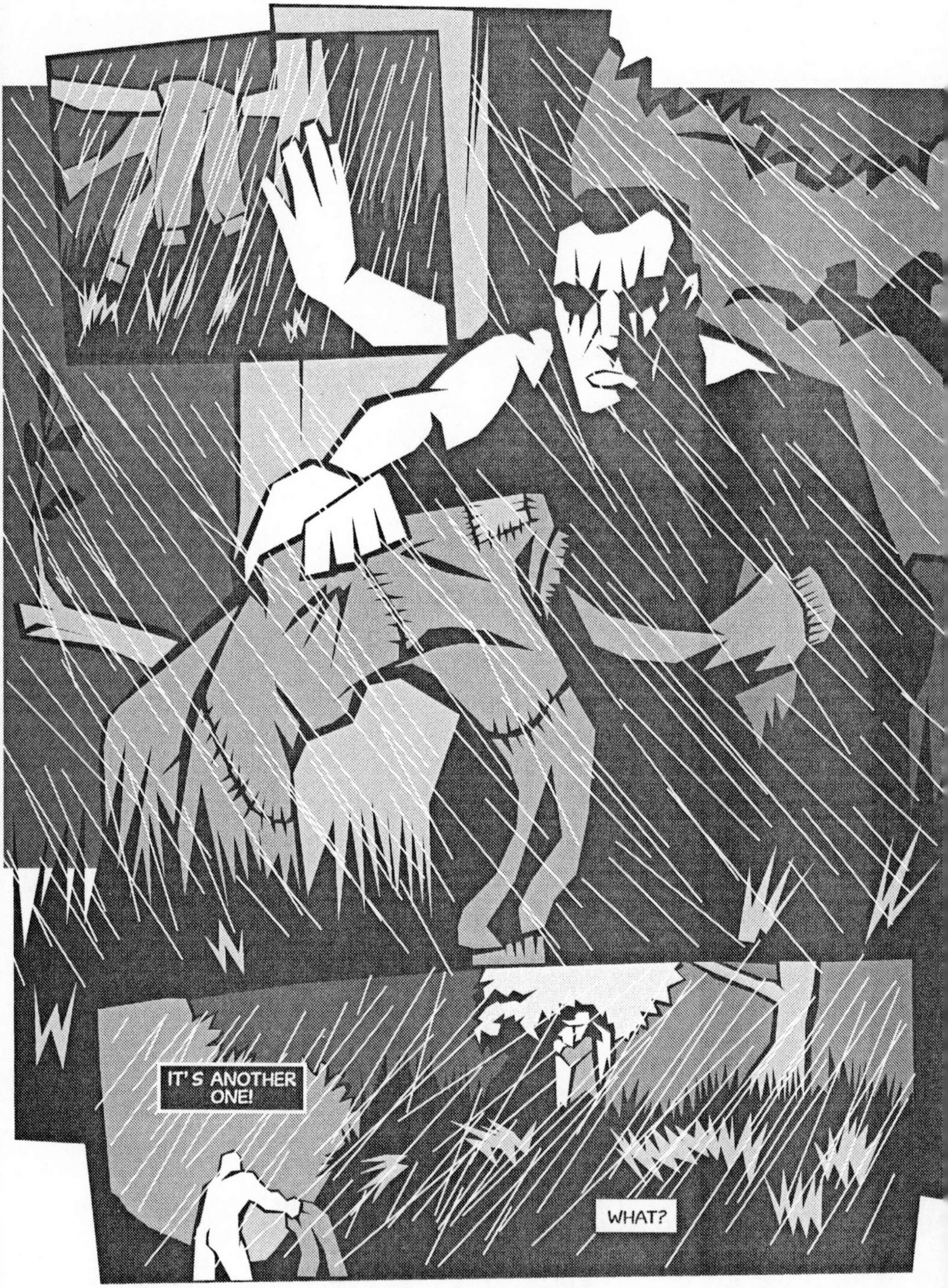
IT'S ANOTHER ONE!
WHAT?

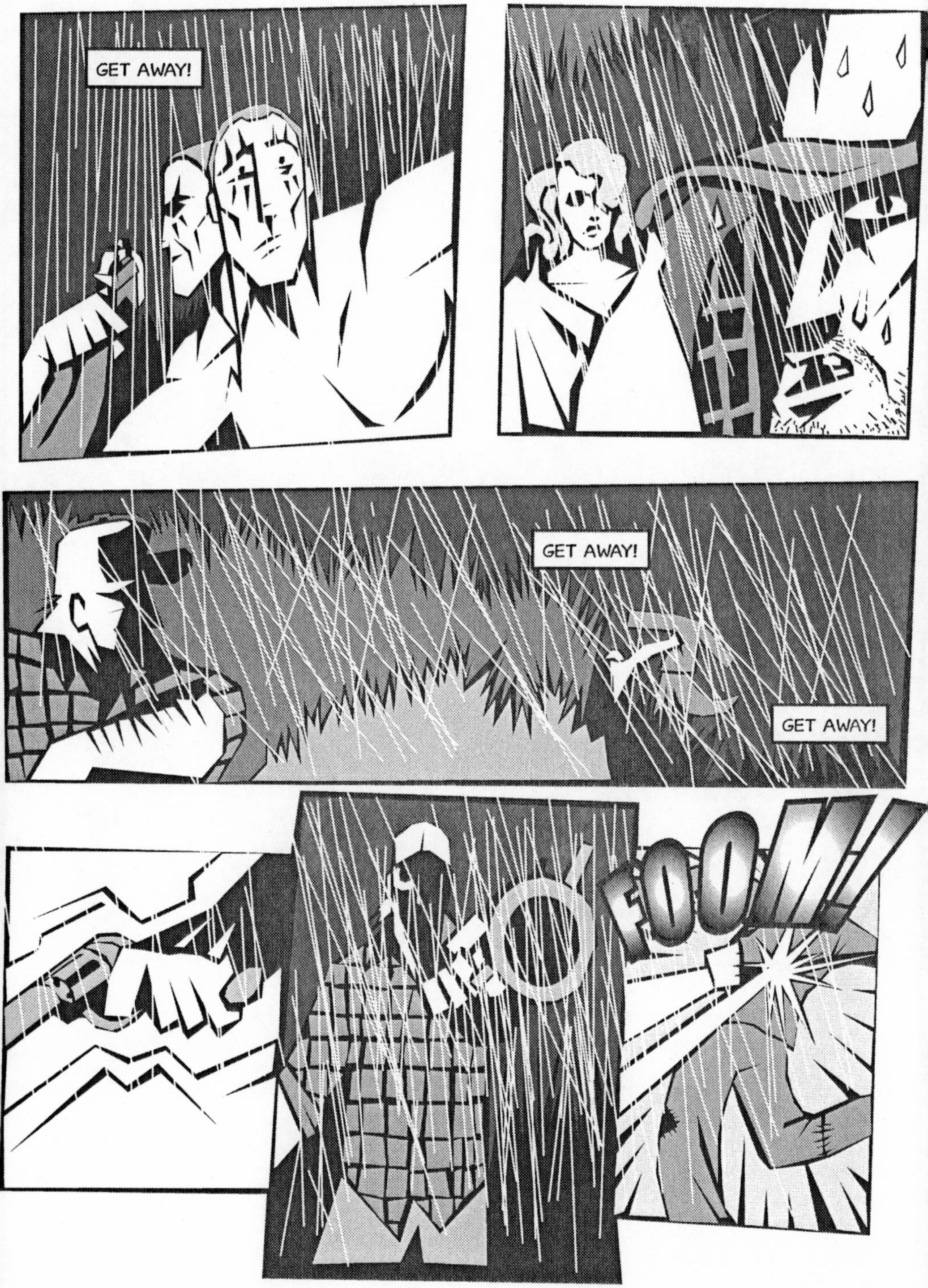
GET AWAY!
GET AWAY!
GET AWAY!
FOOM!

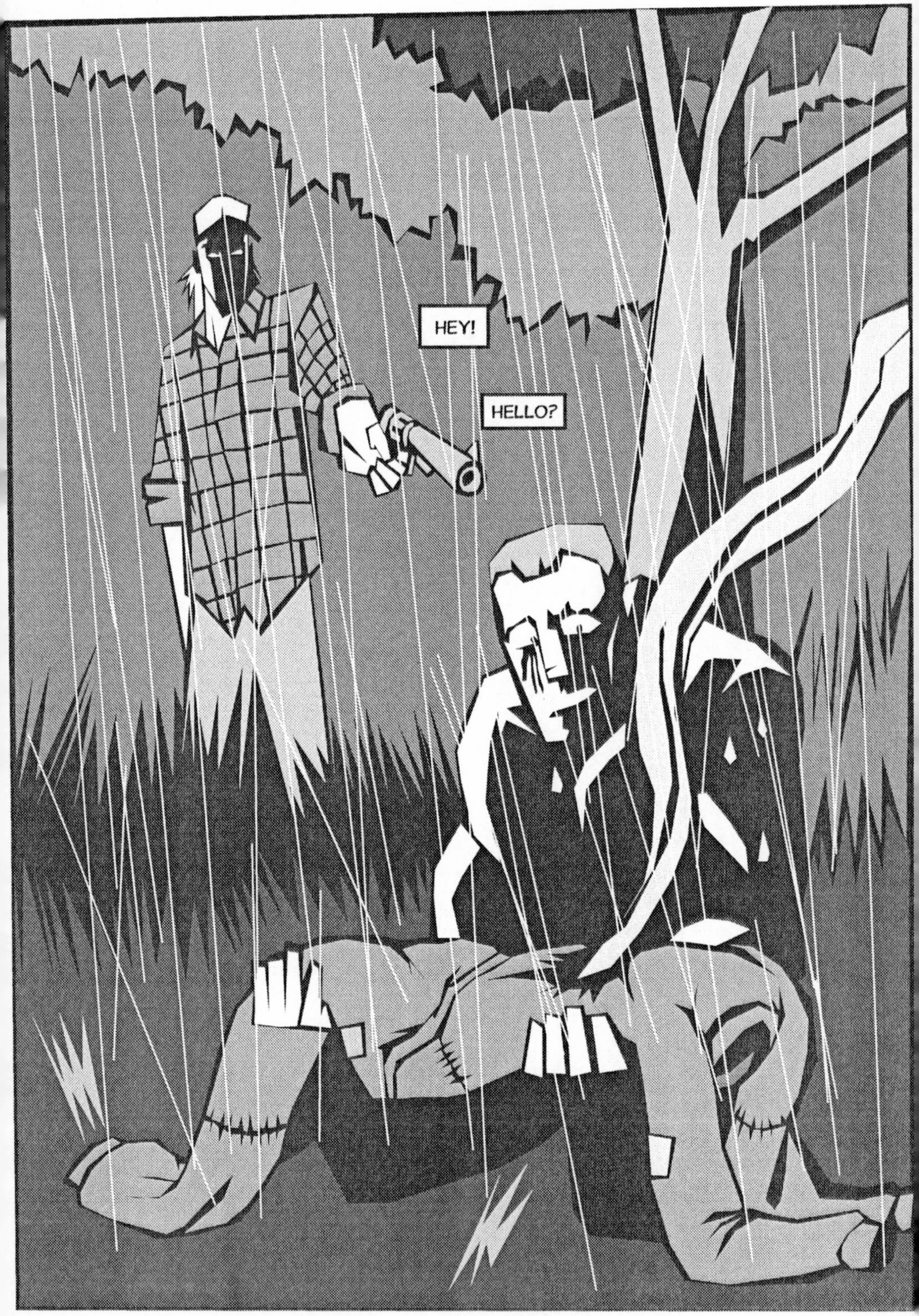
HEY!
HELLO?

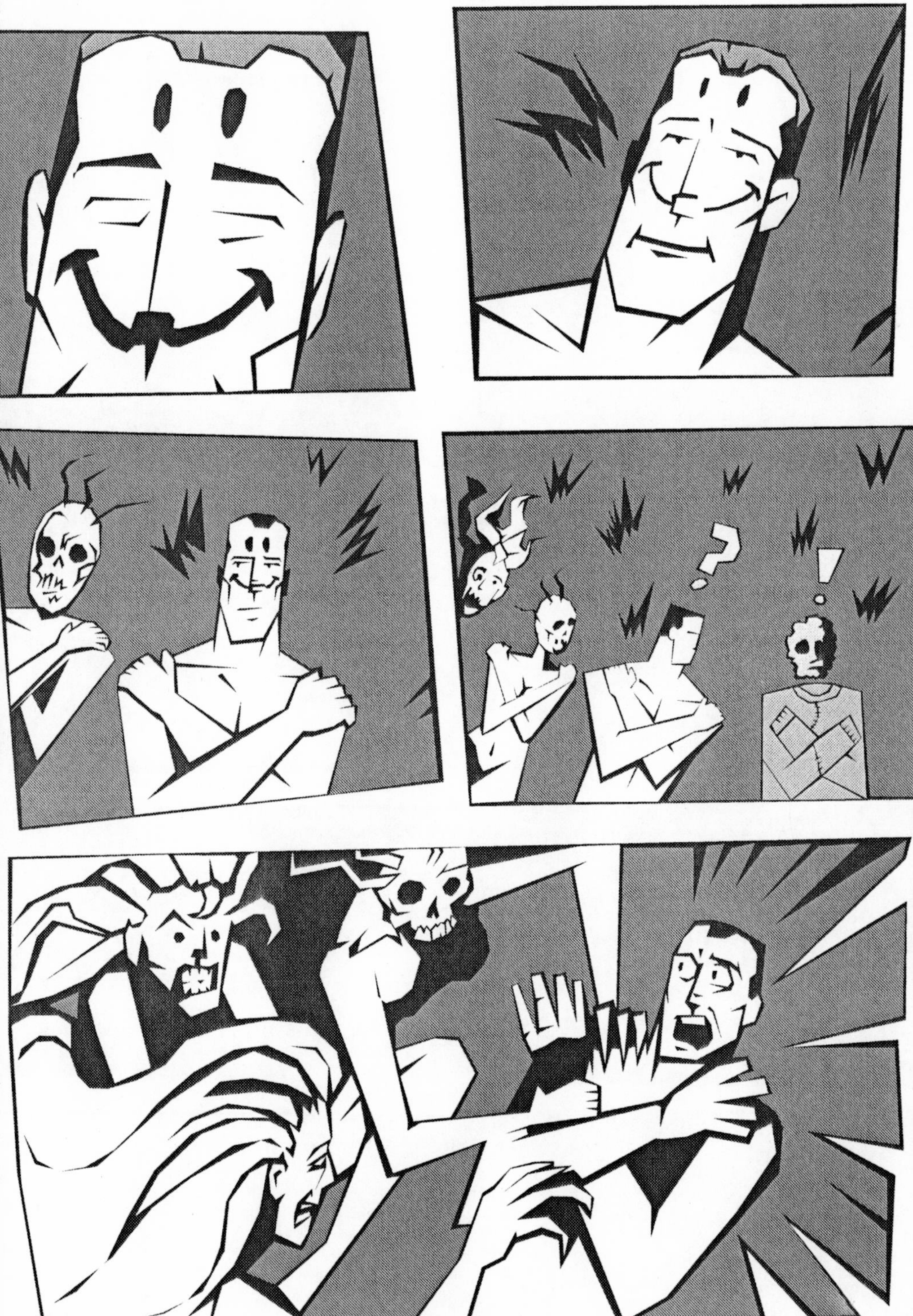
?
!

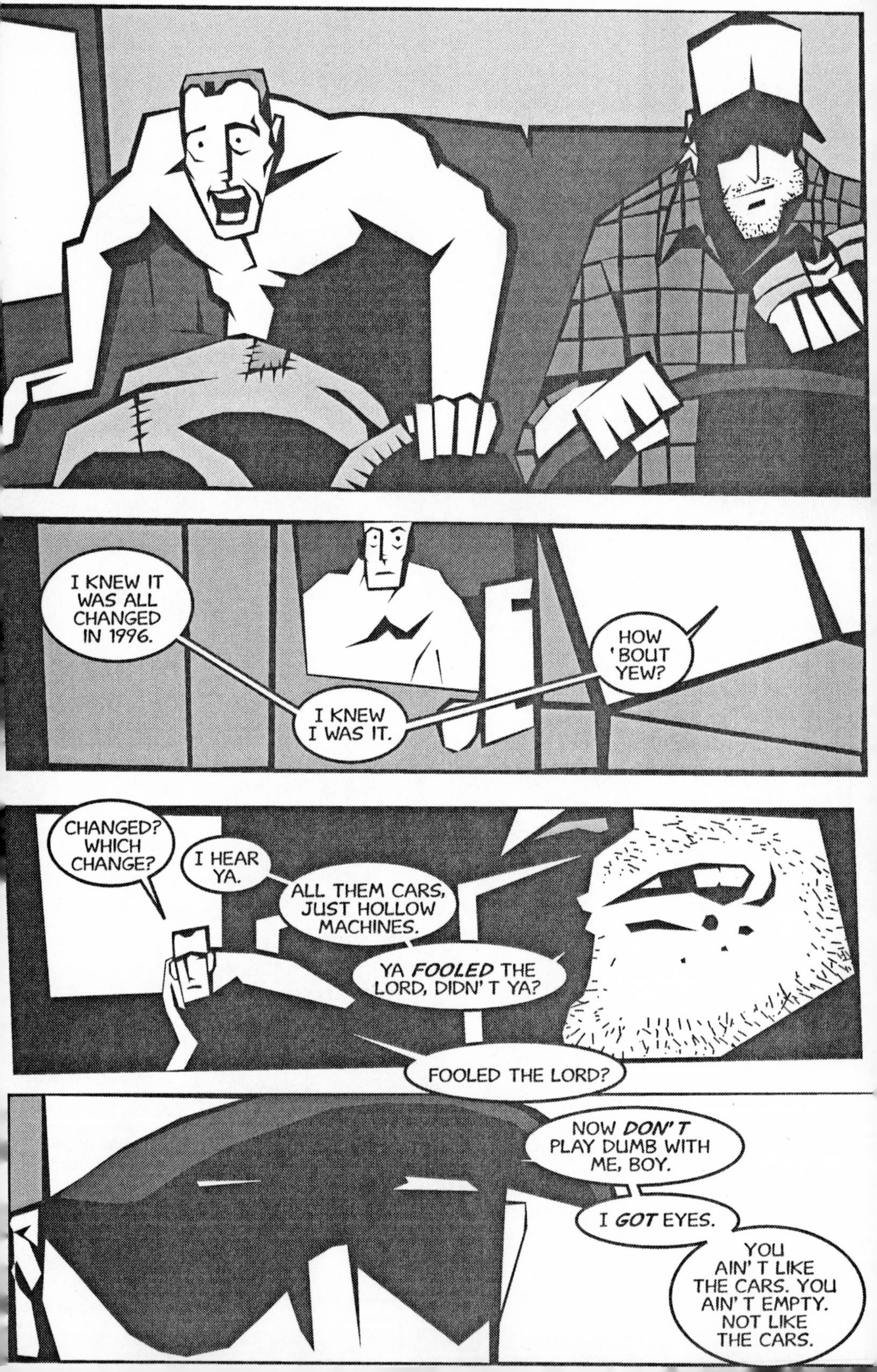

I KNEW IT WAS ALL CHANGED IN 1996.
I KNEW I WAS IT.
HOW 'BOUT YEW?
CHANGED? WHICH CHANGE?
I HEAR YA.
ALL THEM CARS, JUST HOLLOW MACHINES.
YA *FOOLED* THE LORD, DIDN'T YA?
FOOLED THE LORD?
NOW *DON'T* PLAY DUMB WITH ME, BOY.
I *GOT* EYES.
YOU AIN'T LIKE THE CARS. YOU AIN'T EMPTY. NOT LIKE THE CARS.

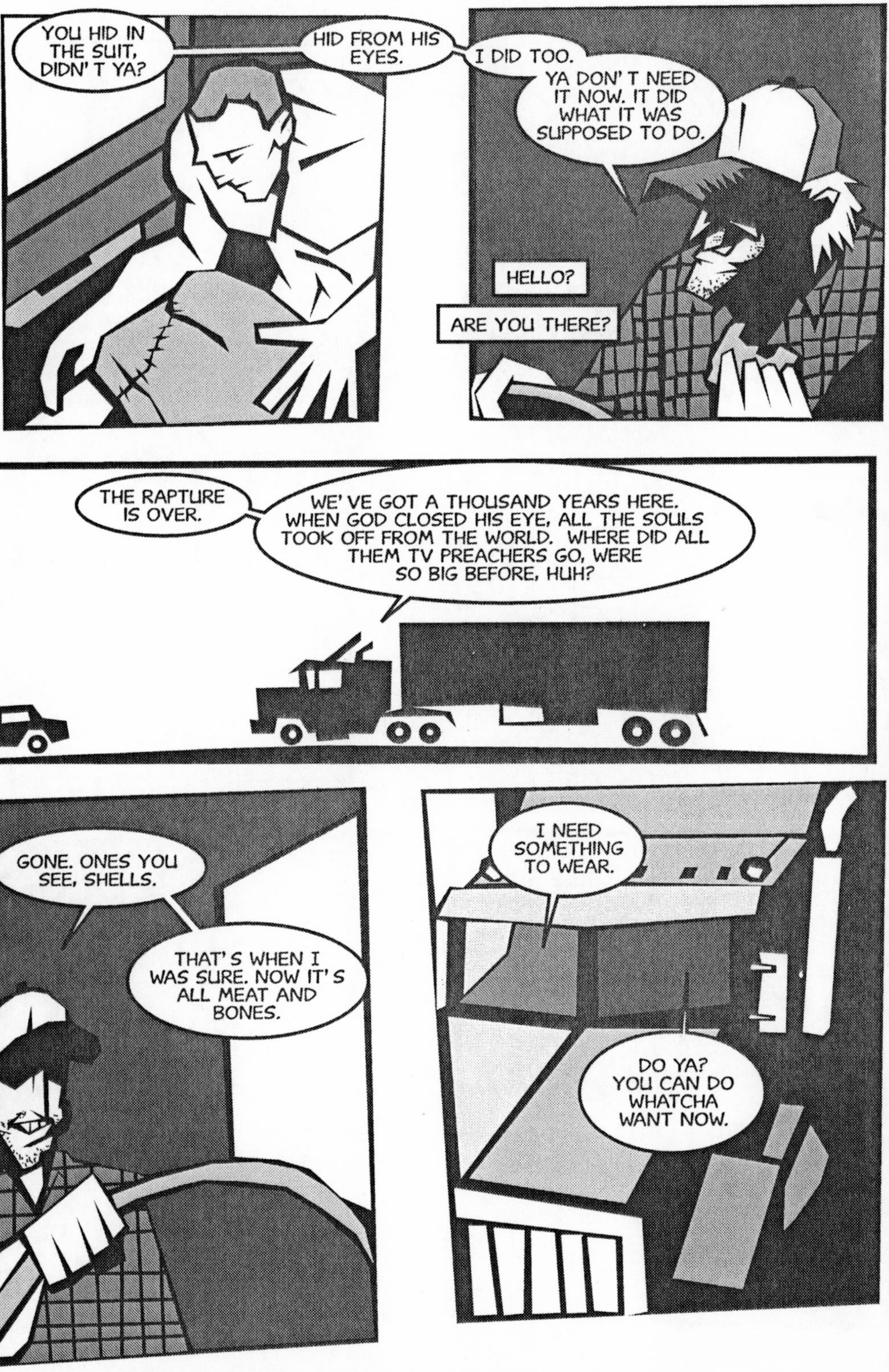
YOU HID IN THE SUIT, DIDN'T YA?
HID FROM HIS EYES.
I DID TOO.
YA DON'T NEED IT NOW. IT DID WHAT IT WAS SUPPOSED TO DO.
HELLO?
ARE YOU THERE?
THE RAPTURE IS OVER.
WE'VE GOT A THOUSAND YEARS HERE. WHEN GOD CLOSED HIS EYE, ALL THE SOULS TOOK OFF FROM THE WORLD. WHERE DID ALL THEM TV PREACHERS GO, WERE SO BIG BEFORE, HUH?
GONE. ONES YOU SEE, SHELLS.
THAT'S WHEN I WAS SURE. NOW IT'S ALL MEAT AND BONES.
I NEED SOMETHING TO WEAR.
DO YA? YOU CAN DO WHATCHA WANT NOW.

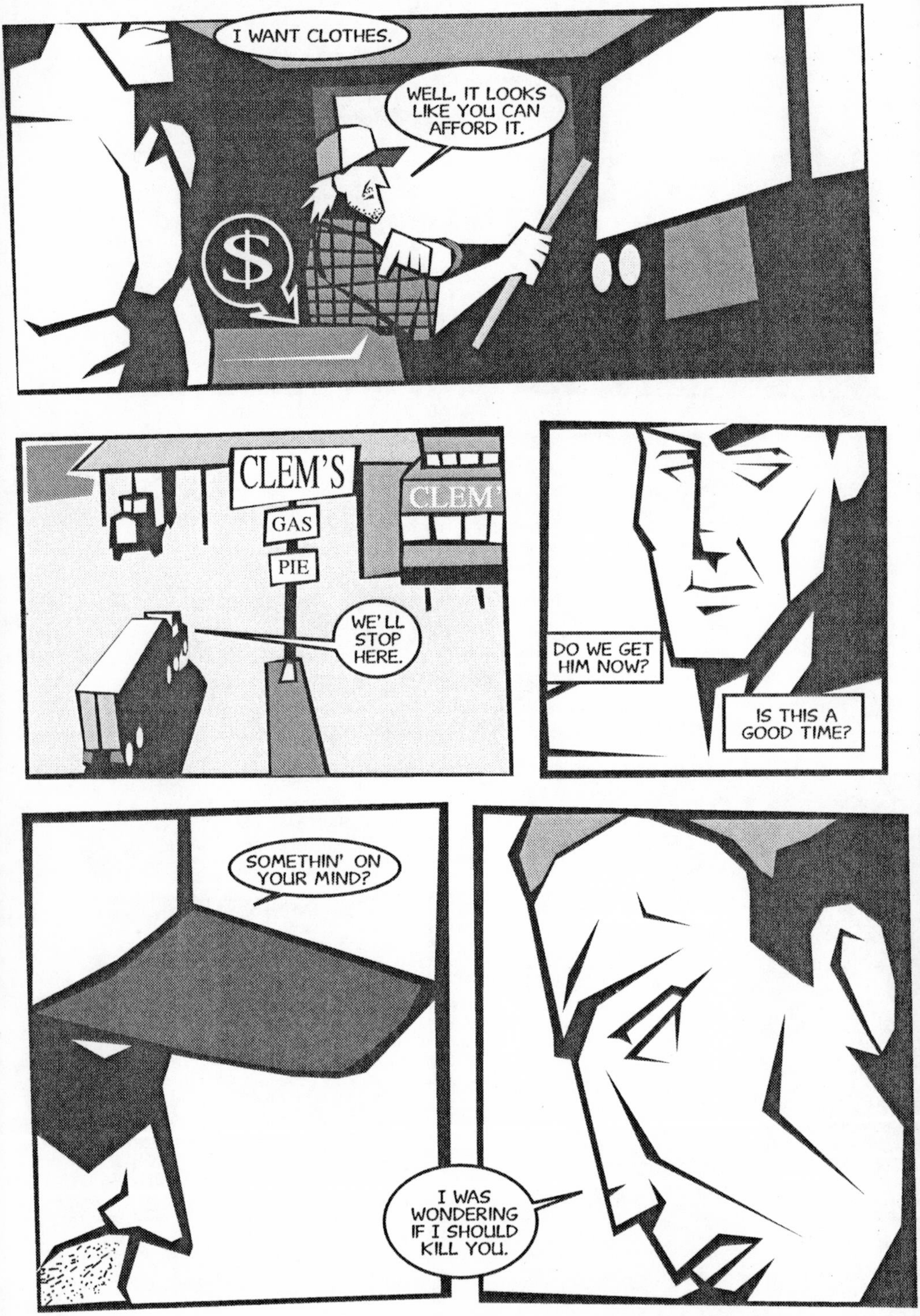
I WANT CLOTHES.
WELL, IT LOOKS LIKE YOU CAN AFFORD IT.
$
CLEM'S
GAS
PIE
CLEM'
WE'LL STOP HERE.
DO WE GET HIM NOW?
IS THIS A GOOD TIME?
SOMETHIN' ON YOUR MIND?
I WAS WONDERING IF I SHOULD KILL YOU.

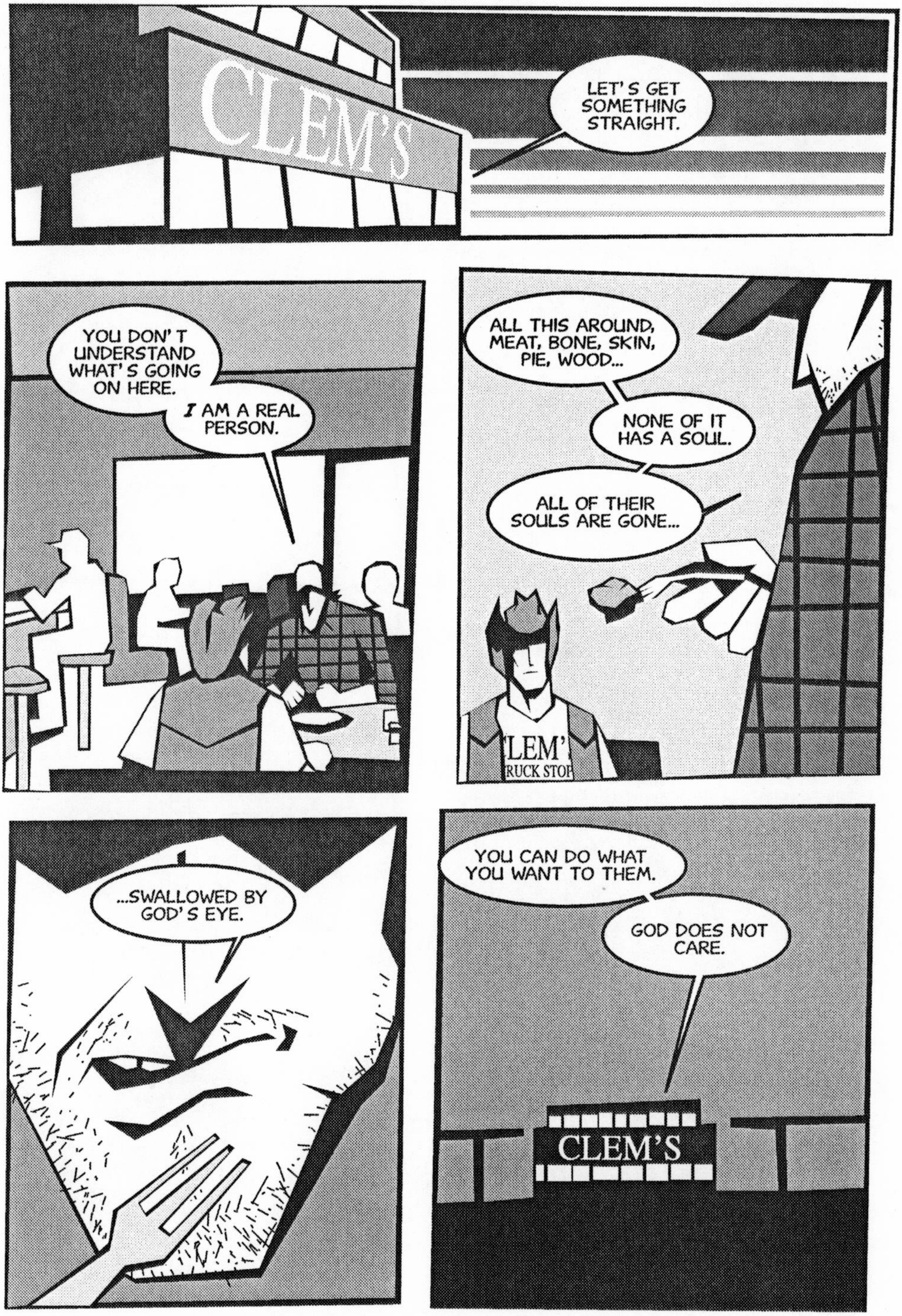
CLEM'S
LET'S GET SOMETHING STRAIGHT.
YOU DON'T UNDERSTAND WHAT'S GOING ON HERE.
I AM A REAL PERSON.
ALL THIS AROUND, MEAT, BONE, SKIN, PIE, WOOD...
NONE OF IT HAS A SOUL.
ALL OF THEIR SOULS ARE GONE...
...SWALLOWED BY GOD'S EYE.
YOU CAN DO WHAT YOU WANT TO THEM.
GOD DOES NOT CARE.
CLEM'S

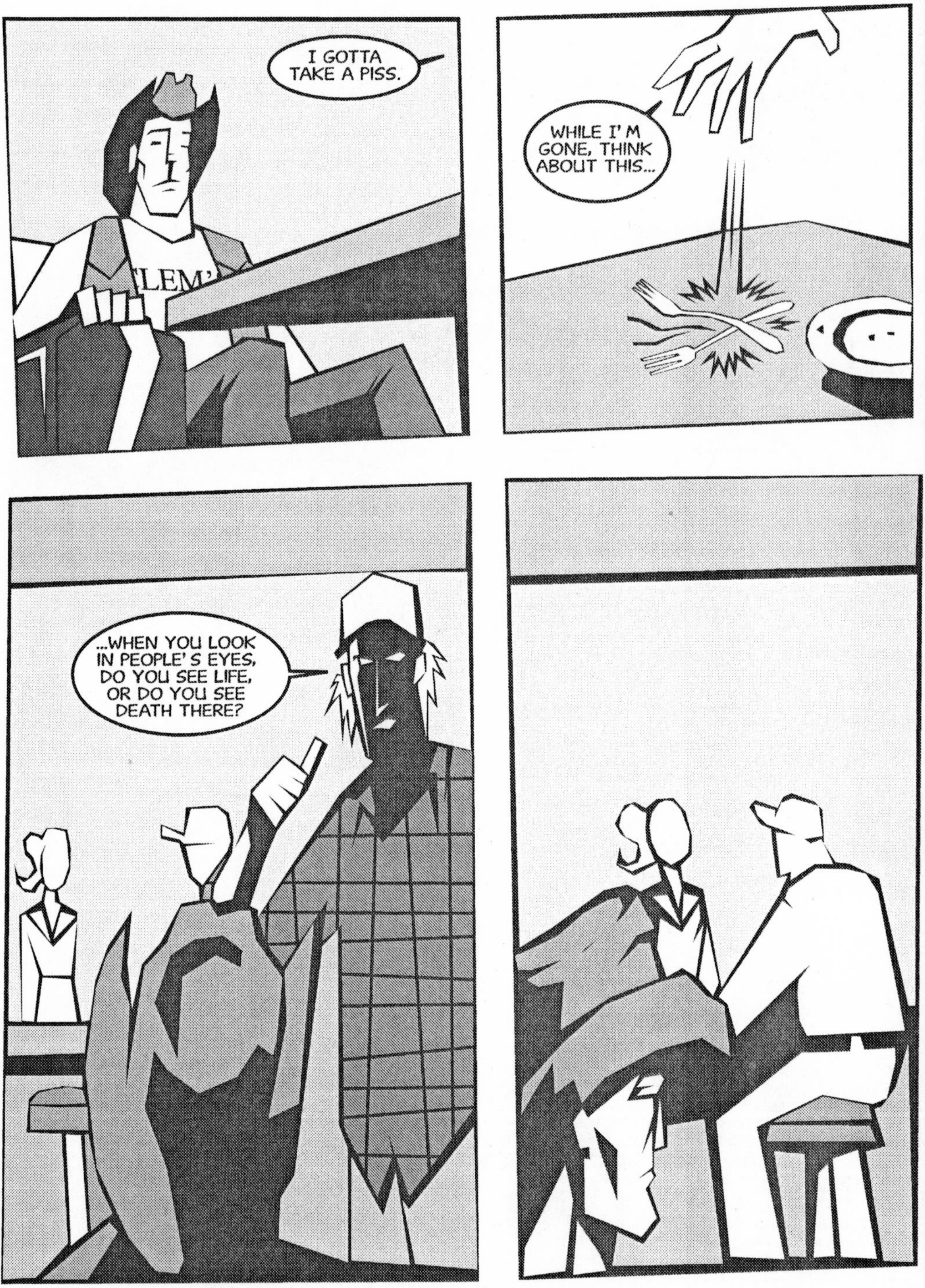
I GOTTA TAKE A PISS.
WHILE I'M GONE, THINK ABOUT THIS...
...WHEN YOU LOOK IN PEOPLE'S EYES, DO YOU SEE LIFE, OR DO YOU SEE DEATH THERE?

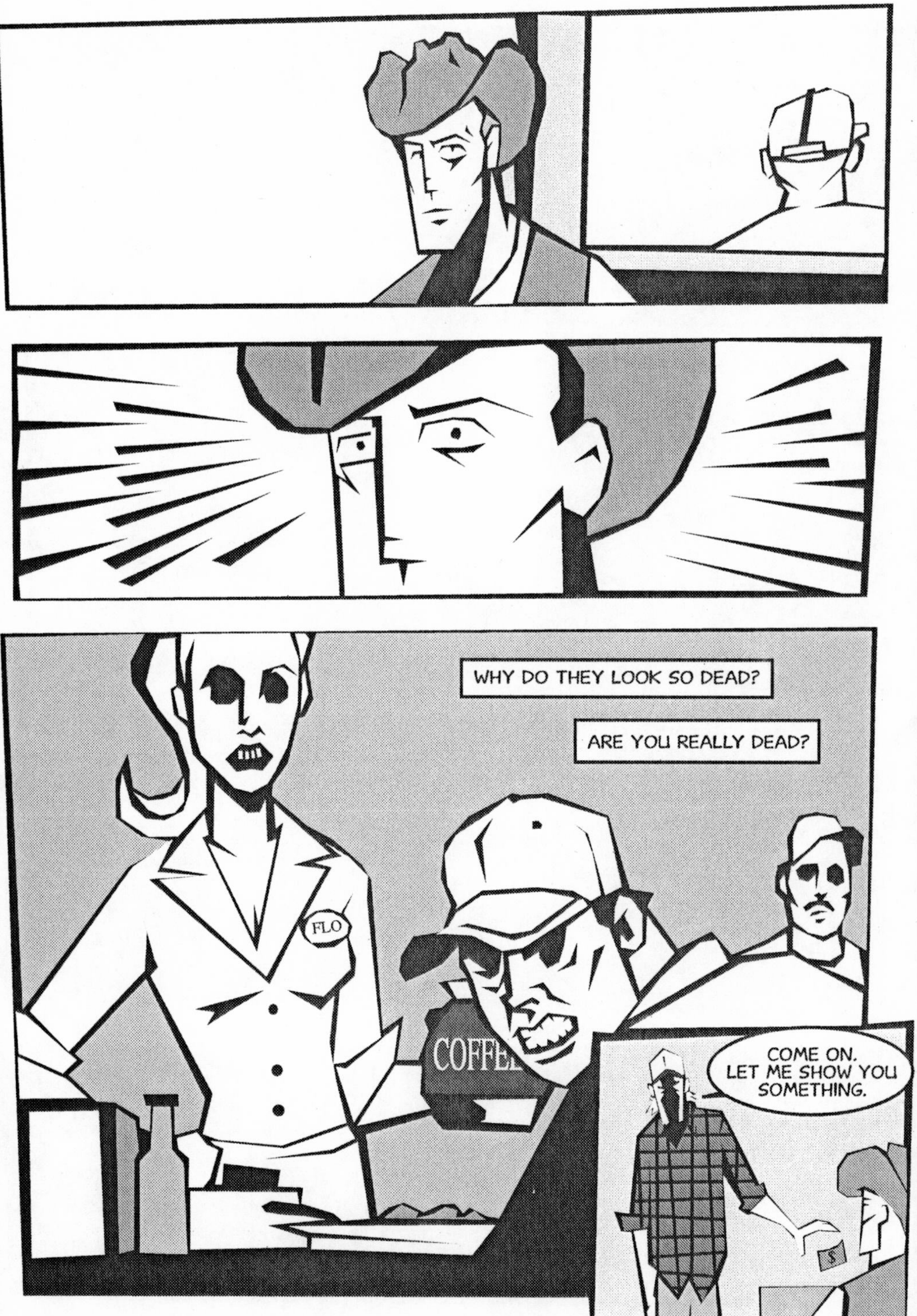
WHY DO THEY LOOK SO DEAD?
ARE YOU REALLY DEAD?
FLO
COFFEE
COME ON. LET ME SHOW YOU SOMETHING.

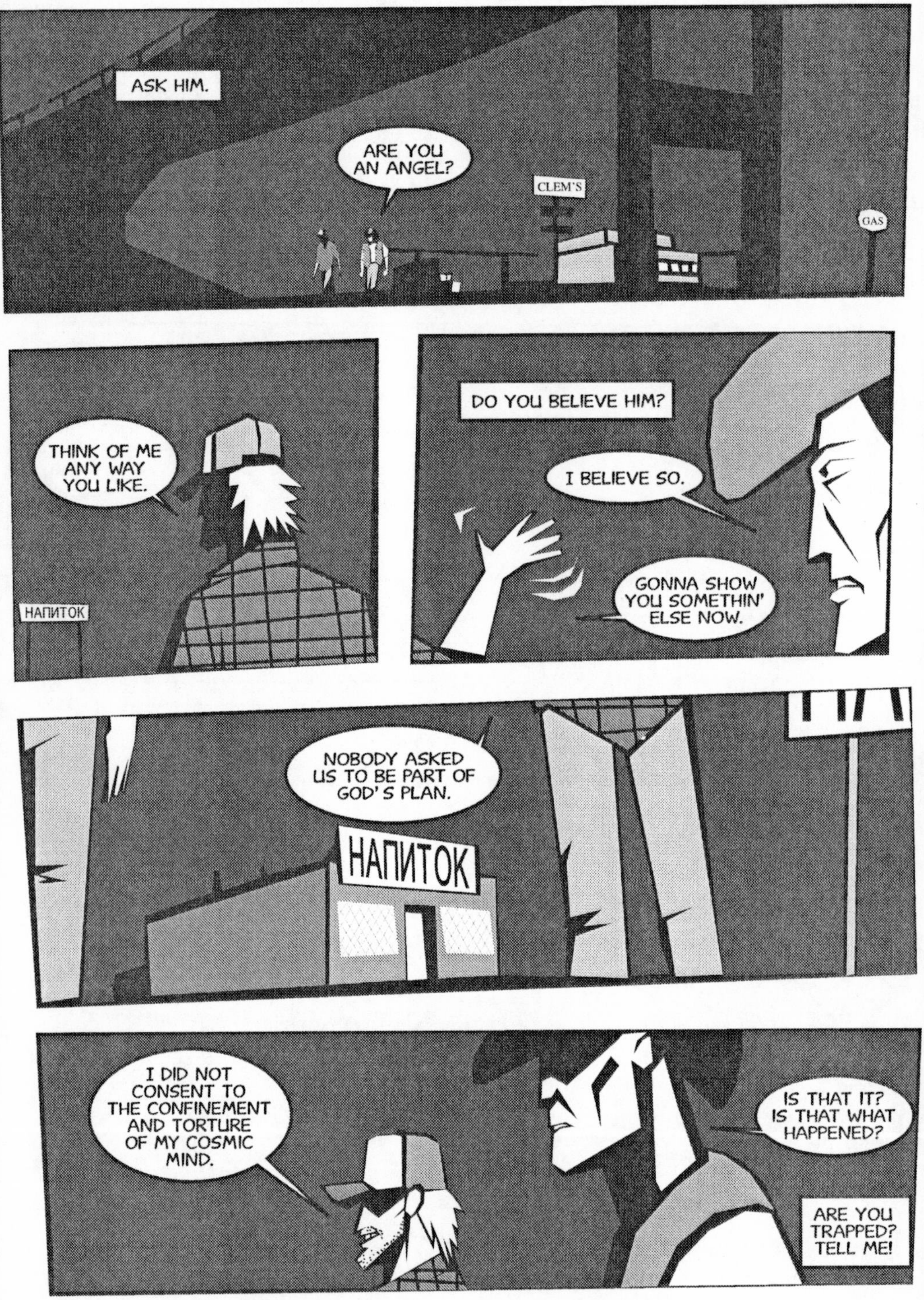
ASK HIM.
ARE YOU AN ANGEL?
CLEM'S
GAS
THINK OF ME ANY WAY YOU LIKE.
НАПИТОК
DO YOU BELIEVE HIM?
I BELIEVE SO.
GONNA SHOW YOU SOMETHIN' ELSE NOW.
NOBODY ASKED US TO BE PART OF GOD'S PLAN.
НАПИТОК
I DID NOT CONSENT TO THE CONFINEMENT AND TORTURE OF MY COSMIC MIND.
IS THAT IT? IS THAT WHAT HAPPENED?
ARE YOU TRAPPED? TELL ME!

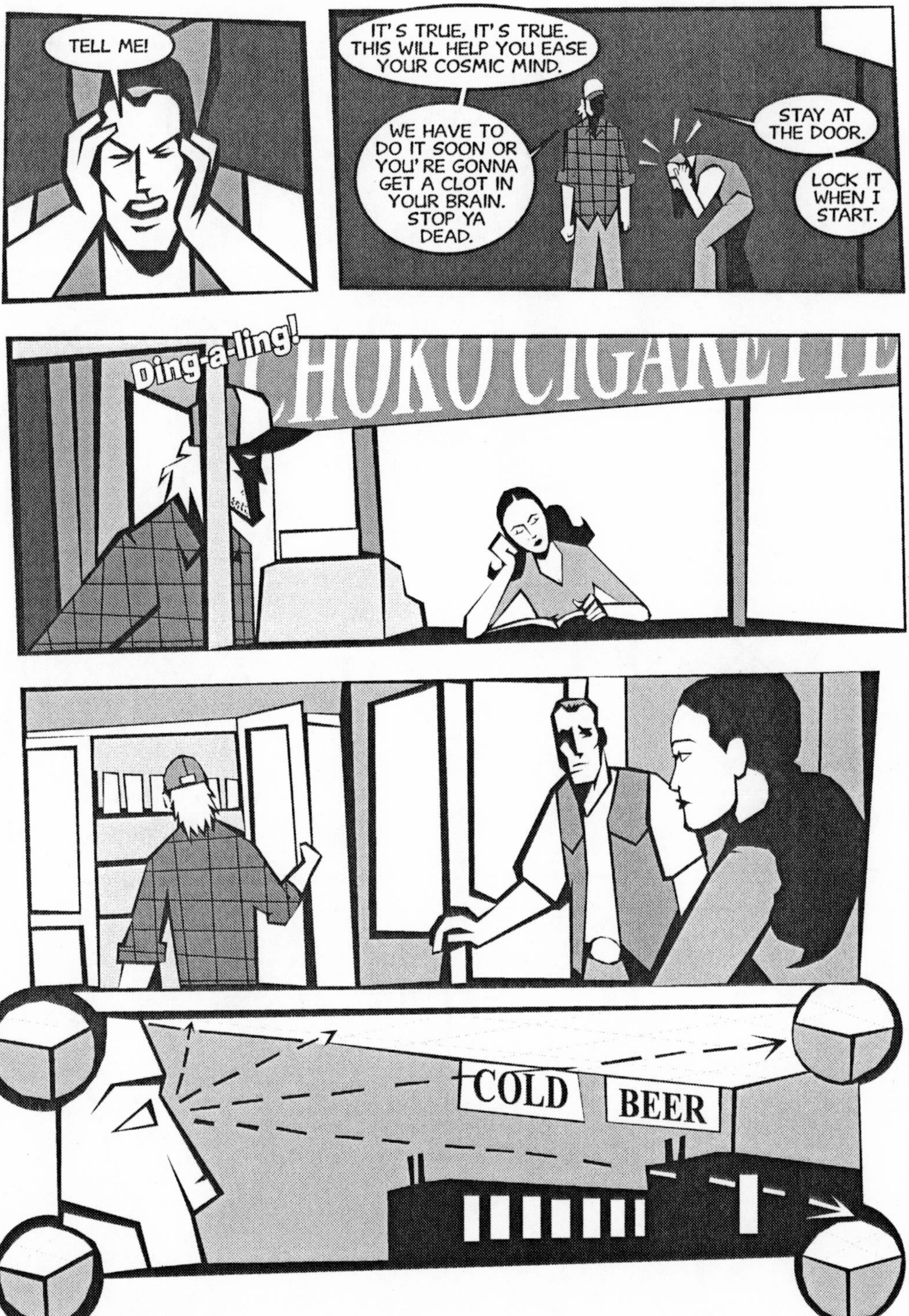
TELL ME!
IT'S TRUE, IT'S TRUE. THIS WILL HELP YOU EASE YOUR COSMIC MIND.
WE HAVE TO DO IT SOON OR YOU'RE GONNA GET A CLOT IN YOUR BRAIN. STOP YA DEAD.
STAY AT THE DOOR.
LOCK IT WHEN I START.
Ding-a-ling!
CHOKO CIGARETTE
COLD
BEER

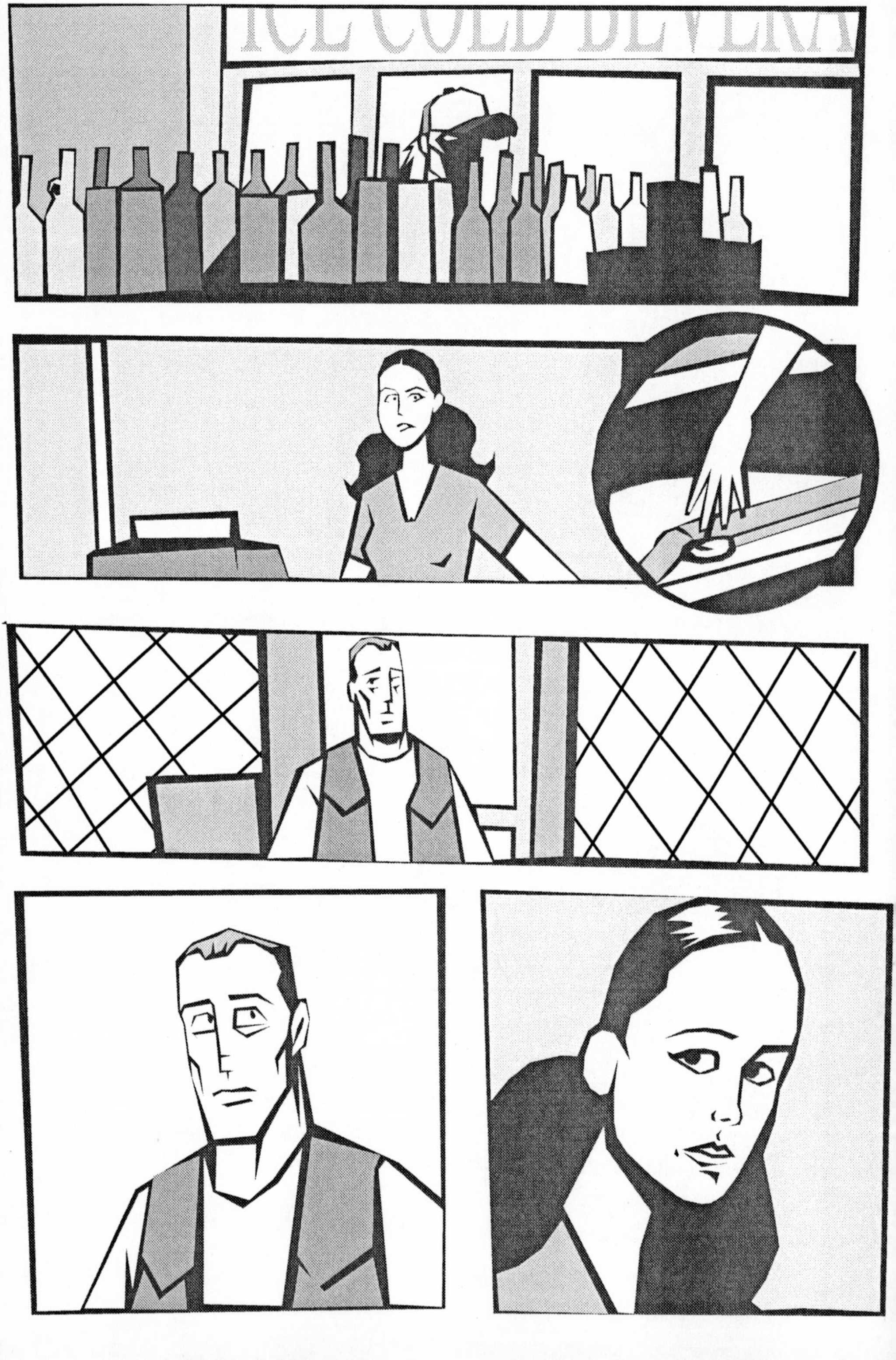
ICE COLD BEVERA

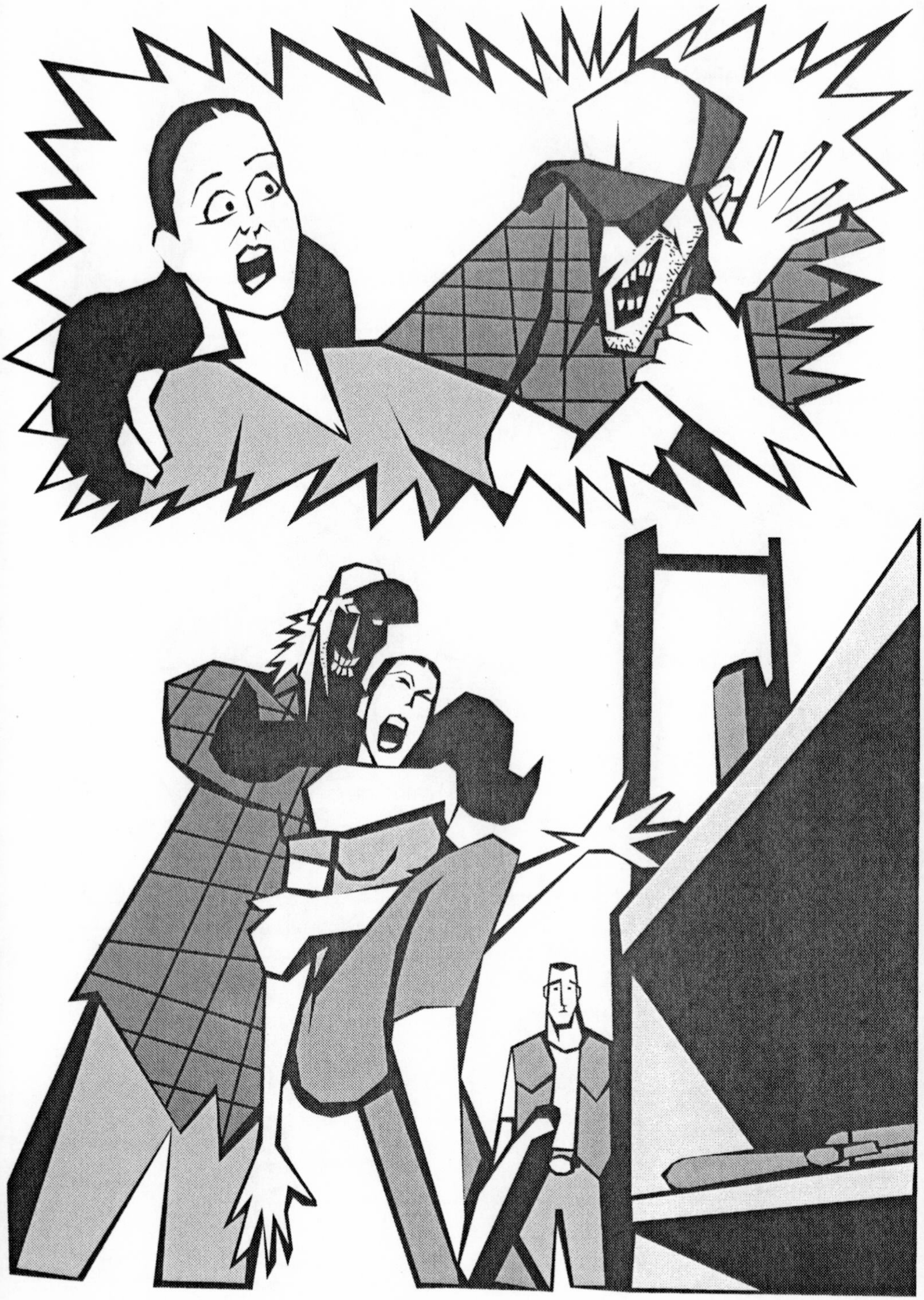

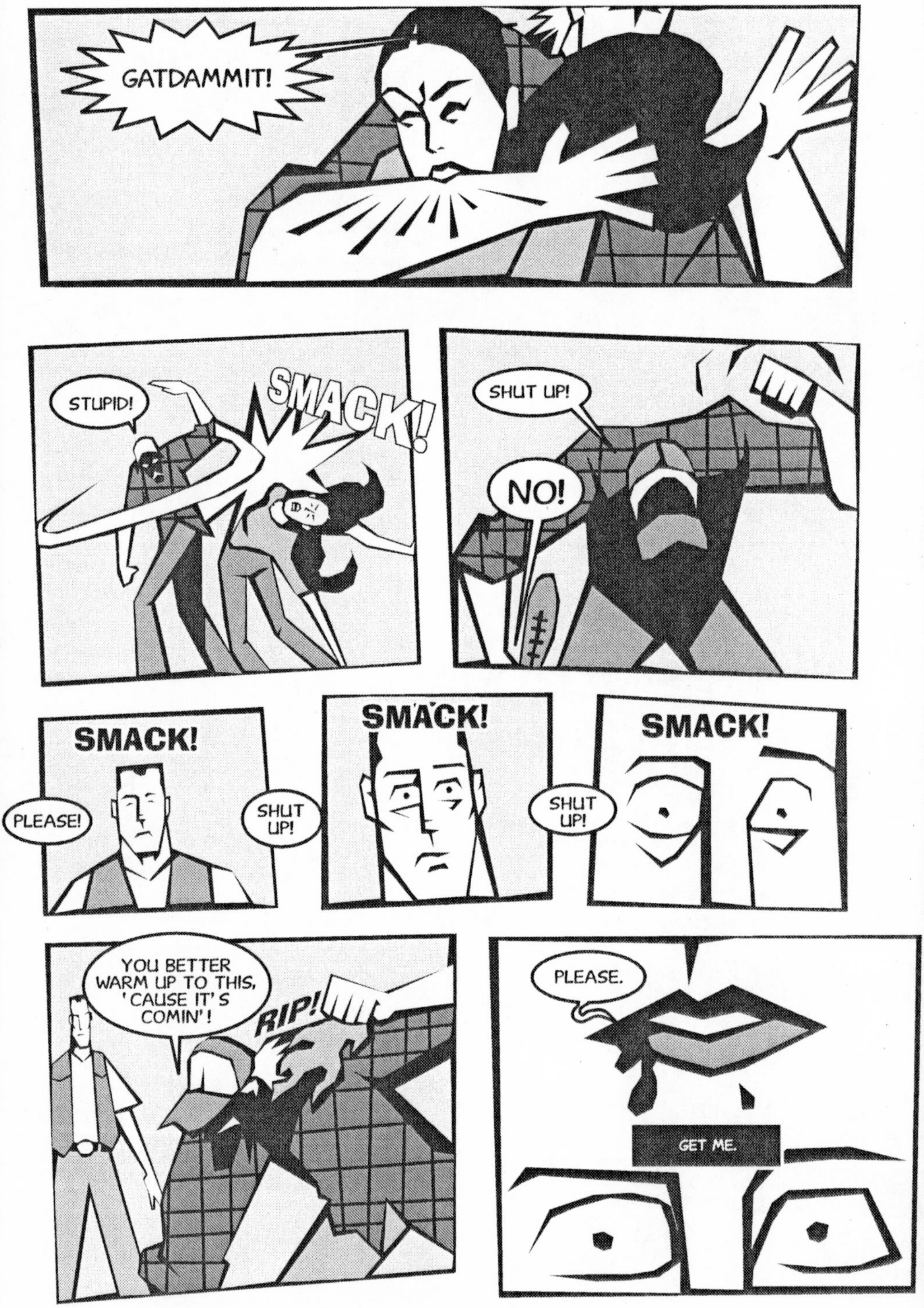
GATDAMMIT!
STUPID!
SMACK!
SHUT UP!
NO!
SMACK!
PLEASE!
SHUT UP!
SMACK!
SHUT UP!
SMACK!
YOU BETTER WARM UP TO THIS, 'CAUSE IT'S COMIN'!
RIP!
PLEASE.
GET ME.

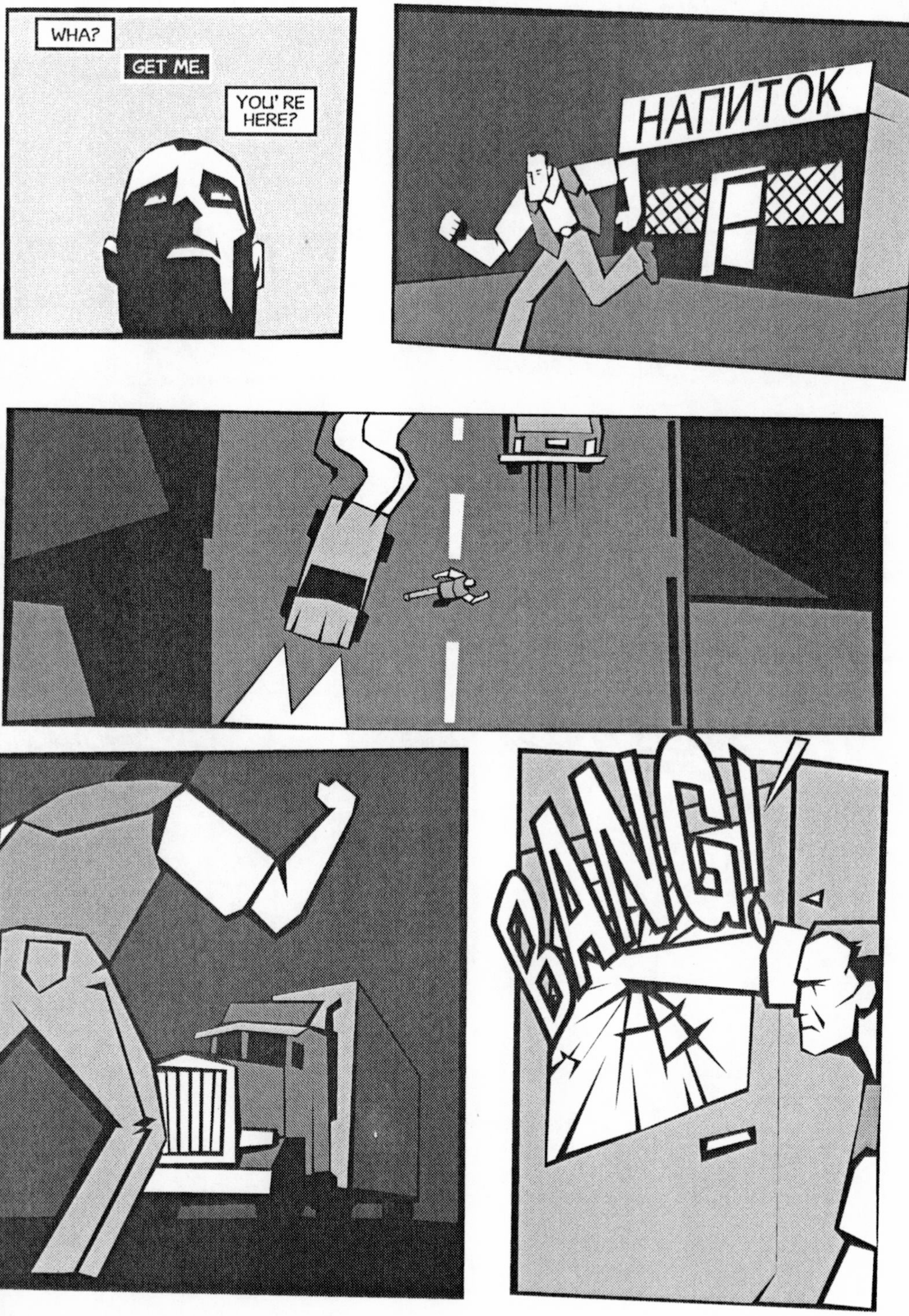
WHA?
GET ME.
YOU'RE HERE?
НАПИТОК
BANG!!

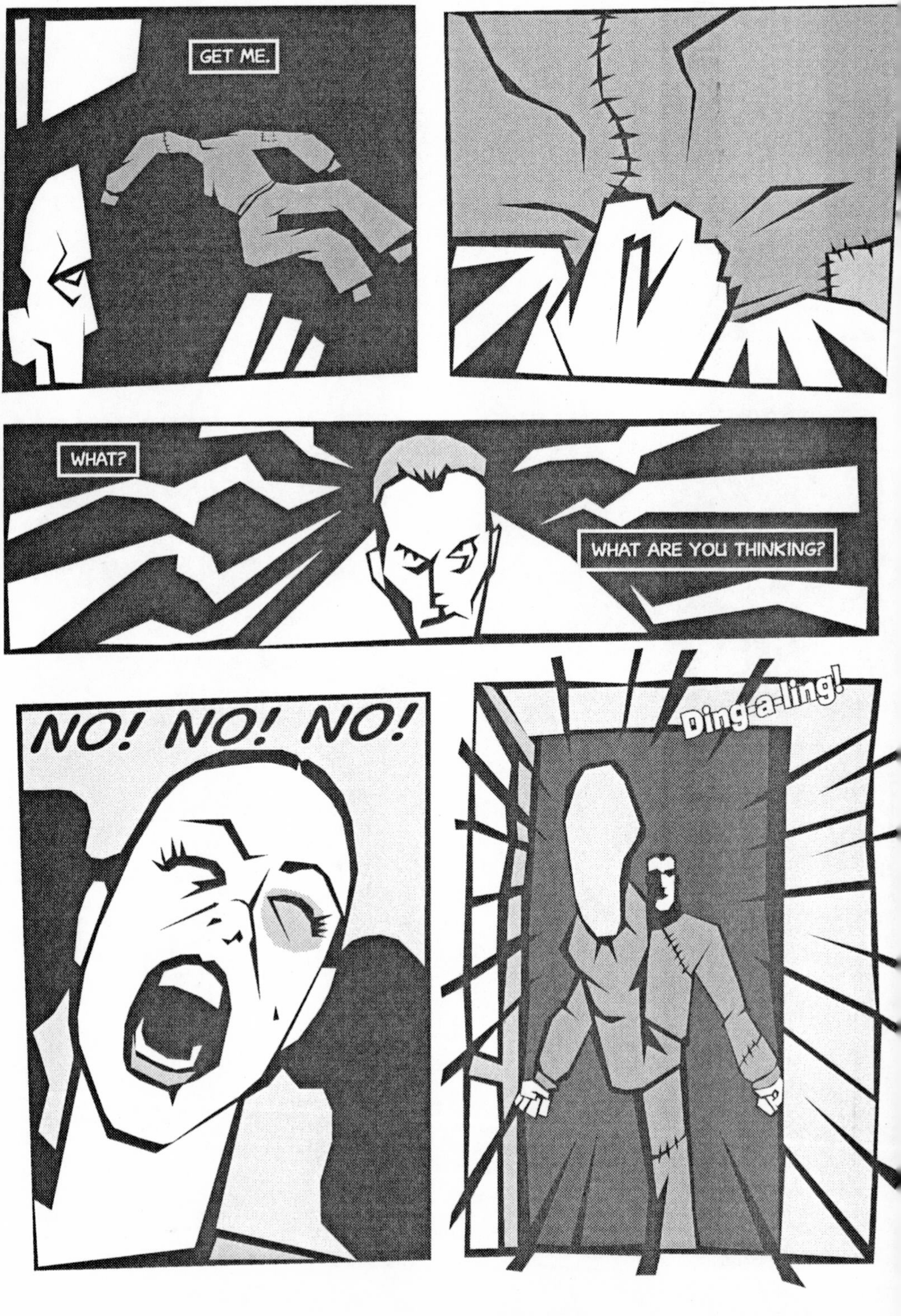
GET ME.
WHAT?
WHAT ARE YOU THINKING?
NO! NO! NO!
Ding-a-ling!

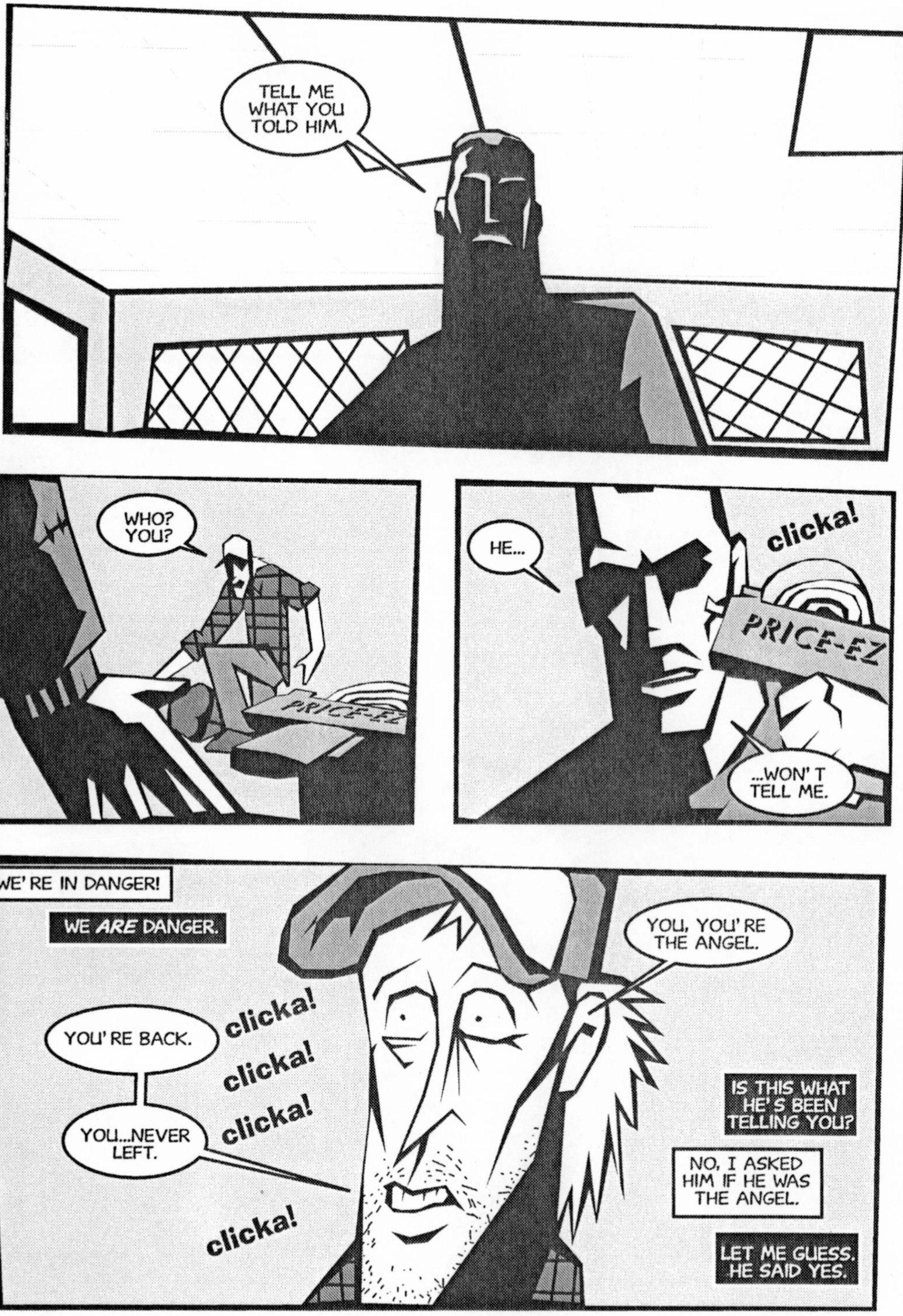

TELL ME WHAT YOU TOLD HIM.
WHO? YOU?
HE...
clicka!
PRICE-EZ
...WON'T TELL ME.
WE'RE IN DANGER!
WE *ARE* DANGER.
YOU, YOU'RE THE ANGEL.
YOU'RE BACK.
clicka!
clicka!
clicka!
YOU...NEVER LEFT.
clicka!
IS THIS WHAT HE'S BEEN TELLING YOU?
NO, I ASKED HIM IF HE WAS THE ANGEL.
LET ME GUESS. HE SAID YES.

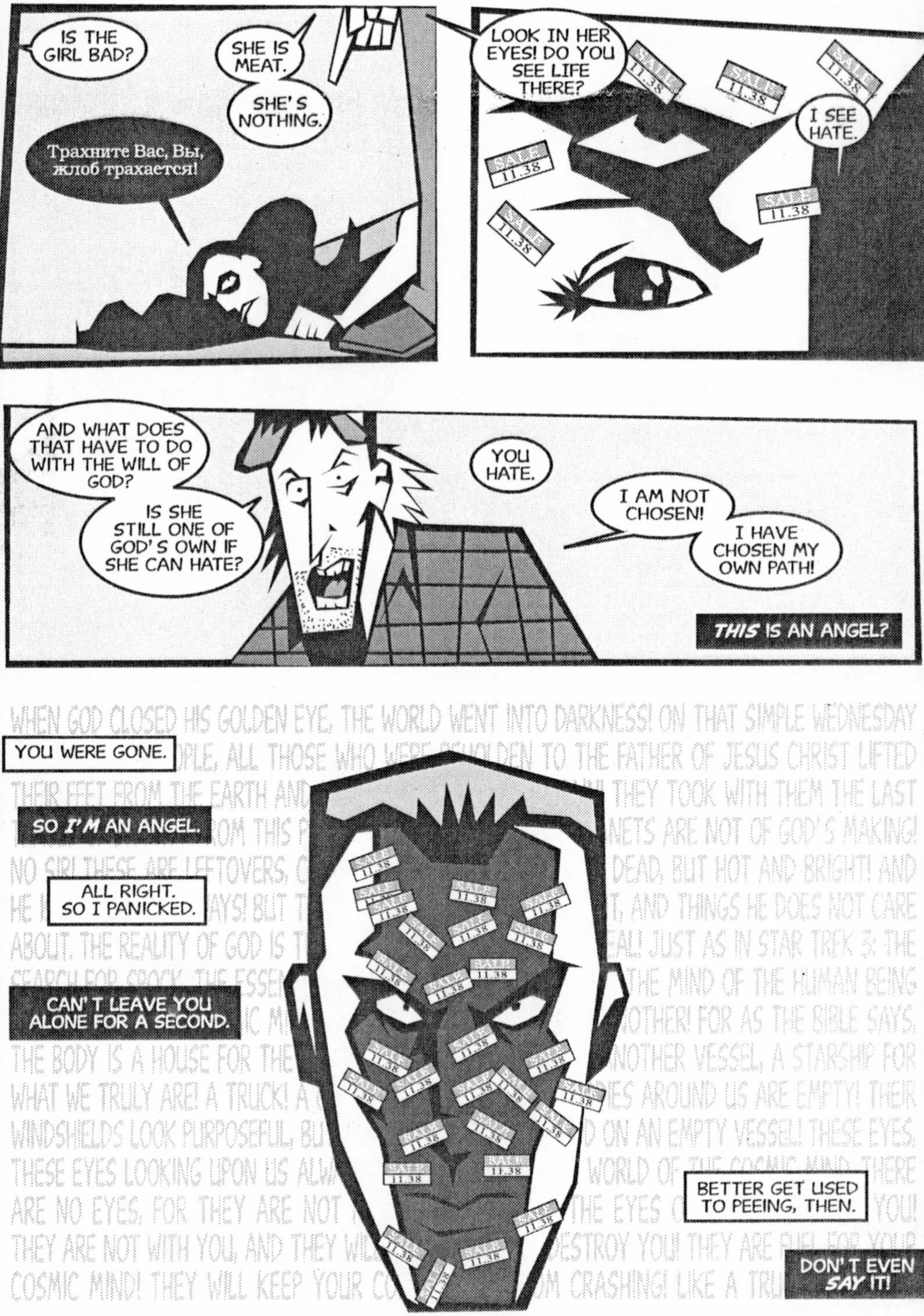
IS THE GIRL BAD?
SHE IS MEAT.
SHE'S NOTHING.
Трахните Вас, Вы, жлоб трахается!
LOOK IN HER EYES! DO YOU SEE LIFE THERE?
I SEE HATE.
SALE 11.38
AND WHAT DOES THAT HAVE TO DO WITH THE WILL OF GOD?
IS SHE STILL ONE OF GOD'S OWN IF SHE CAN HATE?
YOU HATE.
I AM NOT CHOSEN!
I HAVE CHOSEN MY OWN PATH!
THIS IS AN ANGEL?
YOU WERE GONE.
SO I'M AN ANGEL.
ALL RIGHT. SO I PANICKED.
CAN'T LEAVE YOU ALONE FOR A SECOND.
BETTER GET USED TO PEEING, THEN.
DON'T EVEN SAY IT!
WHEN GOD CLOSED HIS GOLDEN EYE, THE WORLD WENT INTO DARKNESS! ON THAT SIMPLE WEDNESDAY
PLE, ALL THOSE WHO WERE BEHOLDEN TO THE FATHER OF JESUS CHRIST LIFTED
THEIR FEET FROM THE EARTH AND
THEY TOOK WITH THEM THE LAST
OM THIS P
NETS ARE NOT OF GOD'S MAKING!
NO SIR! THESE ARE LEFTOVERS,
DEAD, BUT HOT AND BRIGHT! AND
AYS! BUT T
T, AND THINGS HE DOES NOT CARE
ABOUT. THE REALITY OF GOD IS T
EAL! JUST AS IN STAR TREK 3: THE
SEARCH FOR SPOCK, THE ESSEN
THE MIND OF THE HUMAN BEING
NOTHER! FOR AS THE BIBLE SAYS,
THE BODY IS A HOUSE FOR THE
NOTHER VESSEL, A STARSHIP FOR
WHAT WE TRULY ARE! A TRUCK!
ES AROUND US ARE EMPTY! THEIR
WINDSHIELDS LOOK PURPOSEFUL, BU
D ON AN EMPTY VESSEL! THESE EYES,
THESE EYES LOOKING UPON US ALW
WORLD OF THE COSMIC MIND THERE
ARE NO EYES, FOR THEY ARE NOT
THE EYES
YOU!
THEY ARE NOT WITH YOU, AND THEY WIL
DESTROY YOU! THEY ARE FUEL FOR YOUR
COSMIC MIND! THEY WILL KEEP YOUR CO
OM CRASHING! LIKE A TRU

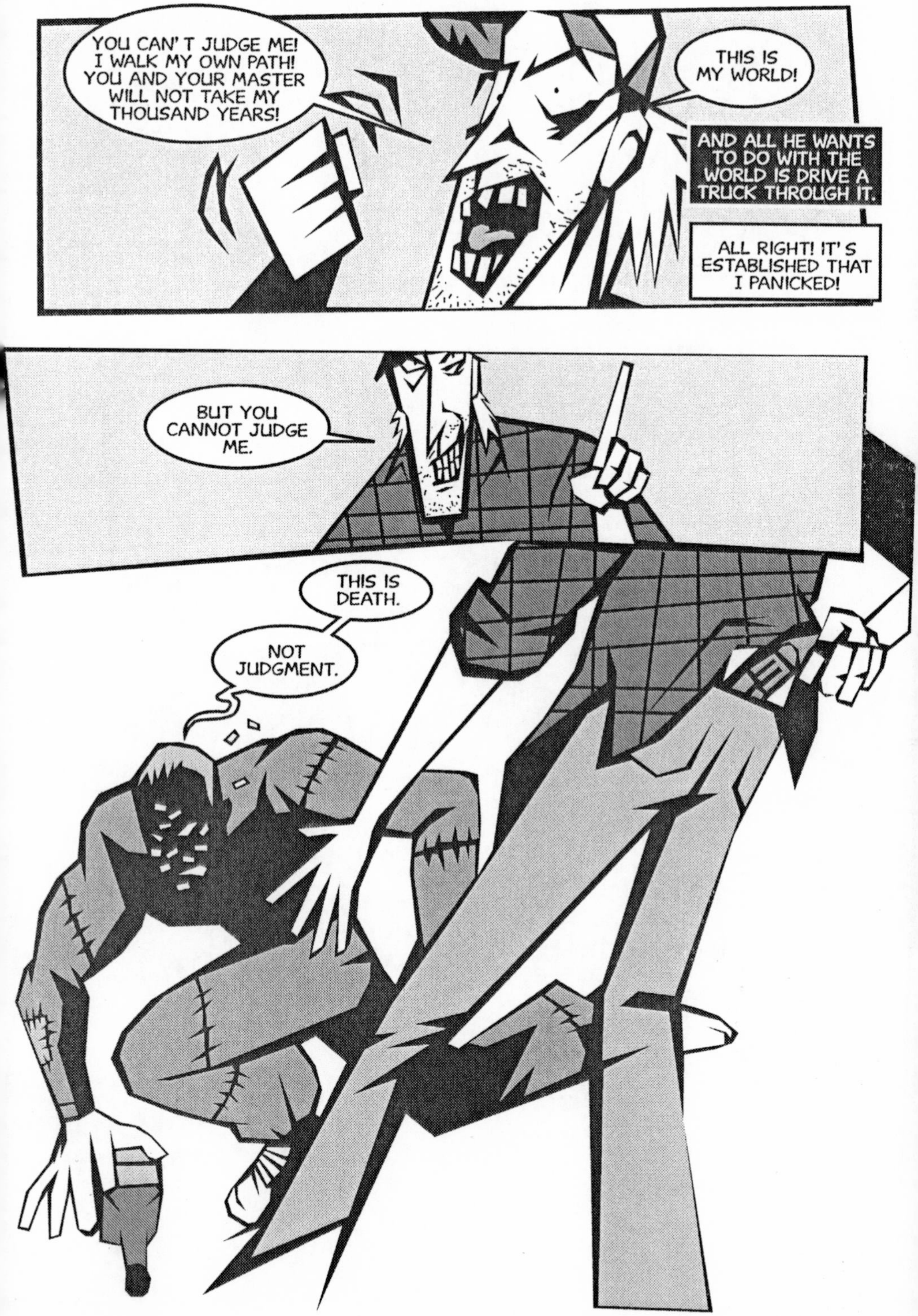
YOU CAN'T JUDGE ME! I WALK MY OWN PATH! YOU AND YOUR MASTER WILL NOT TAKE MY THOUSAND YEARS!
THIS IS MY WORLD!
AND ALL HE WANTS TO DO WITH THE WORLD IS DRIVE A TRUCK THROUGH IT.
ALL RIGHT! IT'S ESTABLISHED THAT I PANICKED!
BUT YOU CANNOT JUDGE ME.
THIS IS DEATH.
NOT JUDGMENT.

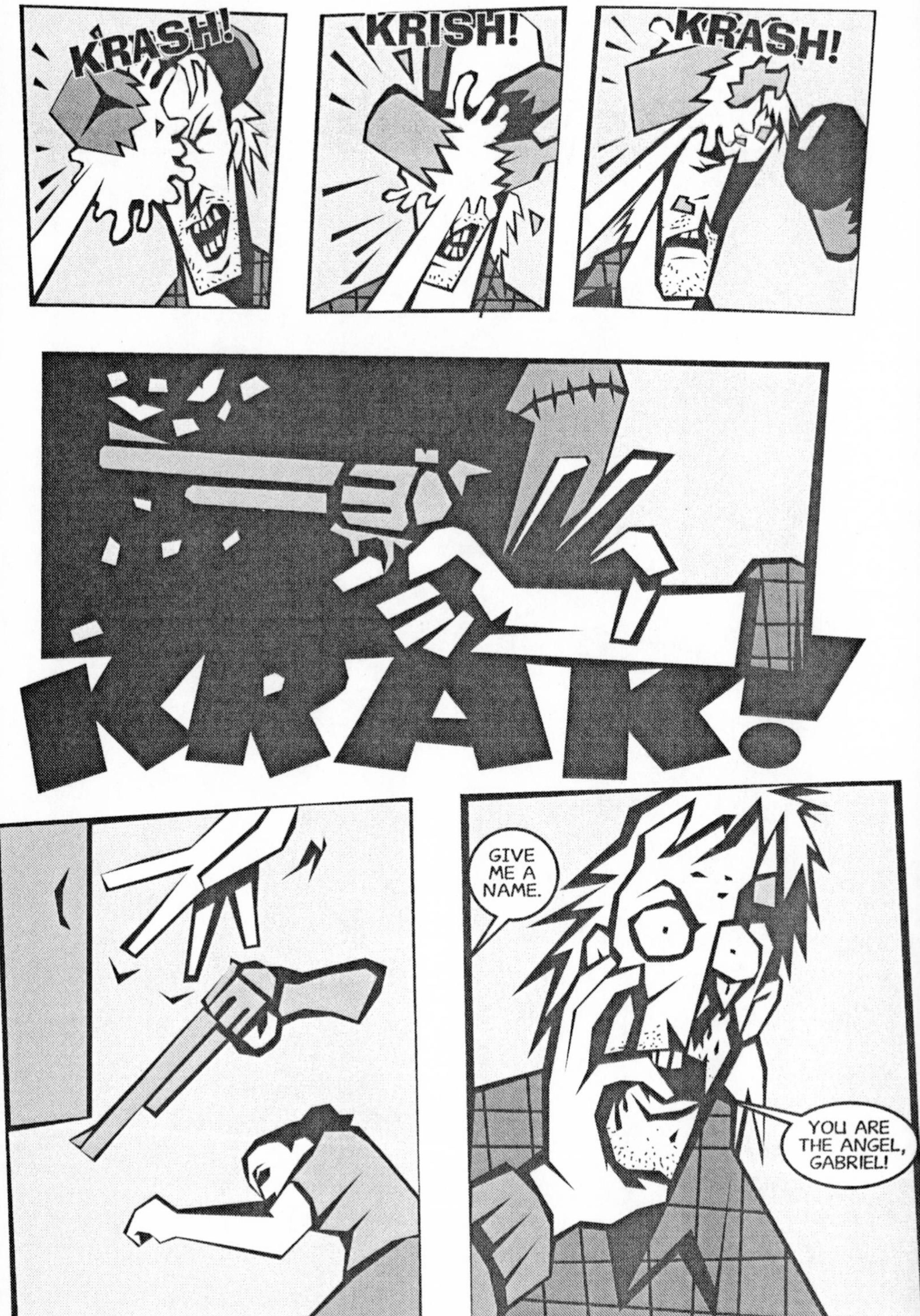
KRASH!
KRISH!
KRASH!
KRAK!
GIVE ME A NAME.
YOU ARE THE ANGEL, GABRIEL!

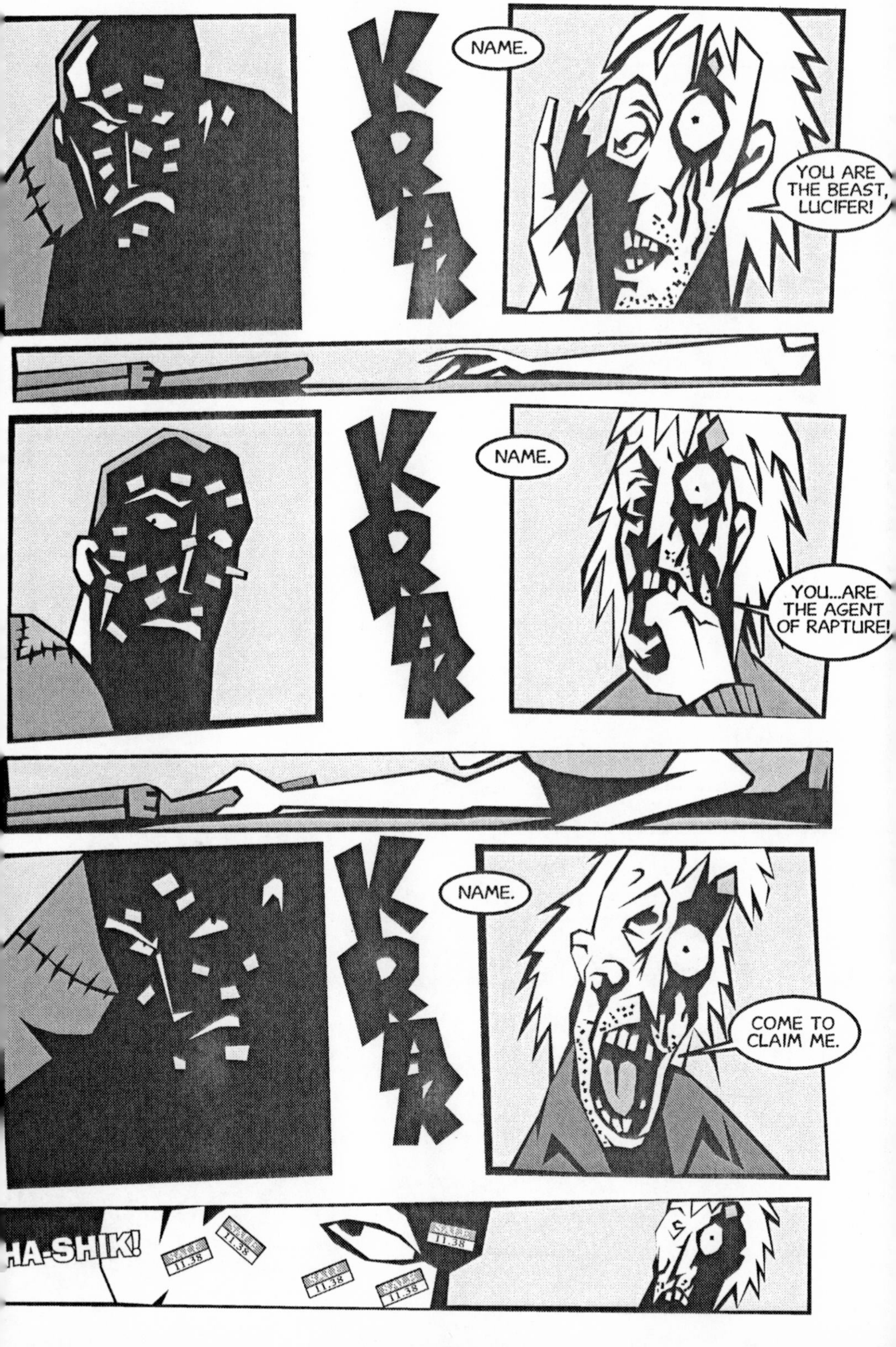
VRAK
NAME.
YOU ARE THE BEAST, LUCIFER!
VRAK
NAME.
YOU...ARE THE AGENT OF RAPTURE!
VRAK
NAME.
COME TO CLAIM ME.
HA-SHIK!

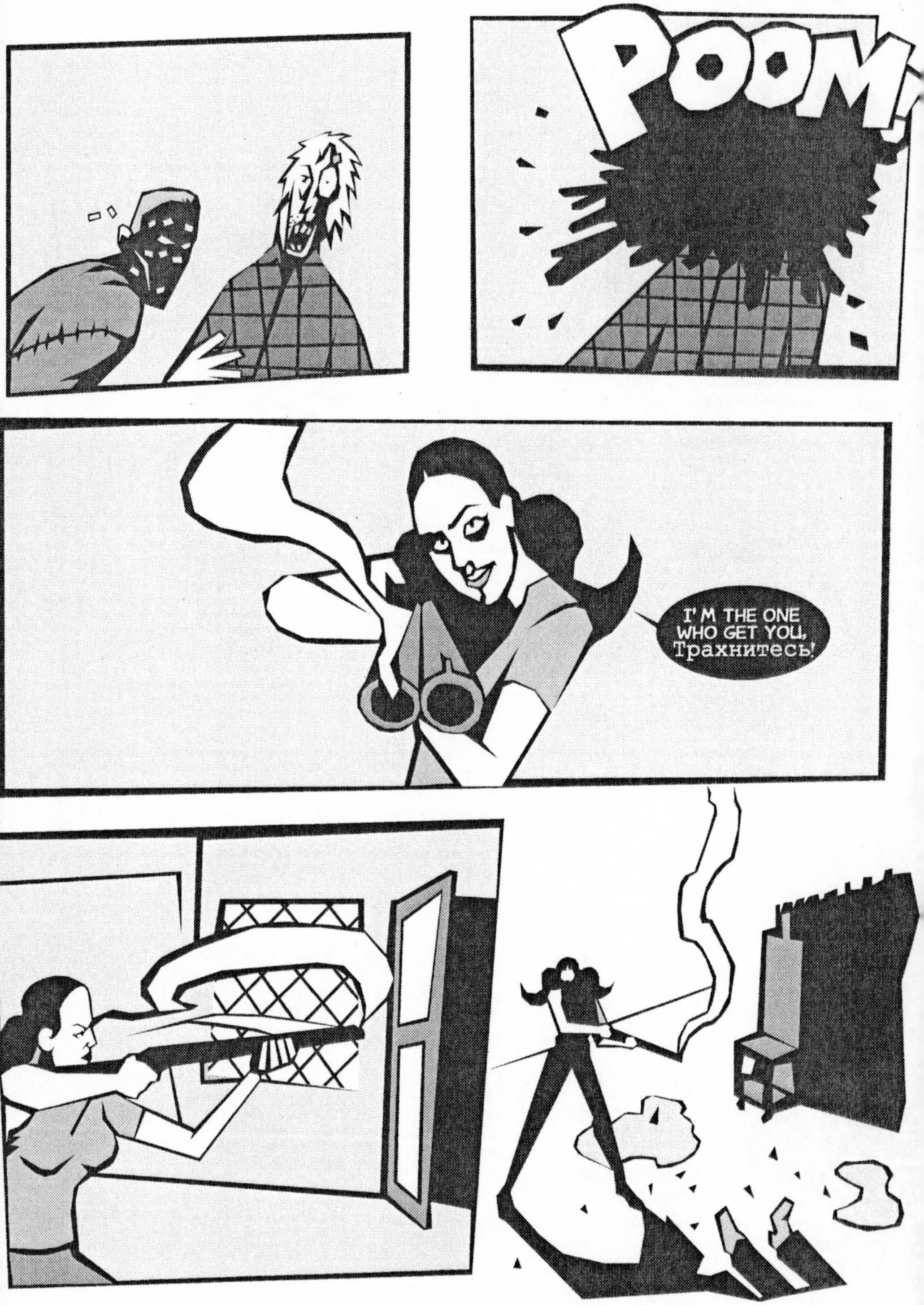
POOM!
I'M THE ONE WHO GET YOU, Трахнитесь!

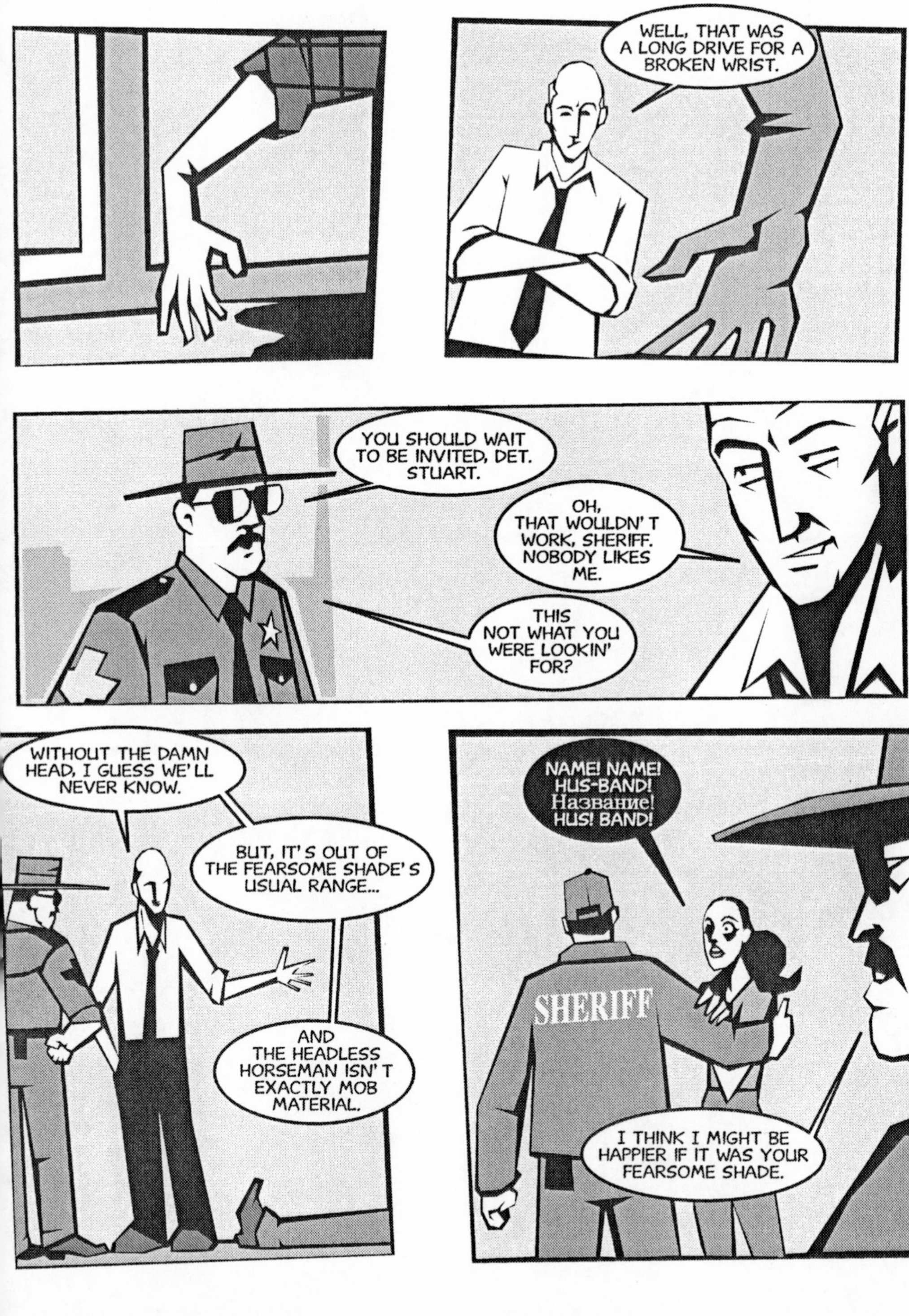
WELL, THAT WAS A LONG DRIVE FOR A BROKEN WRIST.
YOU SHOULD WAIT TO BE INVITED, DET. STUART.
OH, THAT WOULDN'T WORK, SHERIFF. NOBODY LIKES ME.
THIS NOT WHAT YOU WERE LOOKIN' FOR?
WITHOUT THE DAMN HEAD, I GUESS WE'LL NEVER KNOW.
BUT, IT'S OUT OF THE FEARSOME SHADE'S USUAL RANGE...
AND THE HEADLESS HORSEMAN ISN'T EXACTLY MOB MATERIAL.
NAME! NAME! HUS-BAND! Название! HUS! BAND!
SHERIFF
I THINK I MIGHT BE HAPPIER IF IT WAS YOUR FEARSOME SHADE.

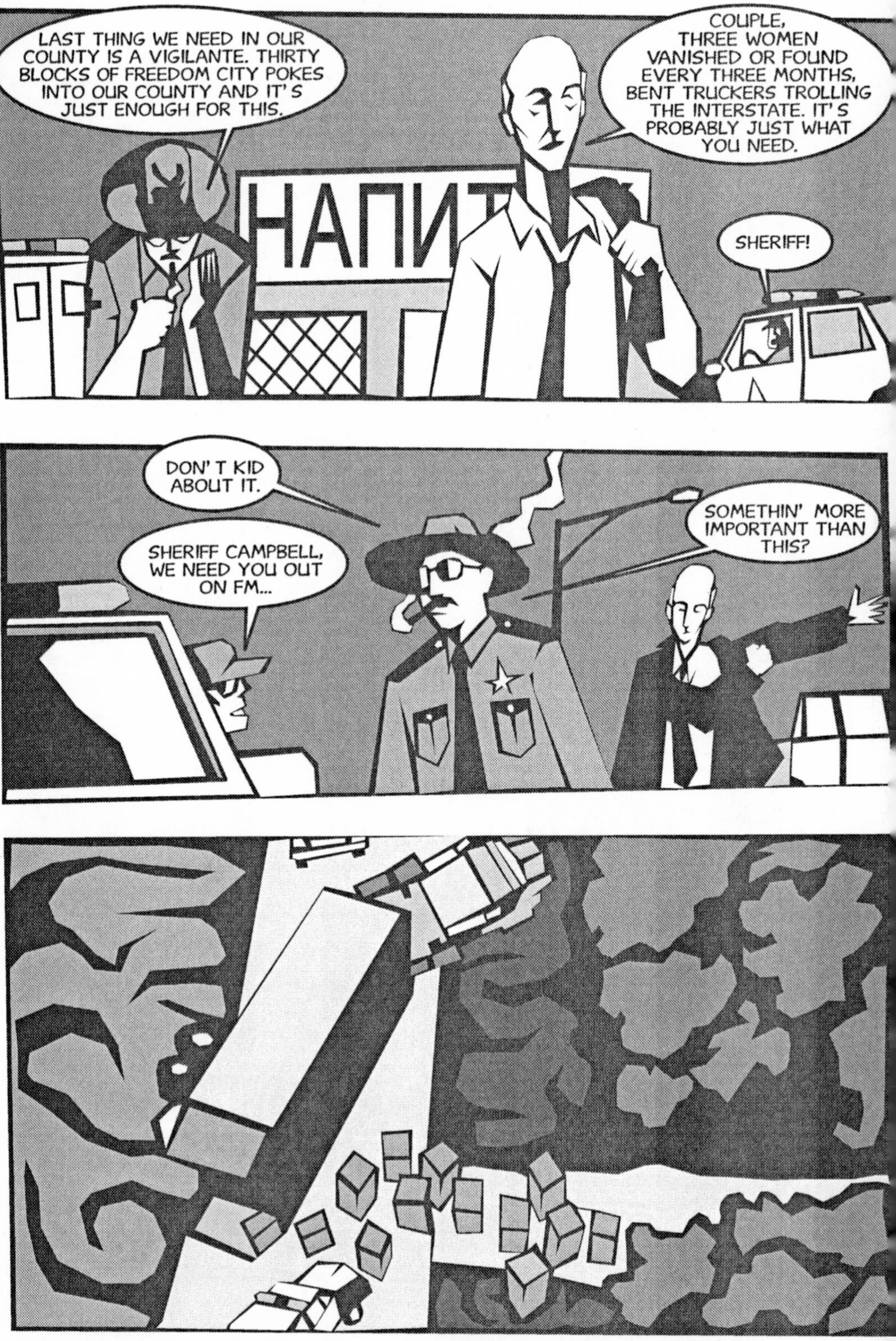
LAST THING WE NEED IN OUR COUNTY IS A VIGILANTE. THIRTY BLOCKS OF FREEDOM CITY POKES INTO OUR COUNTY AND IT'S JUST ENOUGH FOR THIS.
COUPLE, THREE WOMEN VANISHED OR FOUND EVERY THREE MONTHS, BENT TRUCKERS TROLLING THE INTERSTATE. IT'S PROBABLY JUST WHAT YOU NEED.
HANIT
SHERIFF!
DON'T KID ABOUT IT.
SHERIFF CAMPBELL, WE NEED YOU OUT ON FM...
SOMETHIN' MORE IMPORTANT THAN THIS?

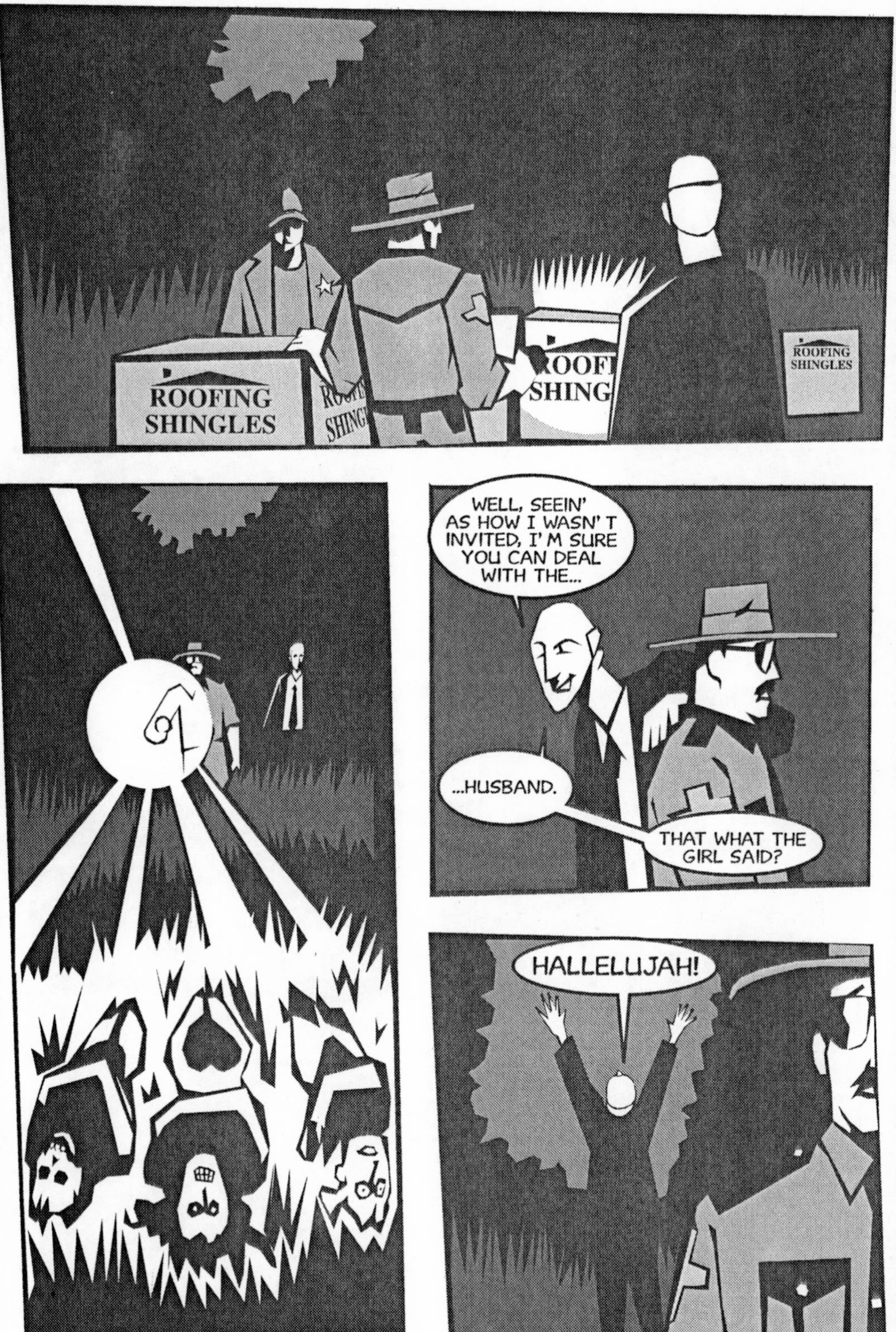
ROOFING SHINGLES
ROOFING SHINGLES
WELL, SEEIN' AS HOW I WASN'T INVITED, I'M SURE YOU CAN DEAL WITH THE...
...HUSBAND.
THAT WHAT THE GIRL SAID?
HALLELUJAH!

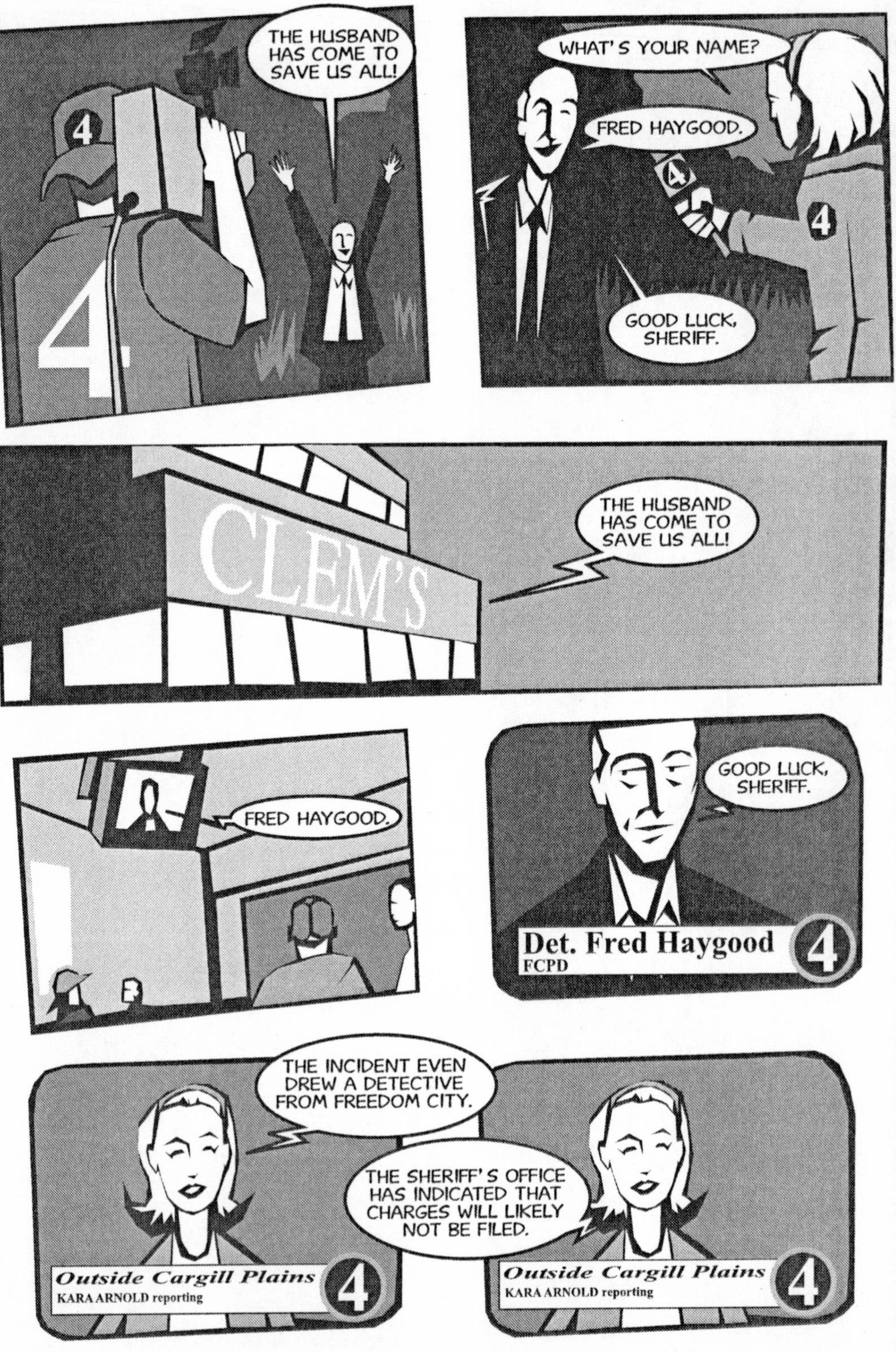
THE HUSBAND HAS COME TO SAVE US ALL!
WHAT'S YOUR NAME?
FRED HAYGOOD.
GOOD LUCK, SHERIFF.
CLEM'S
THE HUSBAND HAS COME TO SAVE US ALL!
FRED HAYGOOD.
GOOD LUCK, SHERIFF.
Det. Fred Haygood
FCPD
THE INCIDENT EVEN DREW A DETECTIVE FROM FREEDOM CITY.
Outside Cargill Plains
KARA ARNOLD reporting
THE SHERIFF'S OFFICE HAS INDICATED THAT CHARGES WILL LIKELY NOT BE FILED.
Outside Cargill Plains
KARA ARNOLD reporting

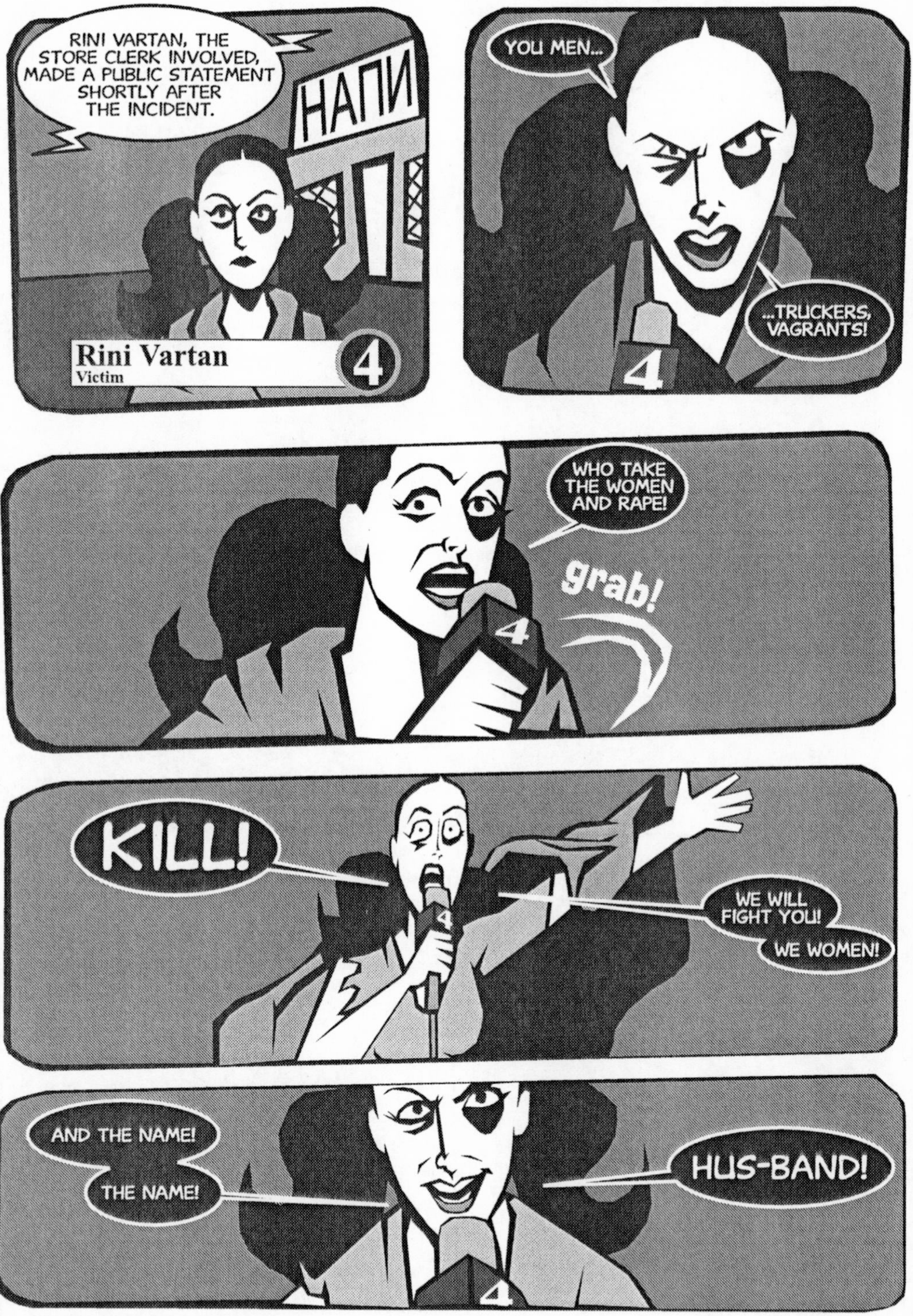
RINI VARTAN, THE STORE CLERK INVOLVED, MADE A PUBLIC STATEMENT SHORTLY AFTER THE INCIDENT.
НАПИ
Rini Vartan
Victim
4
YOU MEN...
...TRUCKERS, VAGRANTS!
4
WHO TAKE THE WOMEN AND RAPE!
grab!
4
KILL!
WE WILL FIGHT YOU!
WE WOMEN!
4
AND THE NAME!
THE NAME!
HUS-BAND!
4

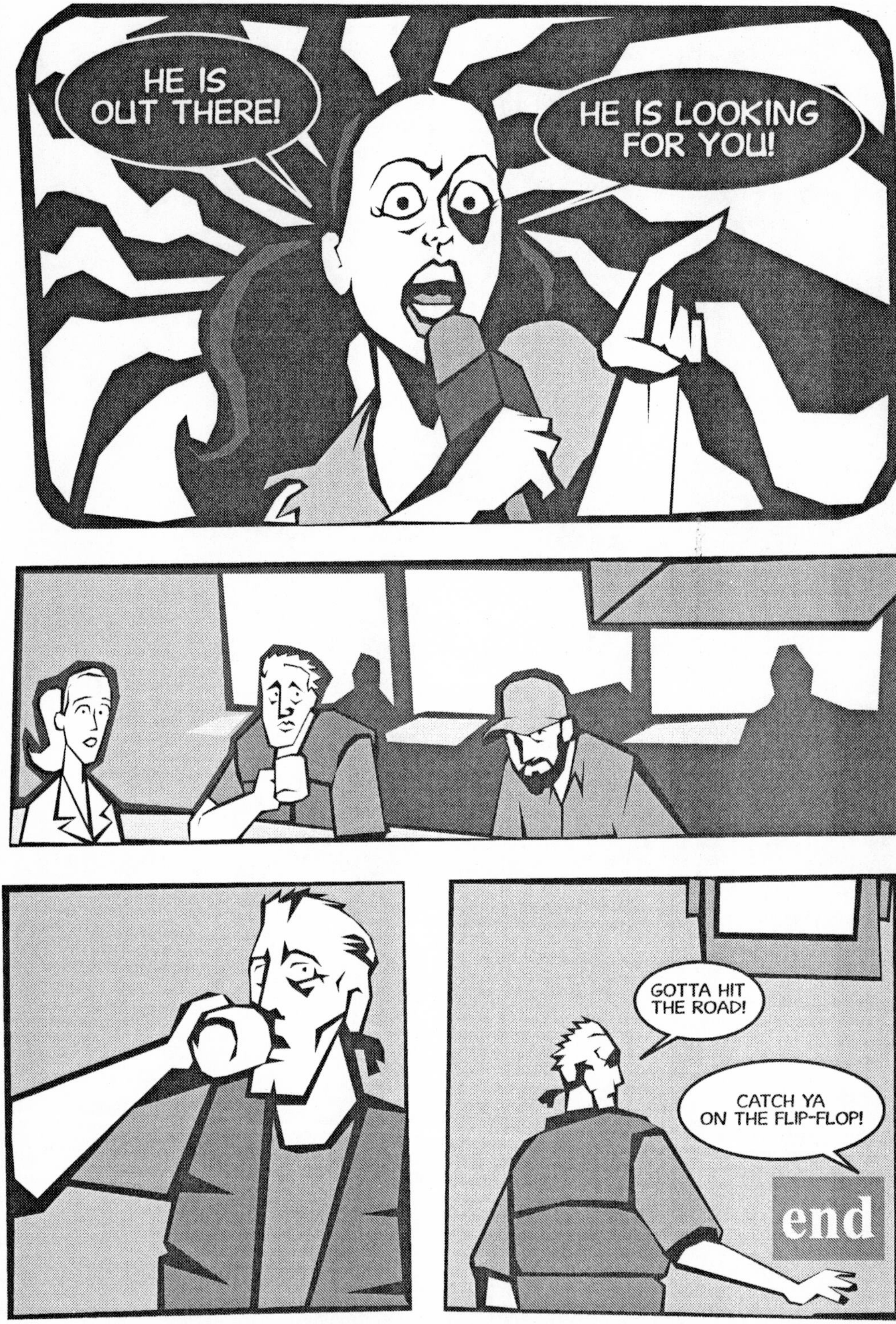
HE IS OUT THERE!
HE IS LOOKING FOR YOU!
GOTTA HIT THE ROAD!
CATCH YA ON THE FLIP-FLOP!
end

CLEM'S
GAS

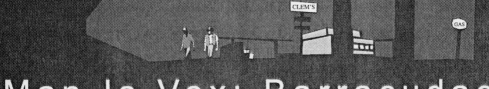

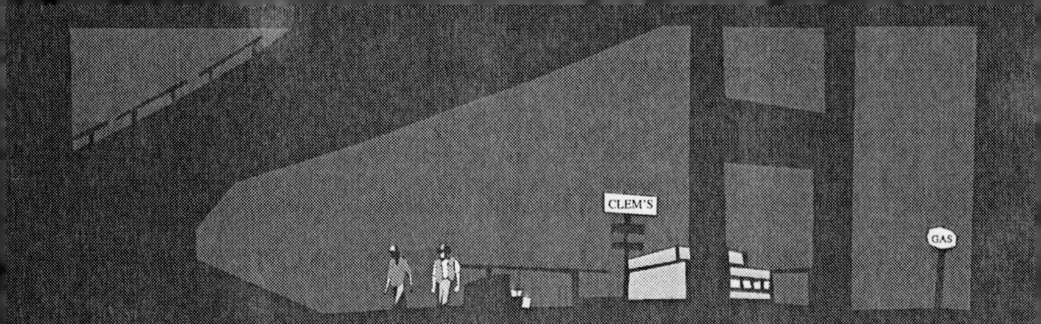

Man Is Vox: Barracudae

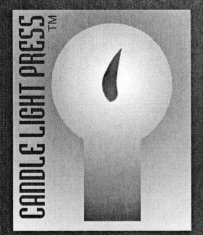

When you talk to yourself all day, you are your own best friend. But even friends fight once in a while. And when you're a bone-breaking psychopath who talks to his underwear, having a friend to see you through the rough times is important. Unless your new friend's a psychopath too.

Join the Fearsome Shade on the road to madness and the truckstops that mark the distance from here to the unthinkable.

CANDLE LIGHT PRESS™

more comics @ www.candlelightpress.com

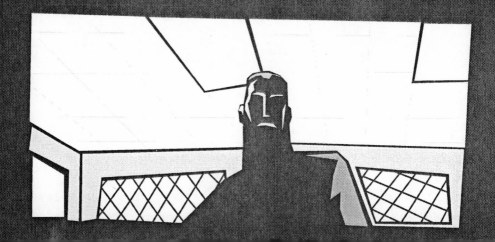

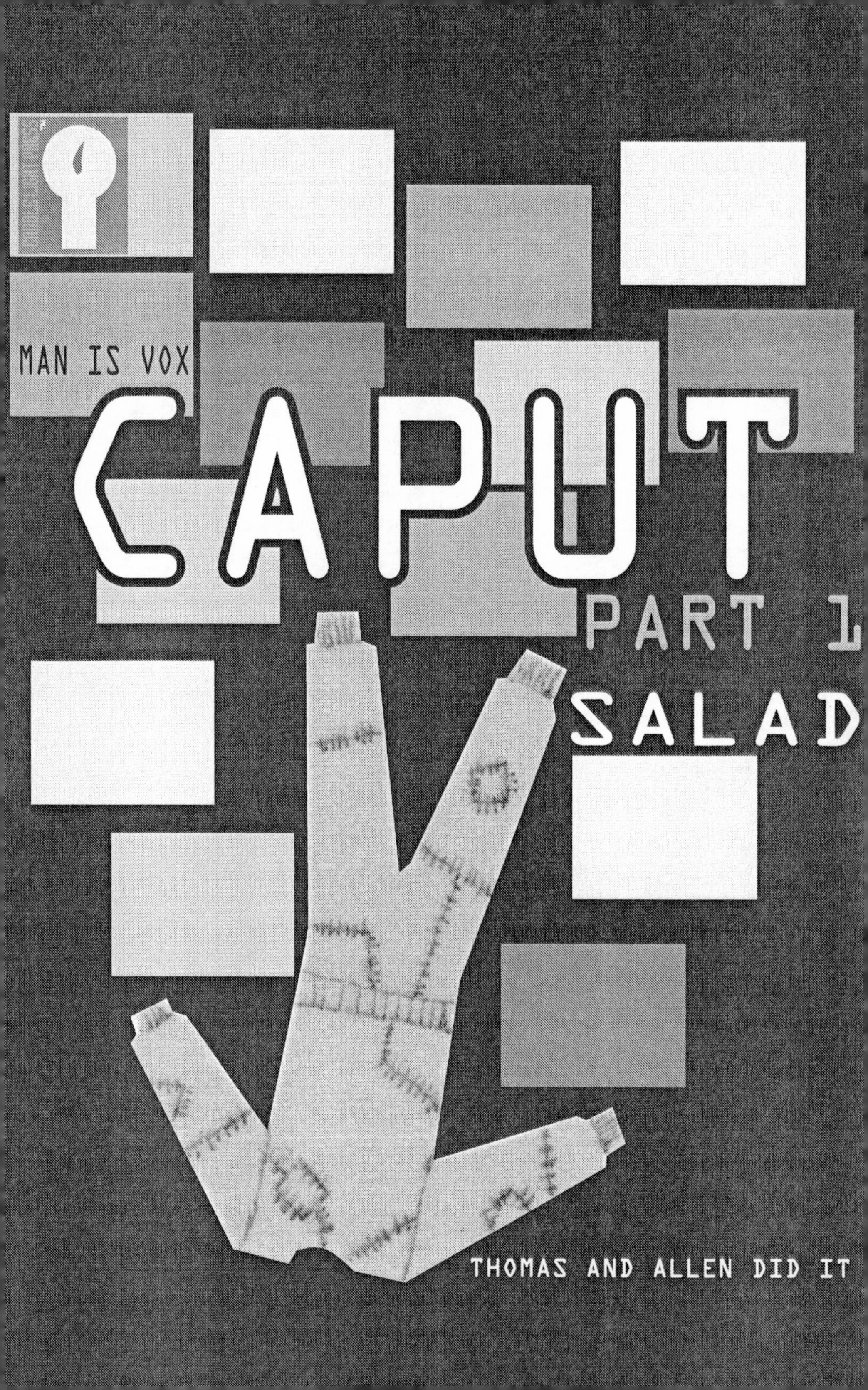
MAN IS VOX
CAPUT
PART 1
SALAD
THOMAS AND ALLEN DID IT

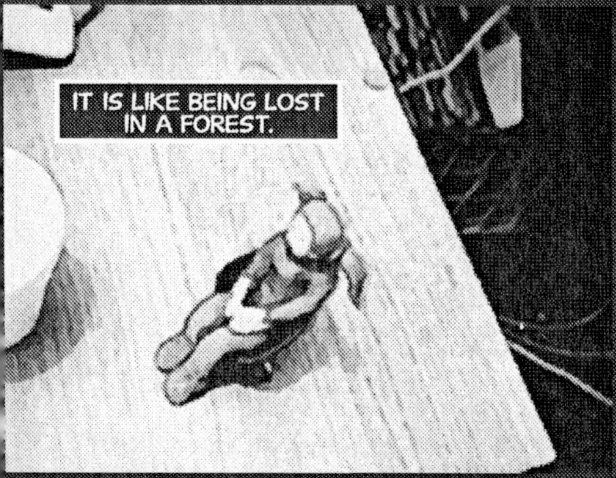
IT IS LIKE BEING LOST IN A FOREST.

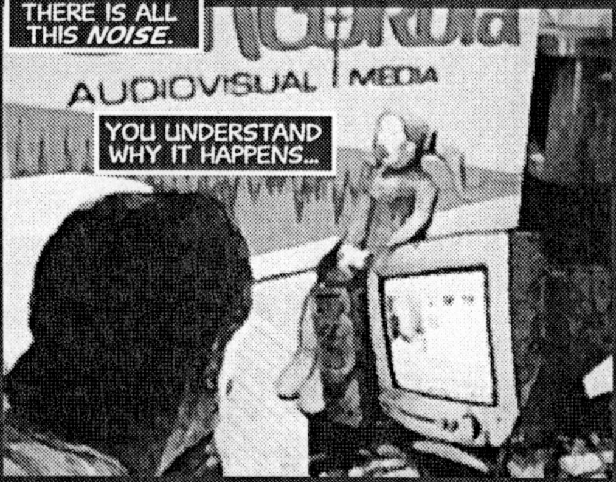
THERE IS ALL THIS *NOISE*.
AUDIOVISUAL MEDIA
YOU UNDERSTAND WHY IT HAPPENS...

MAN IS VOX: CAPUT: PART 1: SALAD

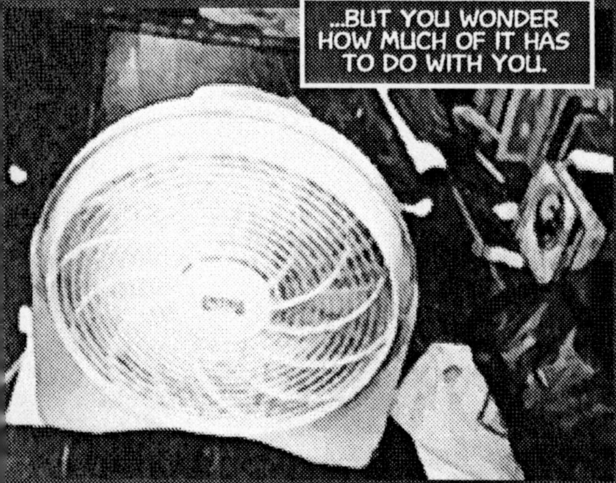
...BUT YOU WONDER HOW MUCH OF IT HAS TO DO WITH YOU.

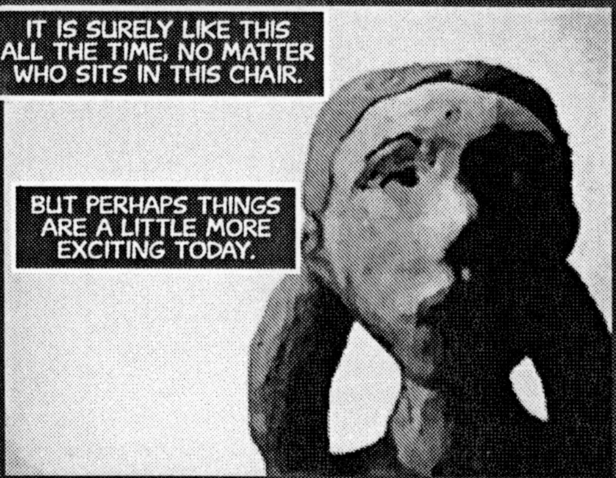
IT IS SURELY LIKE THIS ALL THE TIME, NO MATTER WHO SITS IN THIS CHAIR.
BUT PERHAPS THINGS ARE A LITTLE MORE EXCITING TODAY.

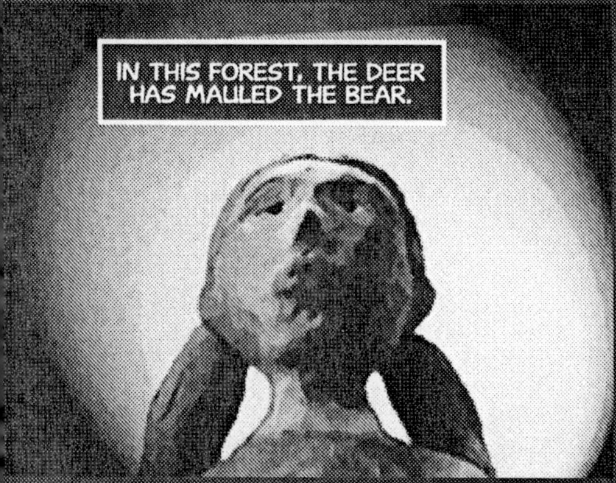
IN THIS FOREST, THE DEER HAS MAULED THE BEAR.

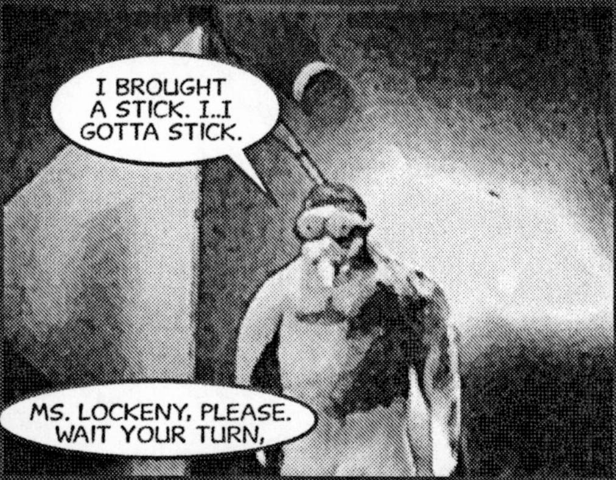
I BROUGHT A STICK. I..I GOTTA STICK.
MS. LOCKENY, PLEASE. WAIT YOUR TURN,

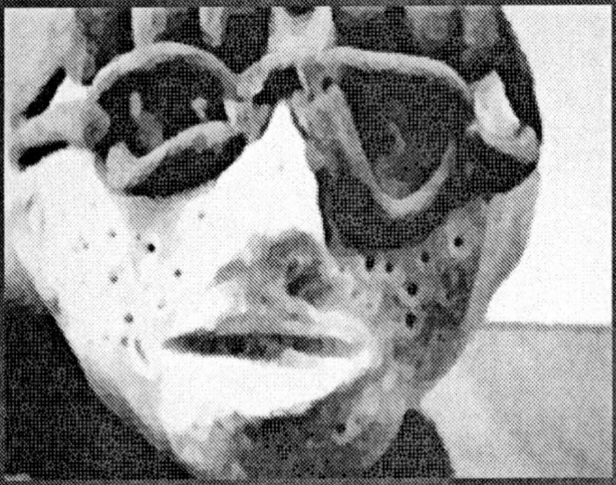

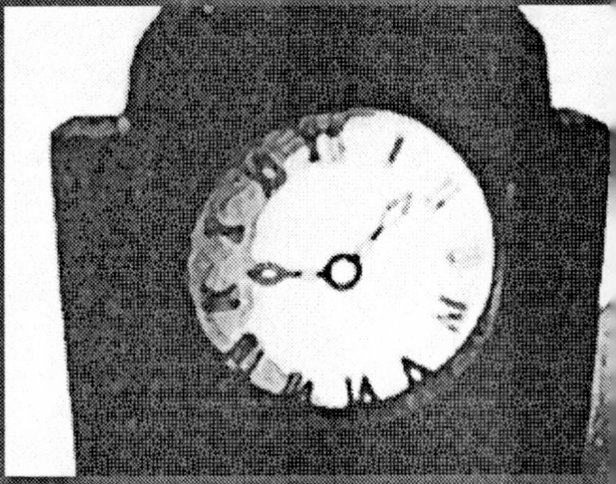

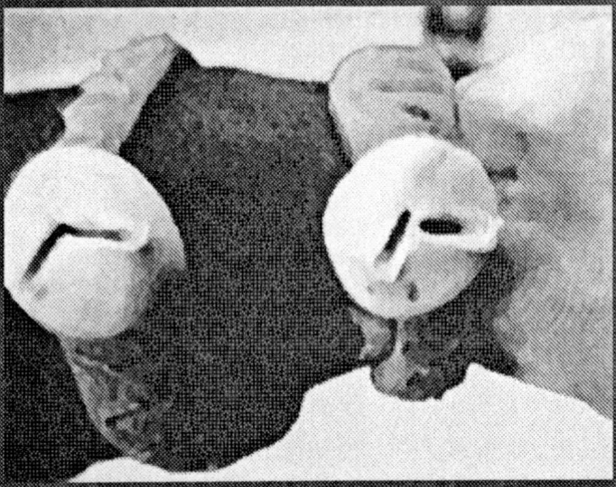

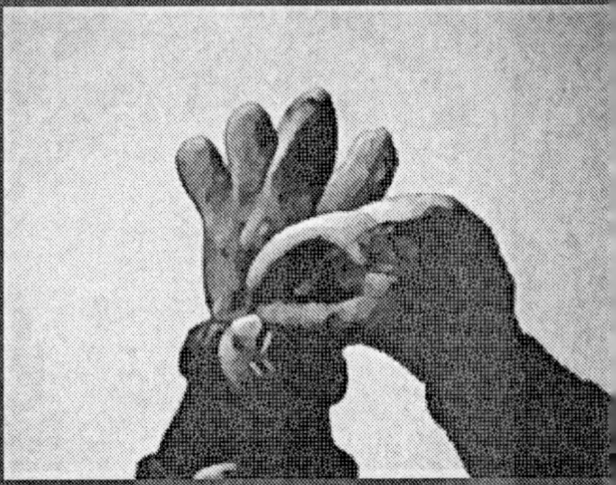

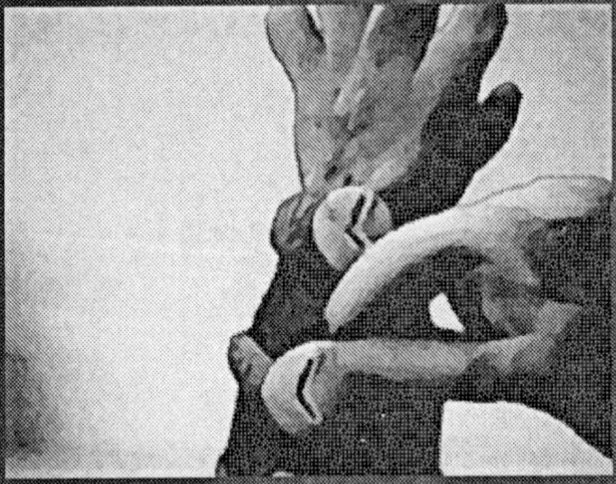

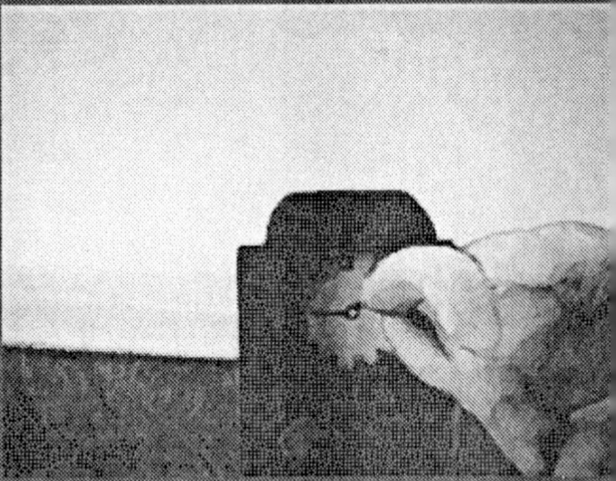

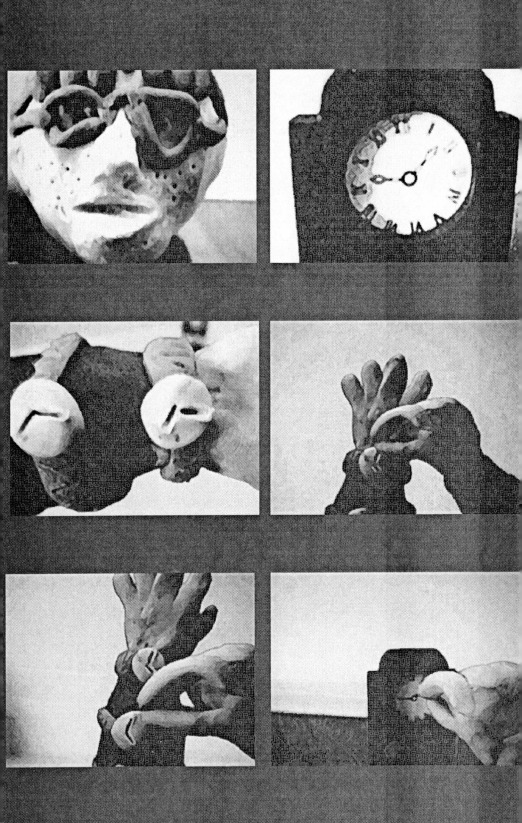

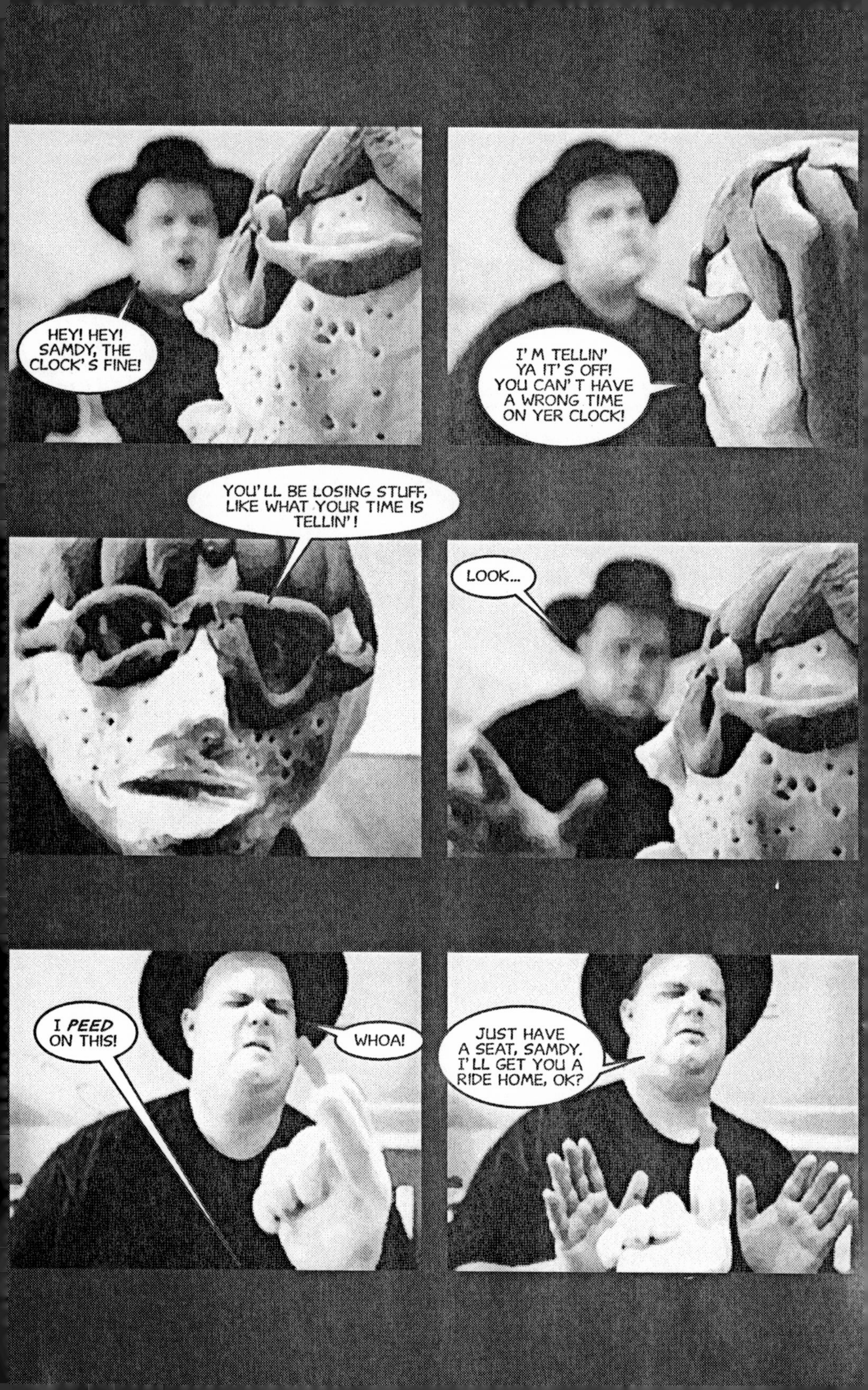
HEY! HEY! SAMDY, THE CLOCK'S FINE!
I'M TELLIN' YA IT'S OFF! YOU CAN'T HAVE A WRONG TIME ON YER CLOCK!
YOU'LL BE LOSING STUFF, LIKE WHAT YOUR TIME IS TELLIN'!
LOOK...
I *PEED* ON THIS!
WHOA!
JUST HAVE A SEAT, SAMDY. I'LL GET YOU A RIDE HOME, OK?

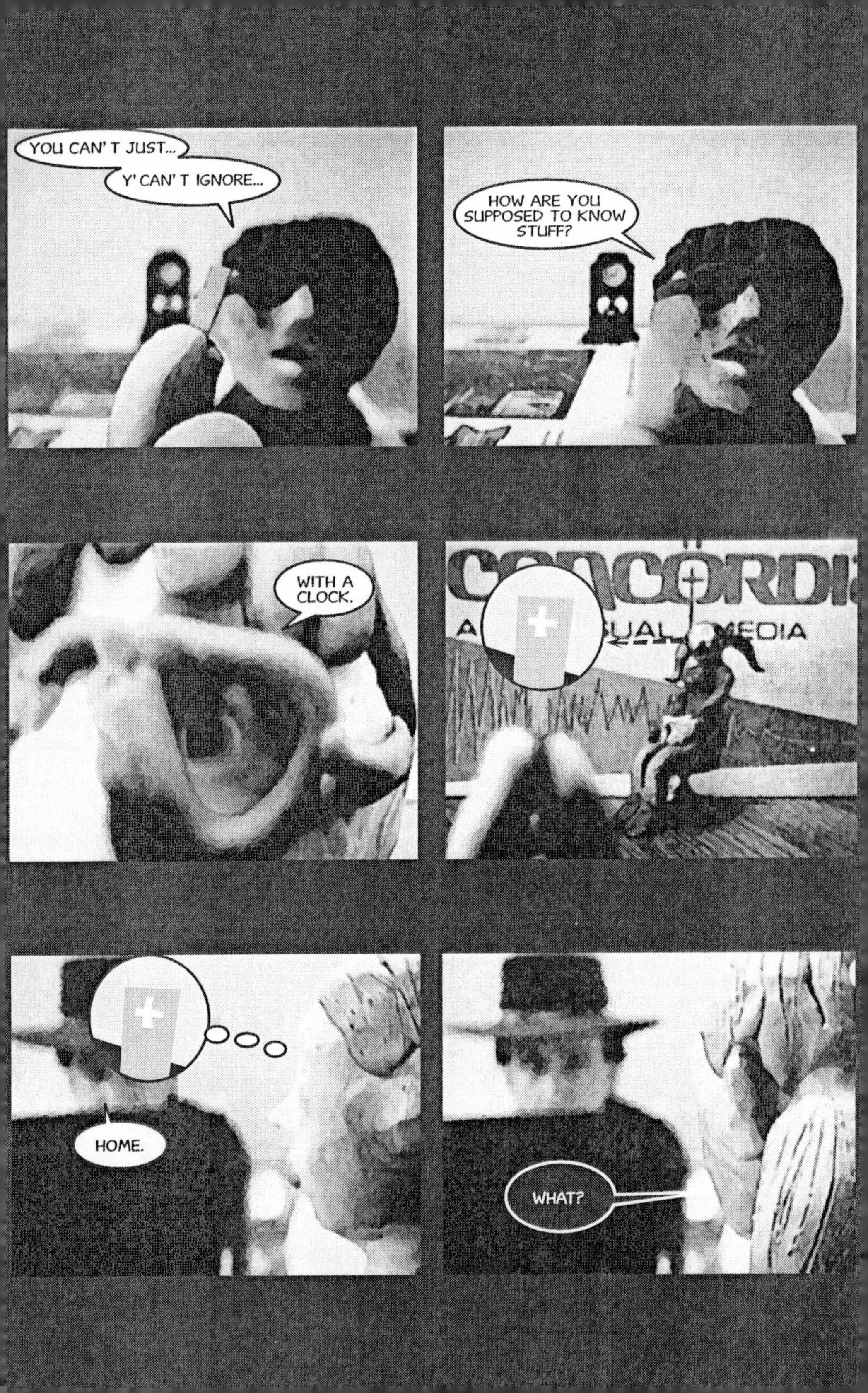
YOU CAN'T JUST...
Y'CAN'T IGNORE...
HOW ARE YOU SUPPOSED TO KNOW STUFF?
WITH A CLOCK.
HOME.
WHAT?

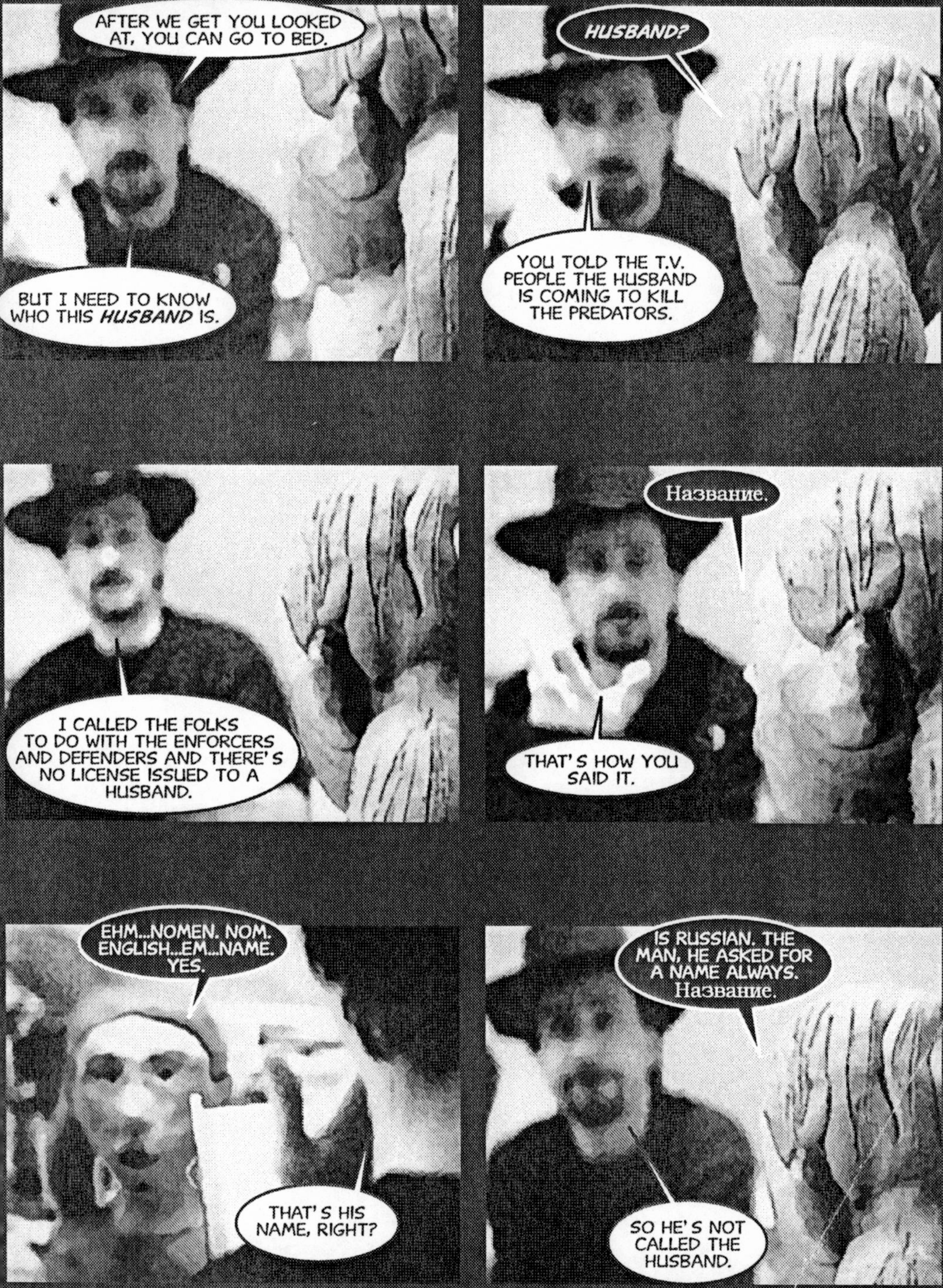
AFTER WE GET YOU LOOKED AT, YOU CAN GO TO BED.
BUT I NEED TO KNOW WHO THIS *HUSBAND* IS.
HUSBAND?
YOU TOLD THE T.V. PEOPLE THE HUSBAND IS COMING TO KILL THE PREDATORS.
I CALLED THE FOLKS TO DO WITH THE ENFORCERS AND DEFENDERS AND THERE'S NO LICENSE ISSUED TO A HUSBAND.
Название.
THAT'S HOW YOU SAID IT.
EHM...NOMEN. NOM. ENGLISH...EM...NAME. YES.
THAT'S HIS NAME, RIGHT?
IS RUSSIAN. THE MAN, HE ASKED FOR A NAME ALWAYS. Название.
SO HE'S NOT CALLED THE HUSBAND.

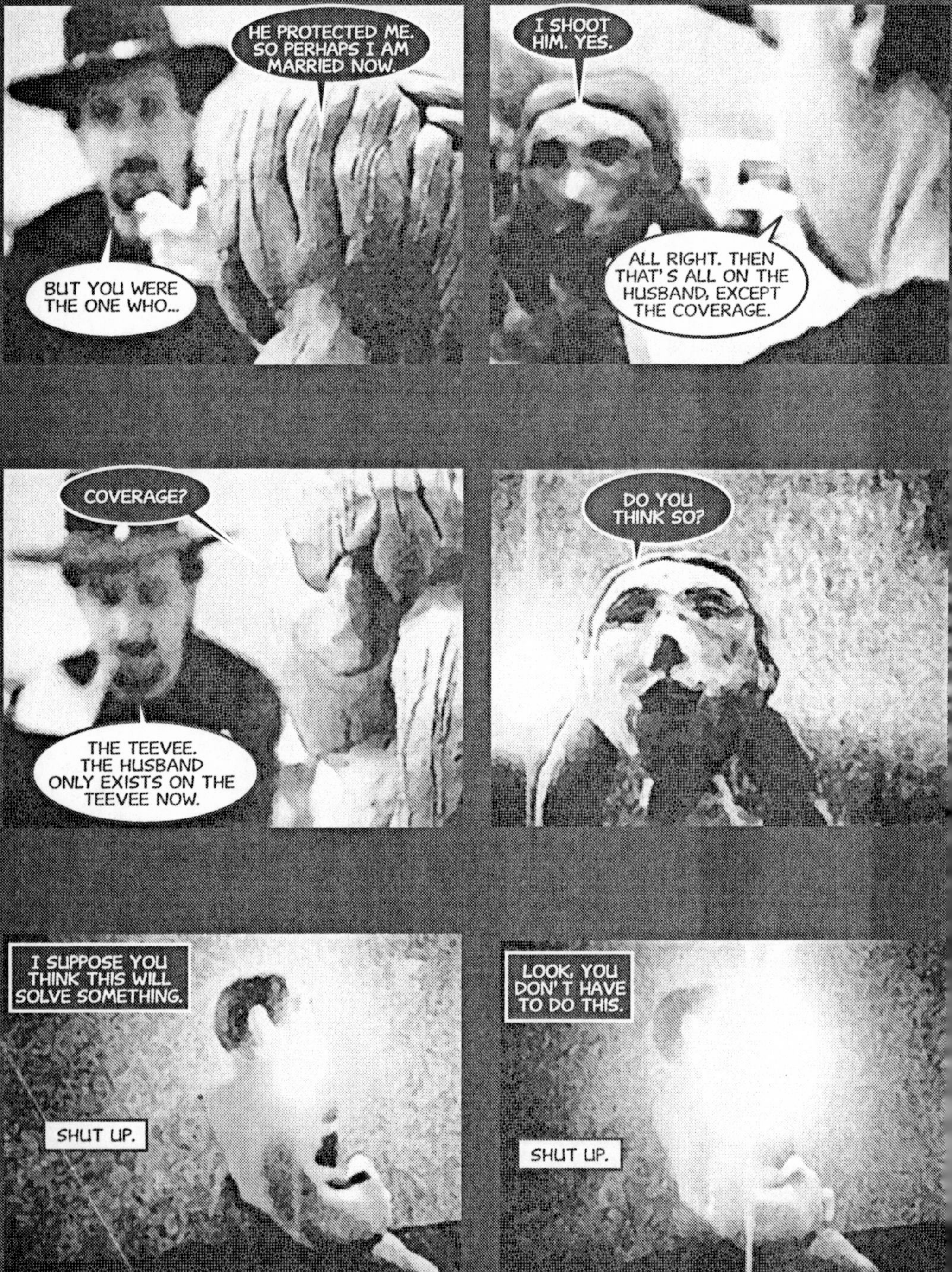
HE PROTECTED ME. SO PERHAPS I AM MARRIED NOW.
BUT YOU WERE THE ONE WHO...
I SHOOT HIM. YES.
ALL RIGHT. THEN THAT'S ALL ON THE HUSBAND, EXCEPT THE COVERAGE.
COVERAGE?
THE TEEVEE. THE HUSBAND ONLY EXISTS ON THE TEEVEE NOW.
DO YOU THINK SO?
I SUPPOSE YOU THINK THIS WILL SOLVE SOMETHING.
SHUT UP.
LOOK, YOU DON'T HAVE TO DO THIS.
SHUT UP.

IT'S NOT YOUR FAULT. YOU JUST SWALLOWED A TOTAL IDIOT'S WORLD-VIEW. COULD HAPPEN TO--
THE HUSBAND.
HELLO, HUSBAND.
HELLO, I'M THE...I AM THE HUSBAND.
WILL YOU BE MY BRIDE?
I TAKE YOU AS MY BRIDE.
I TAKE YOU AS MY WIFE.
HELLO, NICE TO MEET YOU.

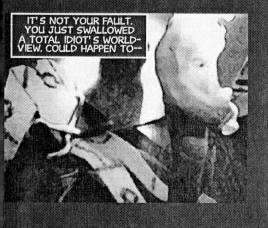

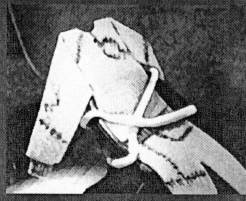

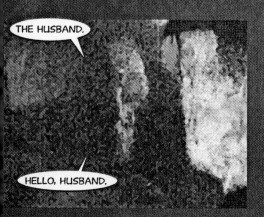

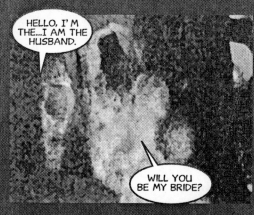

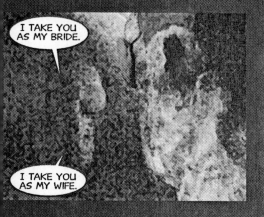

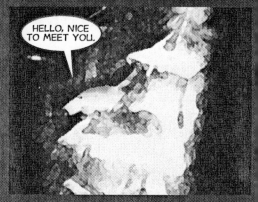

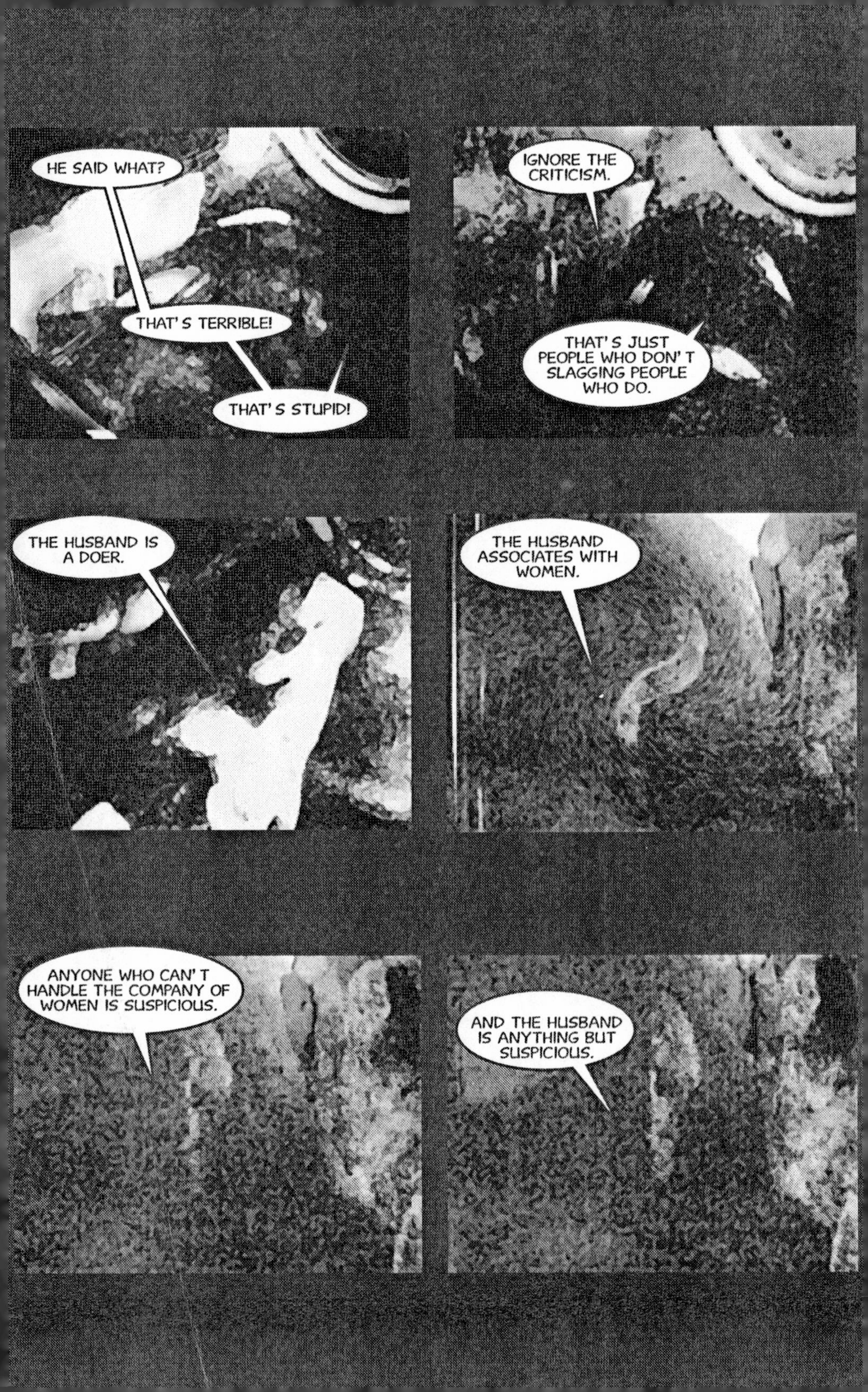
HE SAID WHAT?
THAT'S TERRIBLE!
THAT'S STUPID!
IGNORE THE CRITICISM.
THAT'S JUST PEOPLE WHO DON'T SLAGGING PEOPLE WHO DO.
THE HUSBAND IS A DOER.
THE HUSBAND ASSOCIATES WITH WOMEN.
ANYONE WHO CAN'T HANDLE THE COMPANY OF WOMEN IS SUSPICIOUS.
AND THE HUSBAND IS ANYTHING BUT SUSPICIOUS.

SWEETCAKES.
YOU...YOU RAPE AND MURDER!
THE HUSBAND IS COMING FOR YOU!
NAME.
NAME.
NAME.

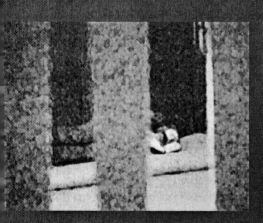

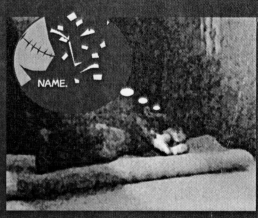

...TO THE, ER, CIRCUMSTANCES.

THE COUNTY ATTORNEY HAS ELECTED NOT TO PROSECUTE YOU.

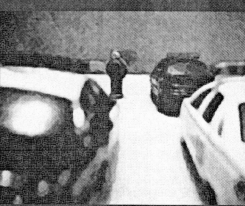

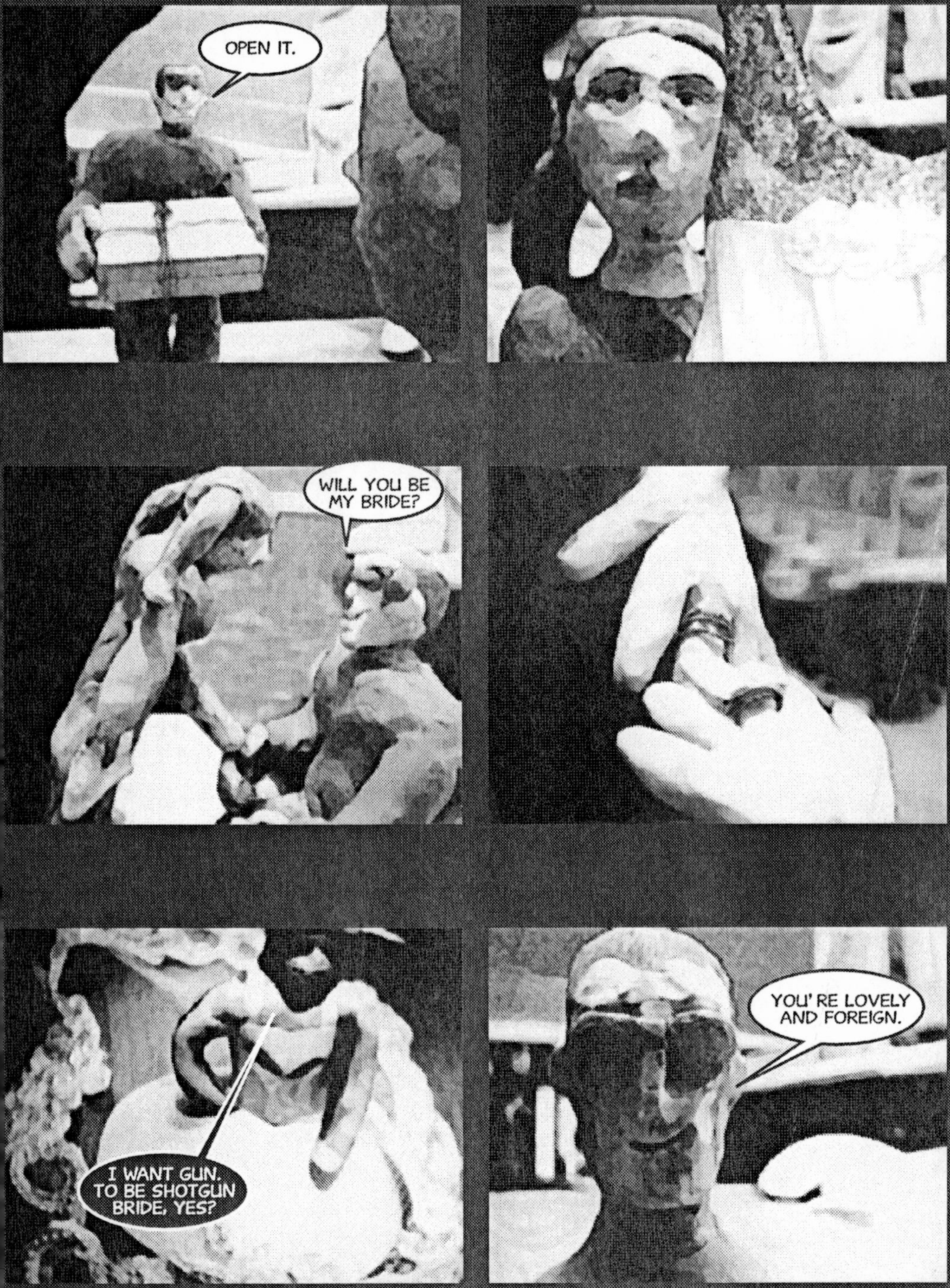
OPEN IT.
WILL YOU BE MY BRIDE?
I WANT GUN. TO BE SHOTGUN BRIDE, YES?
YOU'RE LOVELY AND FOREIGN.

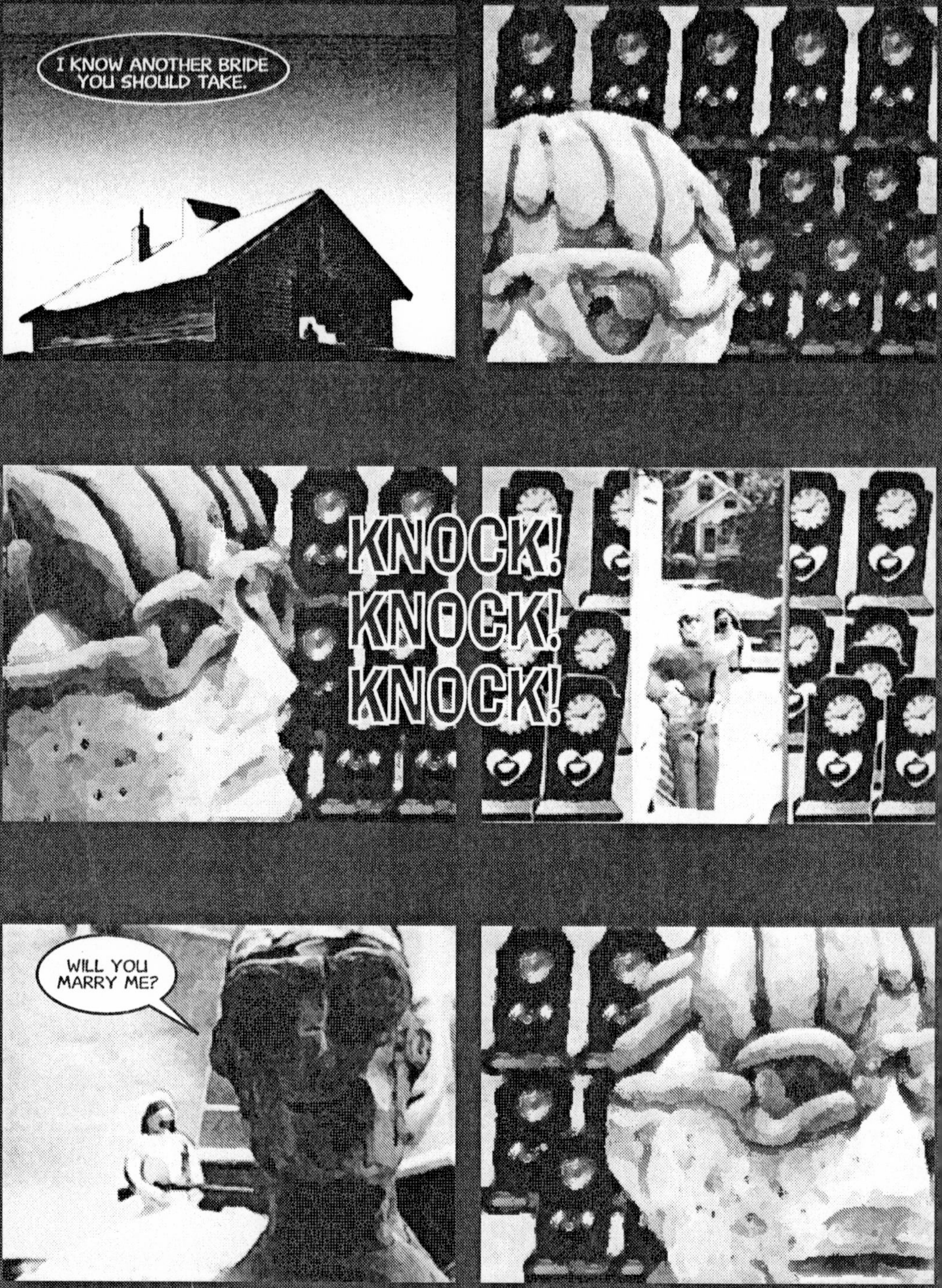
I KNOW ANOTHER BRIDE YOU SHOULD TAKE.
KNOCK! KNOCK! KNOCK!
WILL YOU MARRY ME?

YOU ARE CORDIALLY INVITED TO

THE MARRIAGE

OF

THE HUSBAND (NÉE "THE FEARSOME SHADE")

AND

ALL WOMEN WHO NEED HELP

PART ONE OF <u>CAPUT</u>

When the world's awhirl, and you're not sure if your body's your own anymore, then Man is Vox.

Keep up with the continuing adventures of the Fearsome Shade online at www.candlelightpress.com

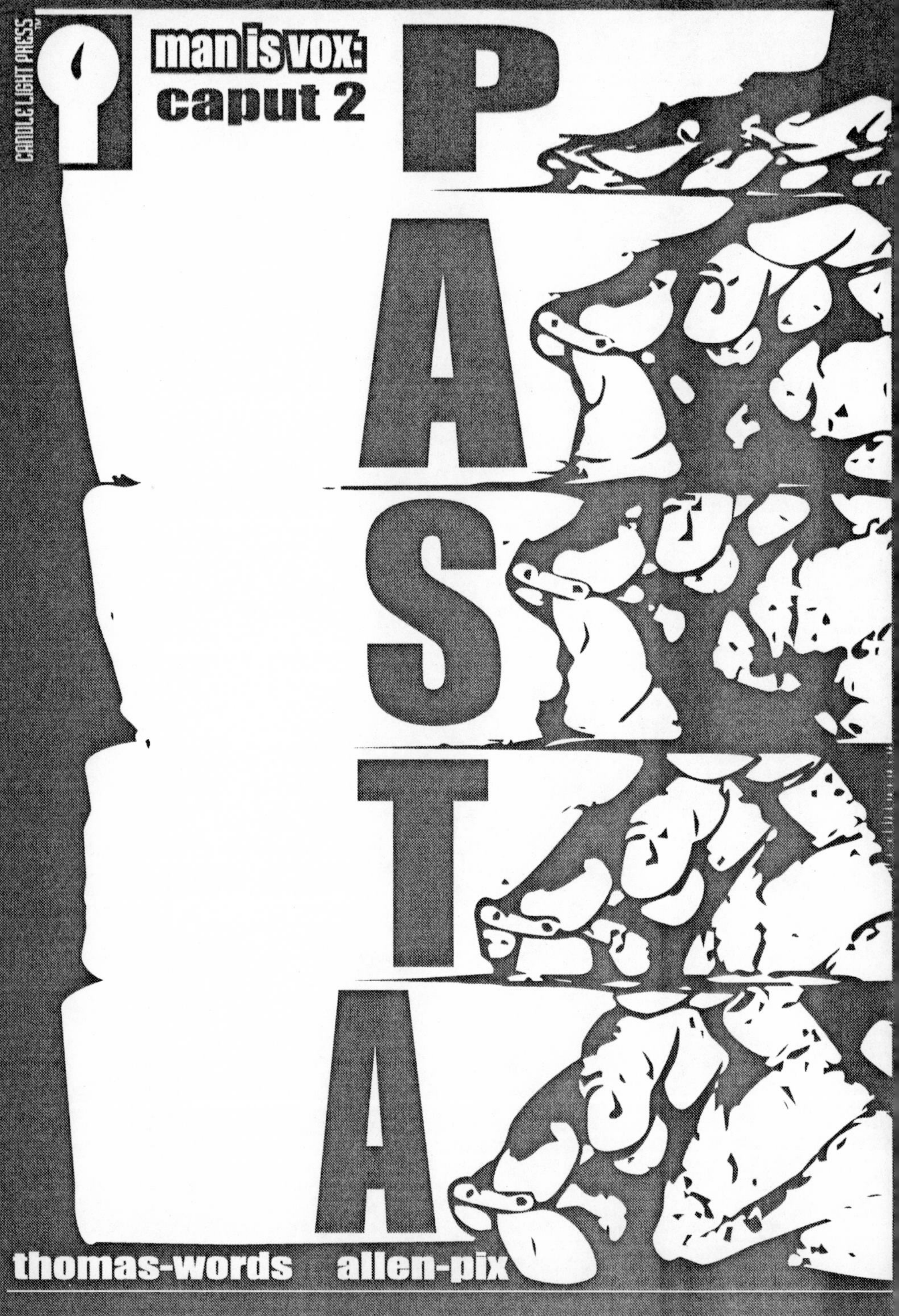
CANDLE LIGHT PRESS
man is vox:
caput 2
PASTA
thomas-words
allen-pix

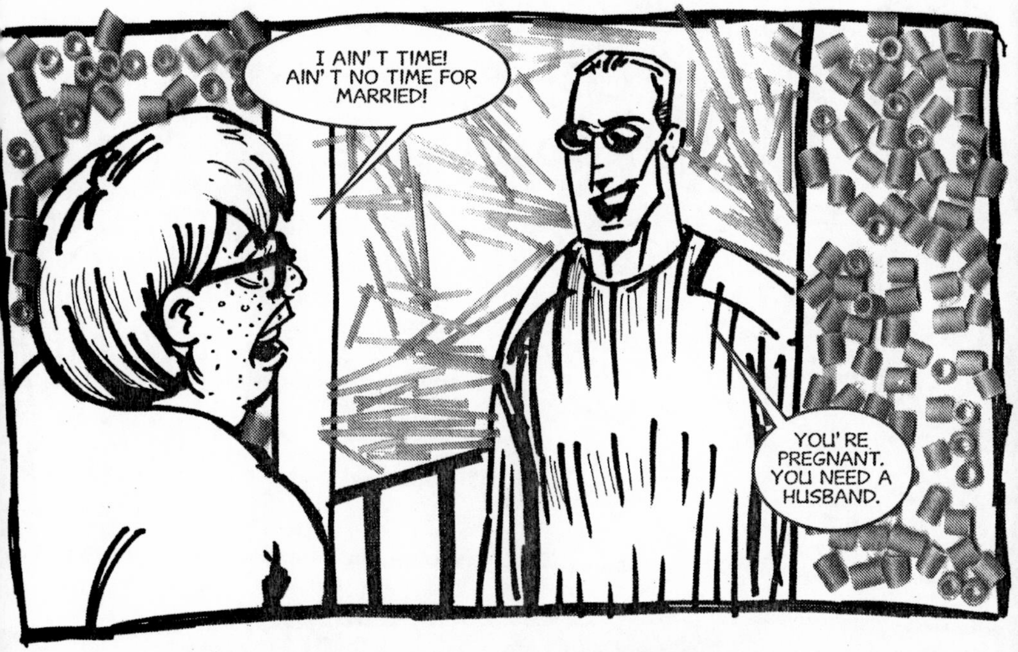
I AIN'T TIME! AIN'T NO TIME FOR MARRIED!
YOU'RE PREGNANT. YOU NEED A HUSBAND.

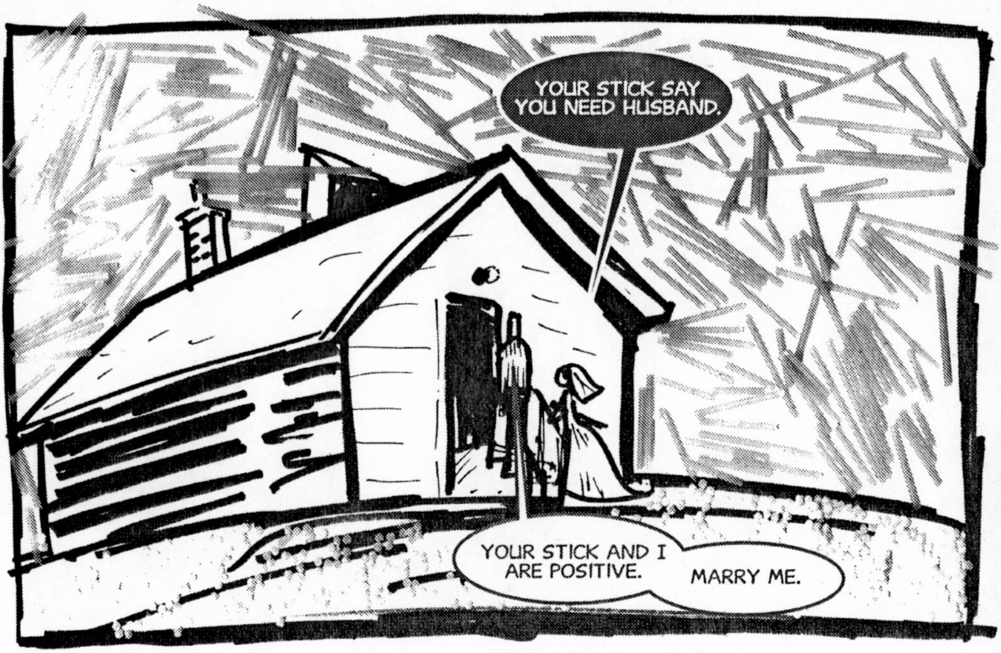
YOUR STICK SAY YOU NEED HUSBAND.
YOUR STICK AND I ARE POSITIVE.
MARRY ME.

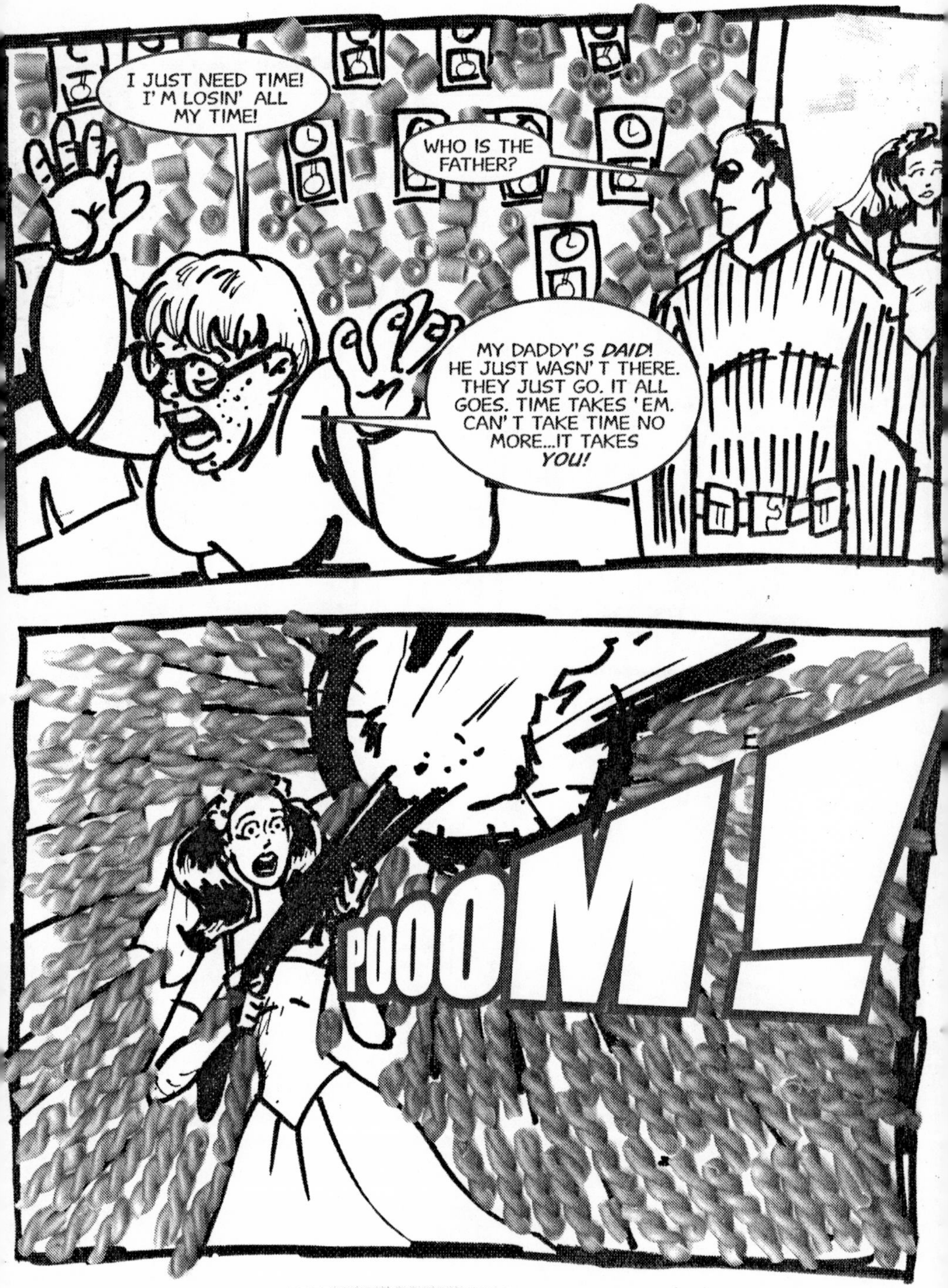
I JUST NEED TIME! I'M LOSIN' ALL MY TIME!
WHO IS THE FATHER?
MY DADDY'S *DAID*! HE JUST WASN'T THERE. THEY JUST GO. IT ALL GOES. TIME TAKES 'EM. CAN'T TAKE TIME NO MORE...IT TAKES *YOU!*
POOOM

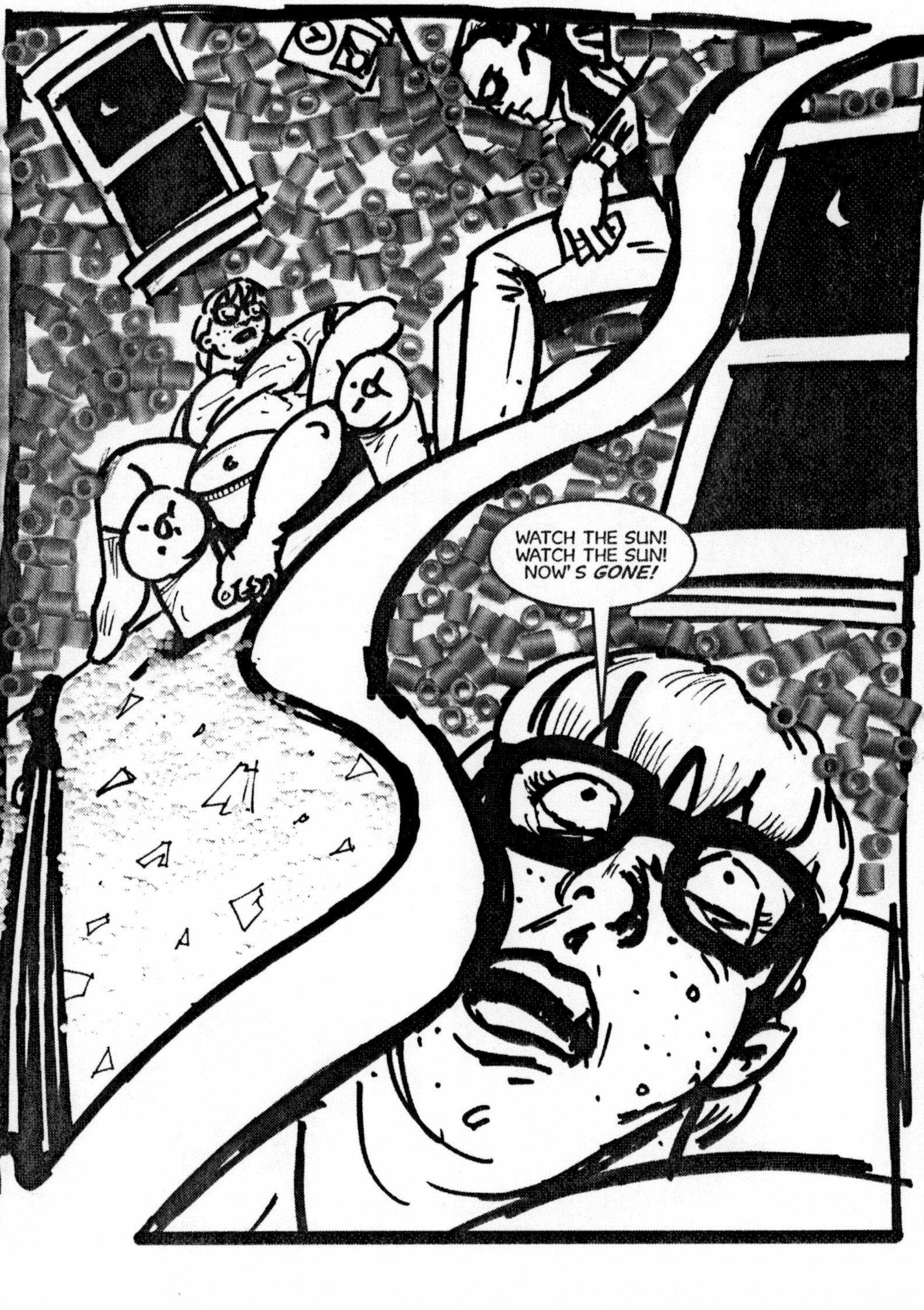
WATCH THE SUN! WATCH THE SUN! NOW'S *GONE!*

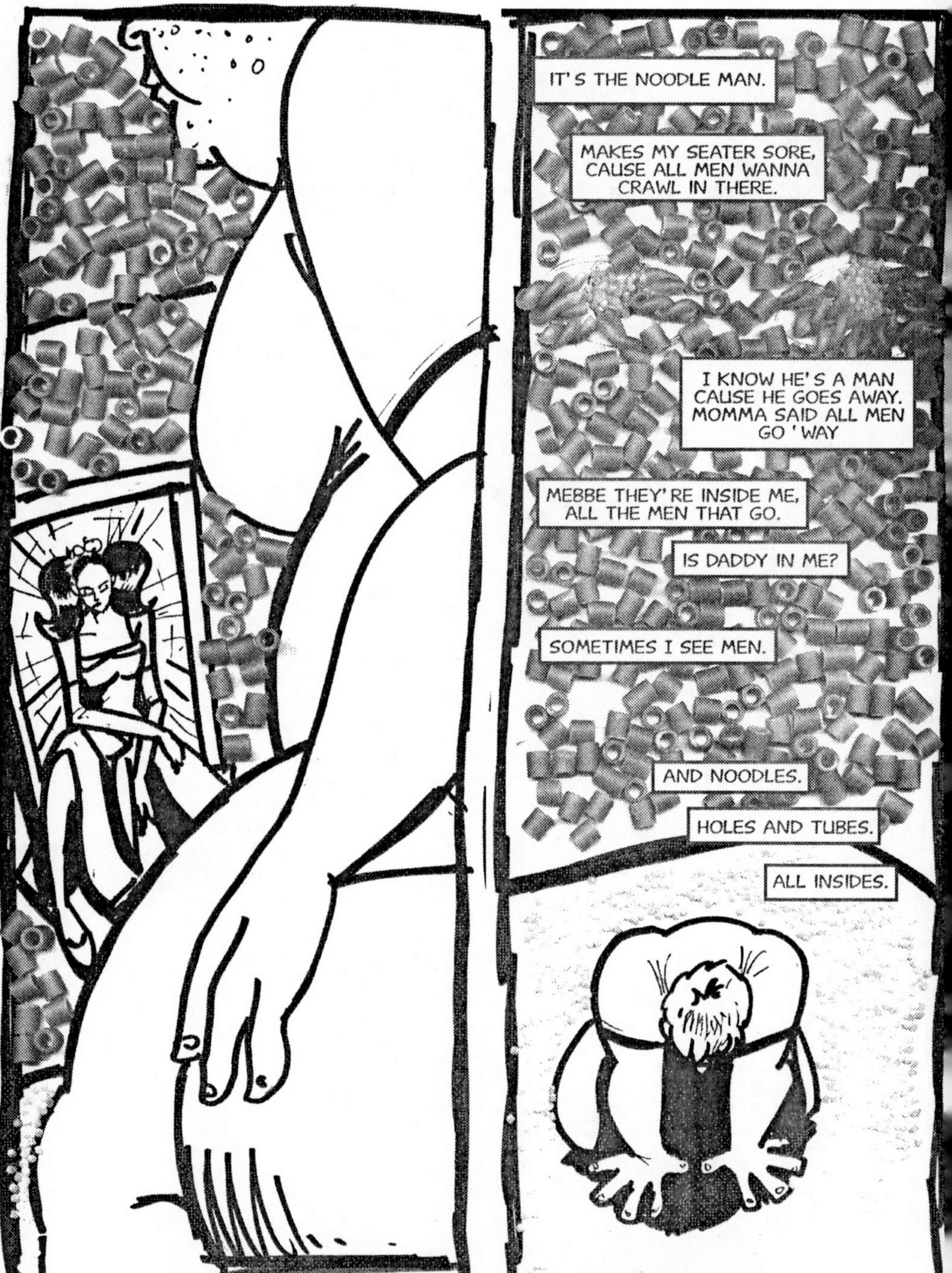
IT'S THE NOODLE MAN.
MAKES MY SEATER SORE, CAUSE ALL MEN WANNA CRAWL IN THERE.
I KNOW HE'S A MAN CAUSE HE GOES AWAY. MOMMA SAID ALL MEN GO 'WAY
MEBBE THEY'RE INSIDE ME, ALL THE MEN THAT GO.
IS DADDY IN ME?
SOMETIMES I SEE MEN.
AND NOODLES.
HOLES AND TUBES.
ALL INSIDES.

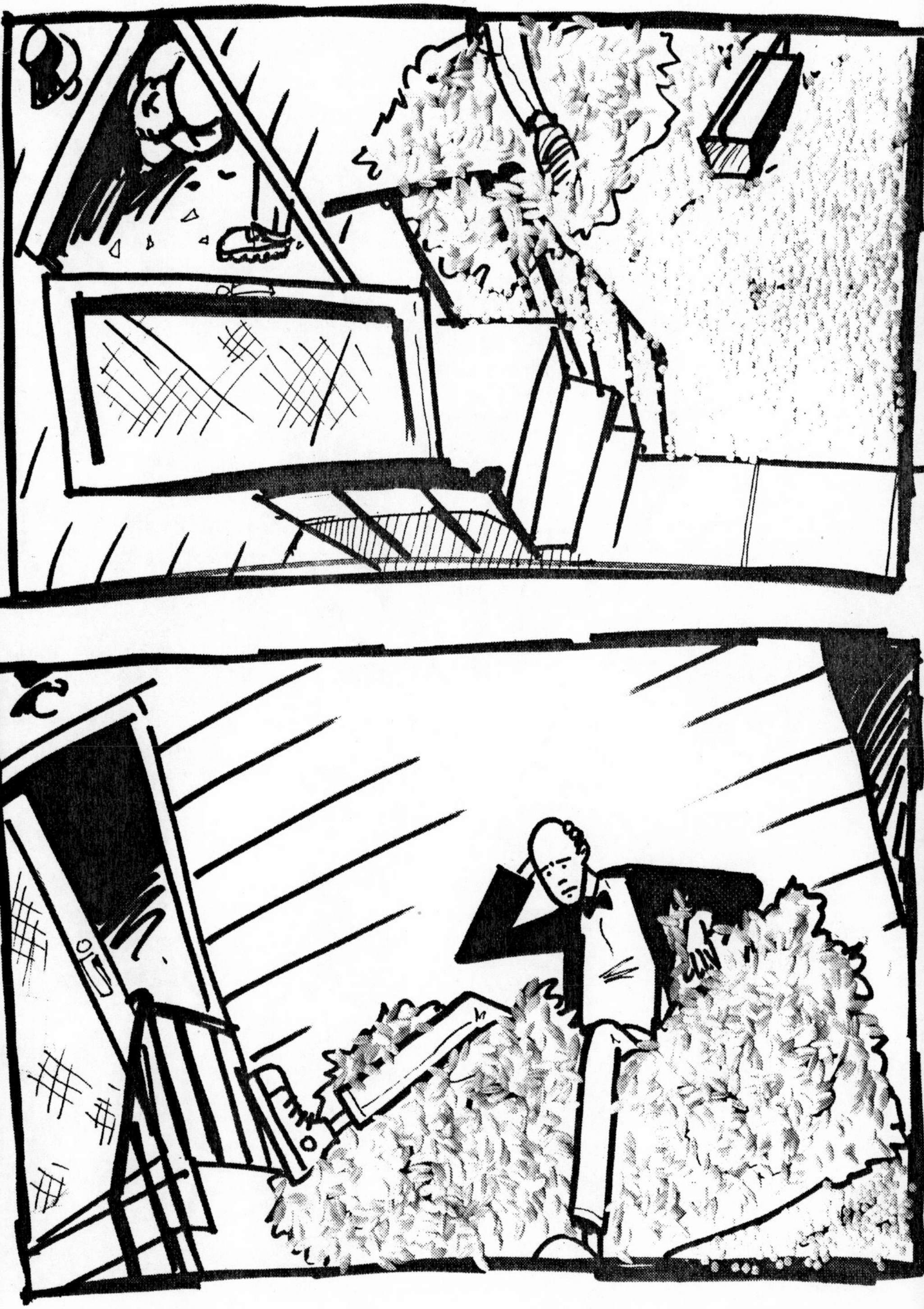

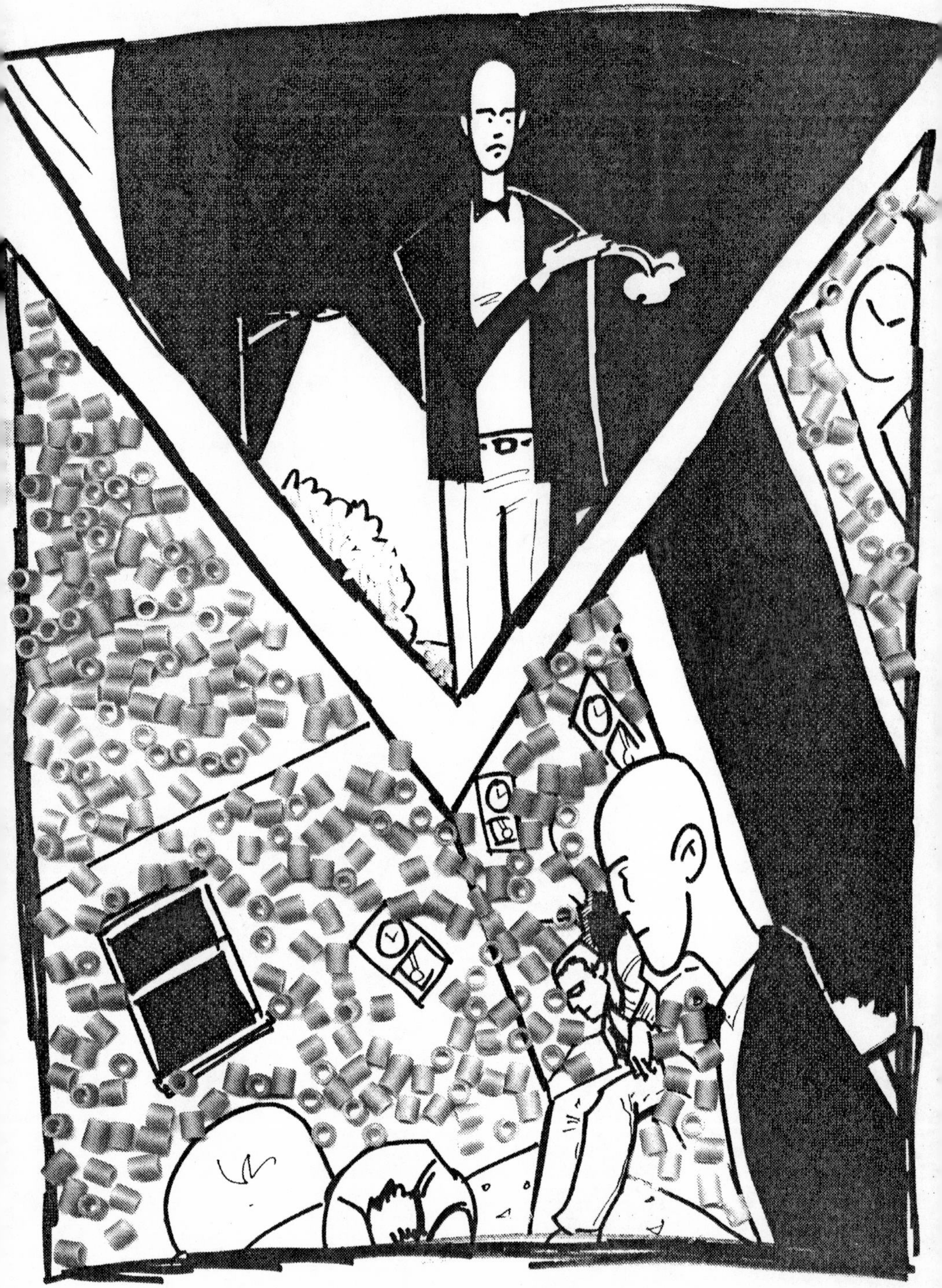

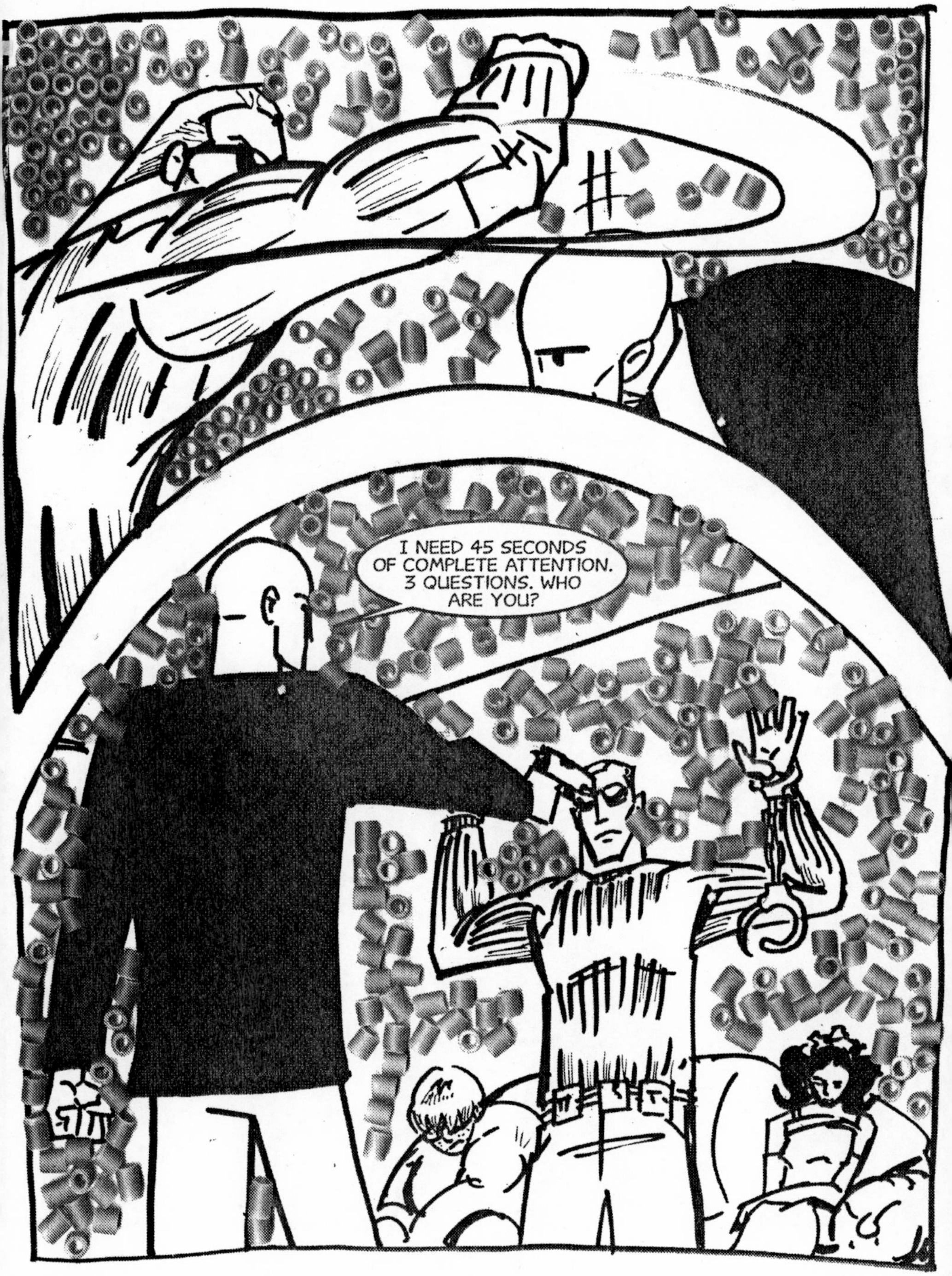
I NEED 45 SECONDS OF COMPLETE ATTENTION. 3 QUESTIONS. WHO ARE YOU?

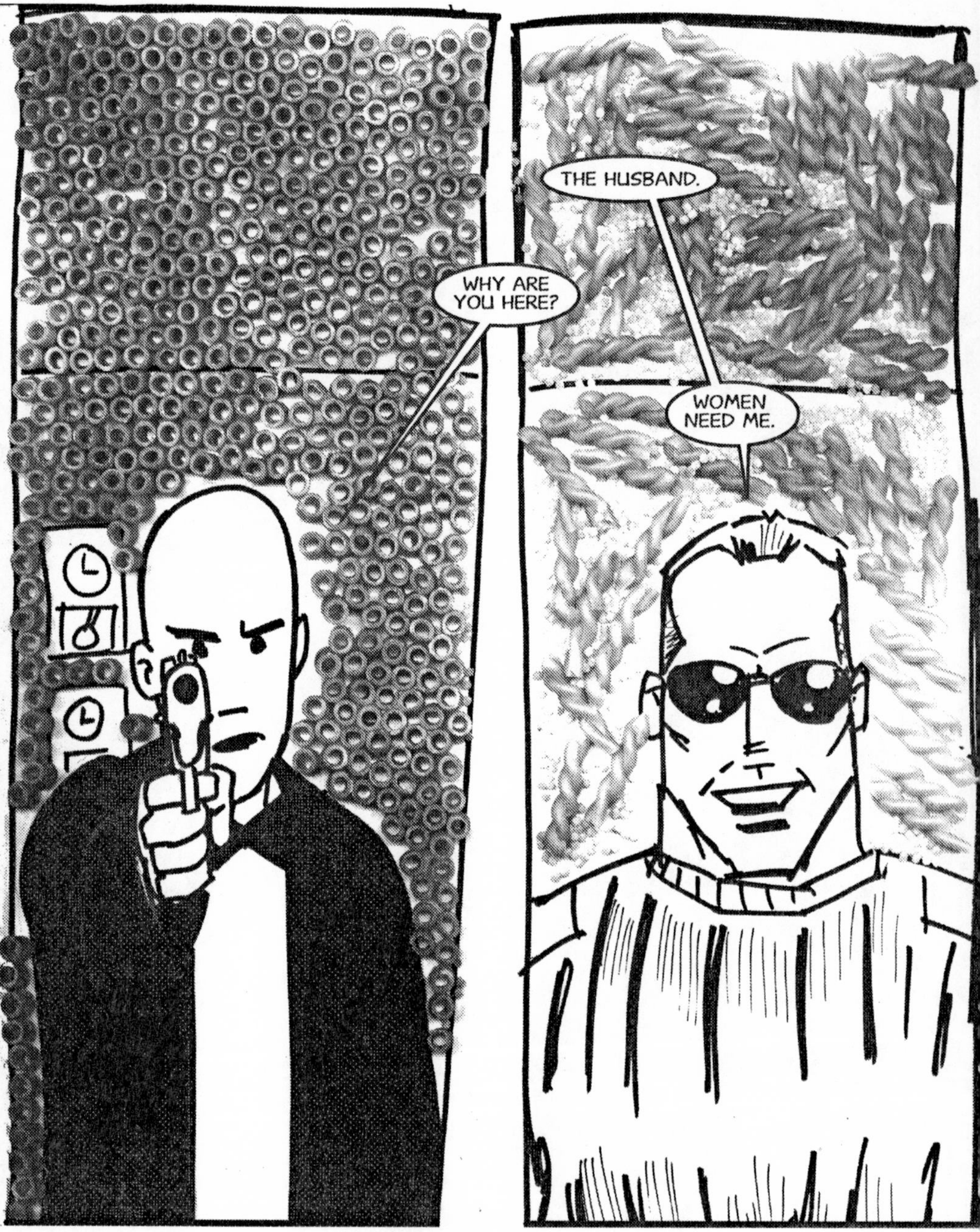
WHY ARE YOU HERE?
THE HUSBAND.
WOMEN NEED ME.

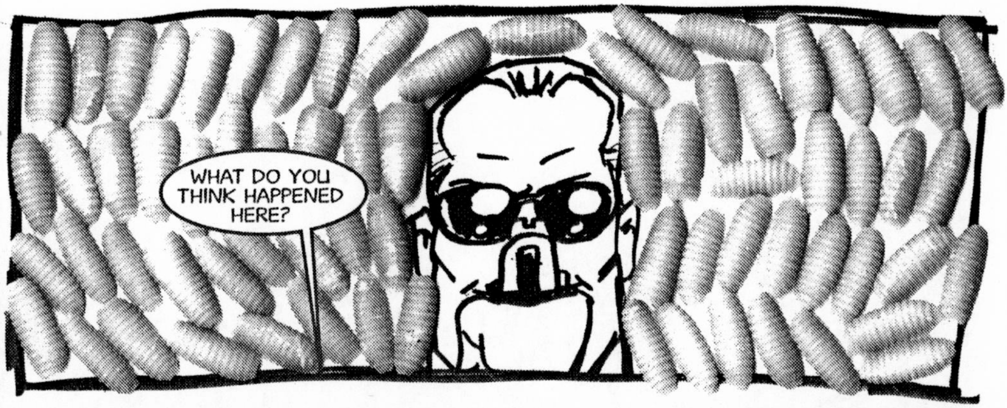
WHAT DO YOU THINK HAPPENED HERE?

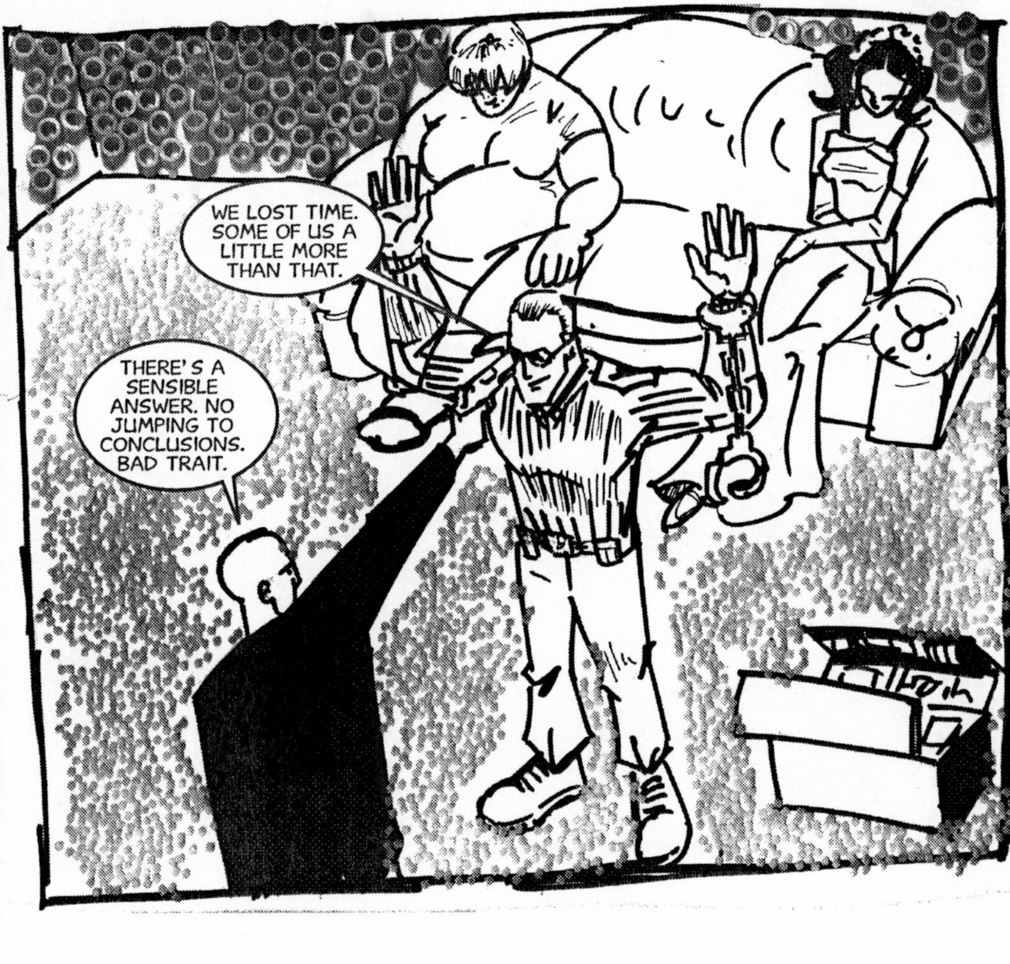
WE LOST TIME. SOME OF US A LITTLE MORE THAN THAT.
THERE'S A SENSIBLE ANSWER. NO JUMPING TO CONCLUSIONS. BAD TRAIT.

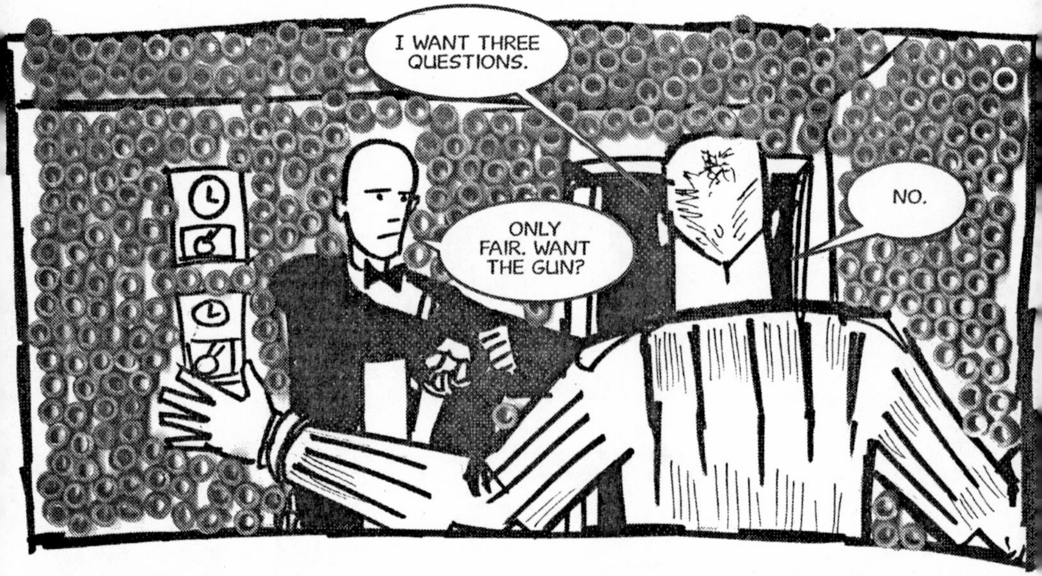
I WANT THREE QUESTIONS.
ONLY FAIR. WANT THE GUN?
NO.

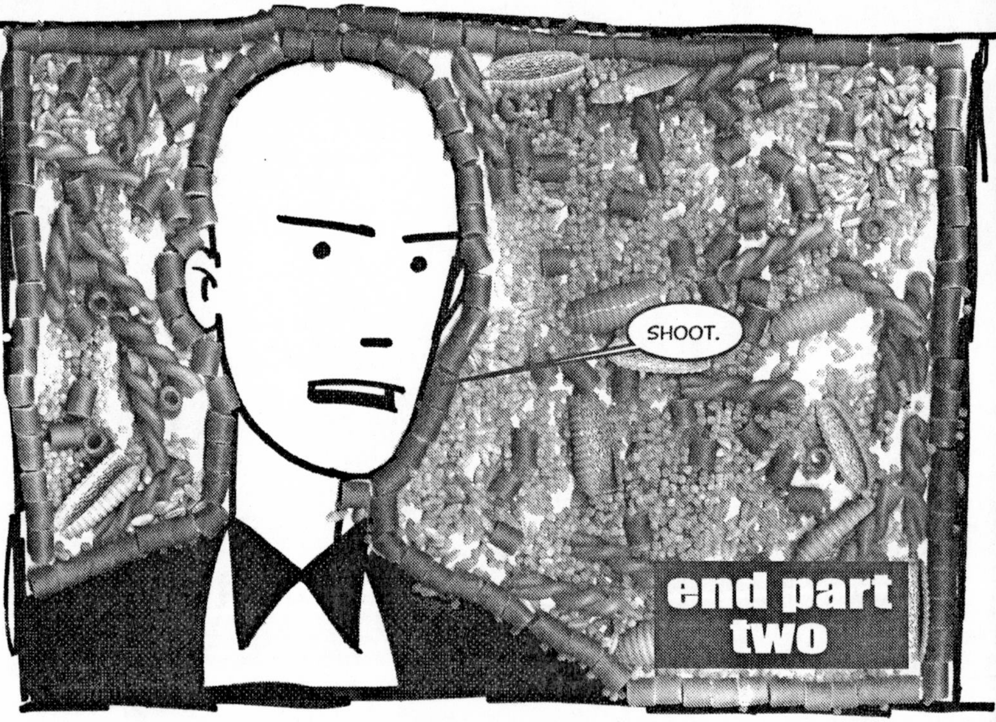
SHOOT.
end part two

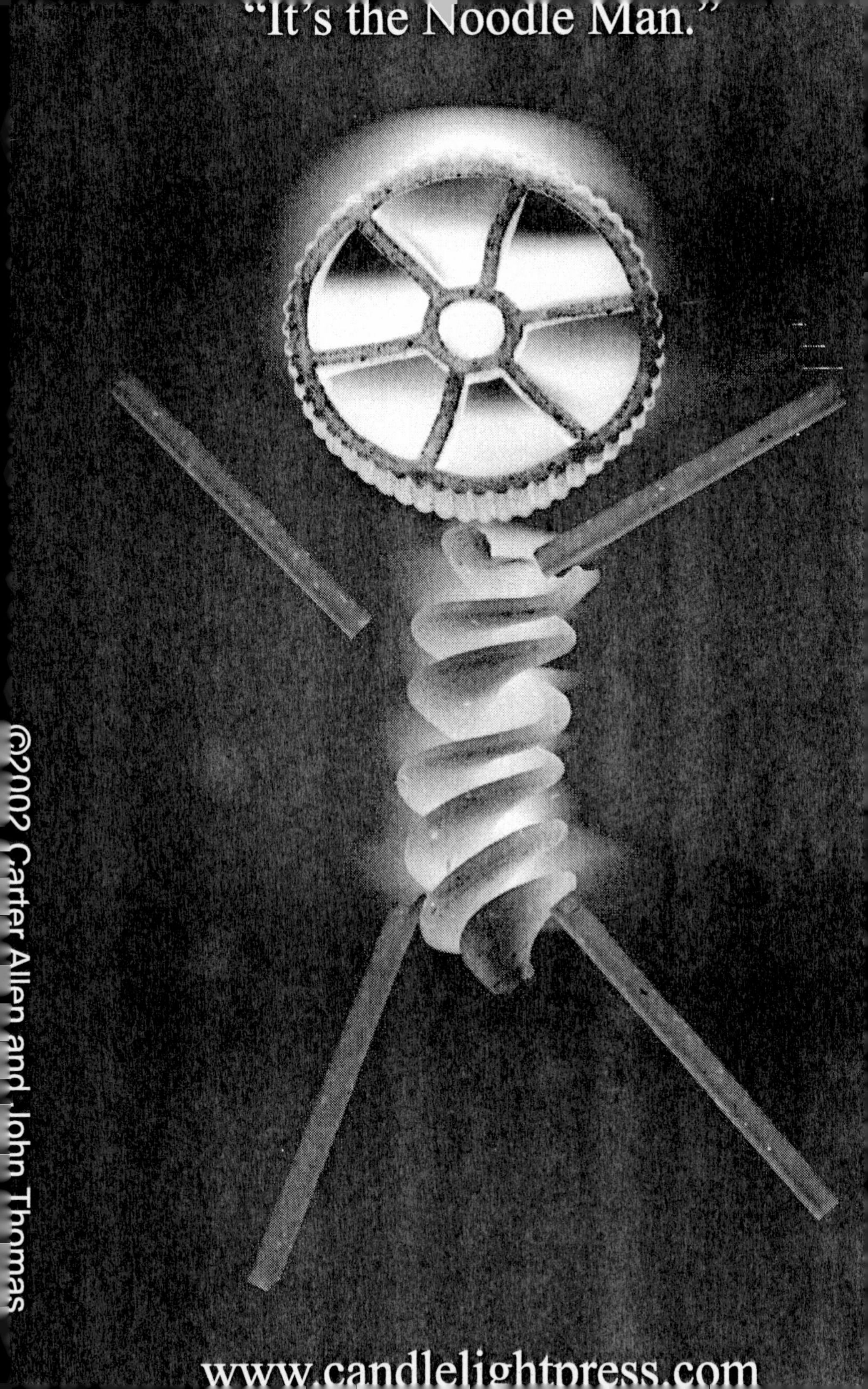
"It's the Noodle Man."
©2002 Carter Allen and John Thomas
www.candlelightpress.com

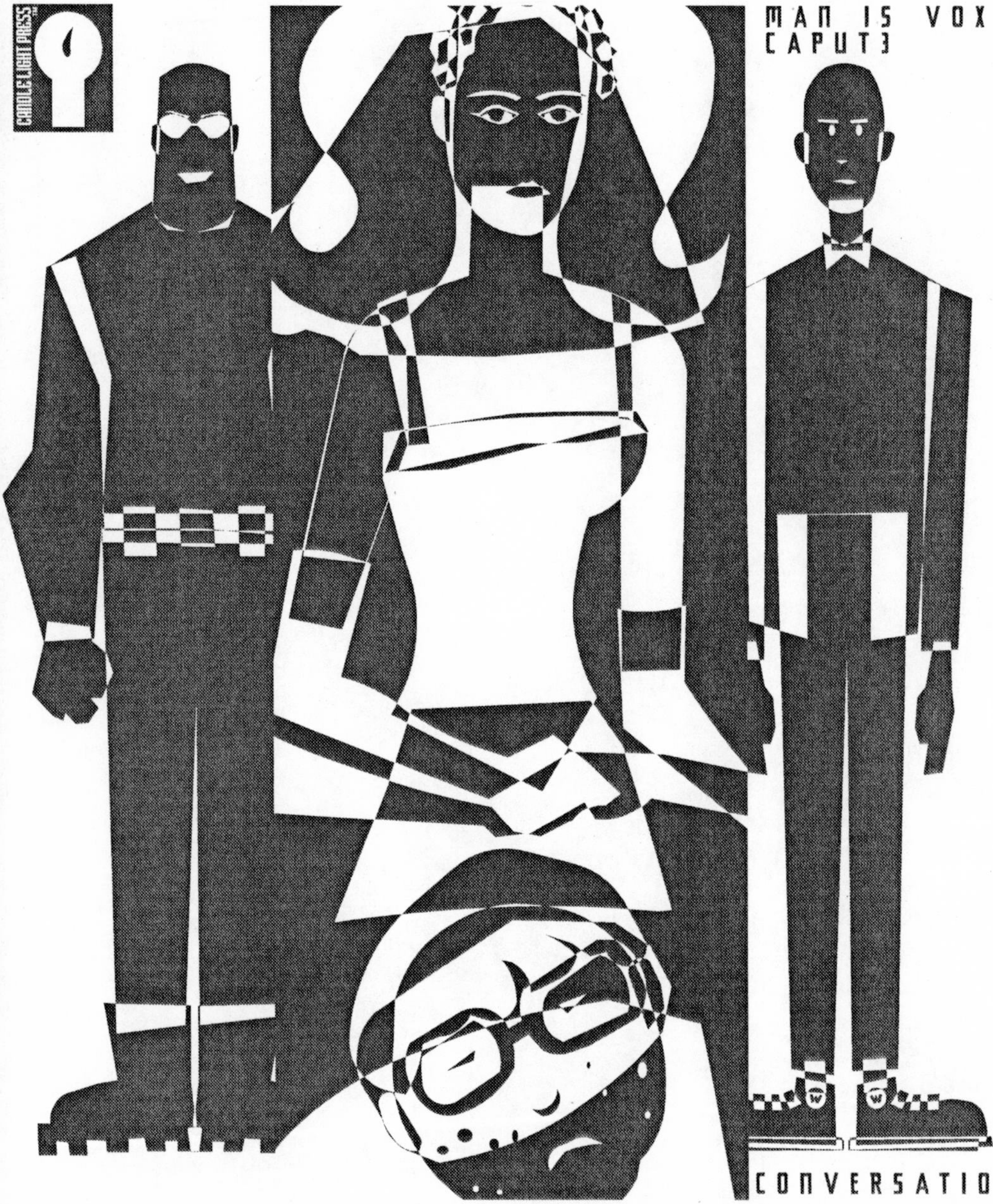
CANDLELIGHT PRESS
MAN IS VOX:
CAPUT3
CONVERSATION

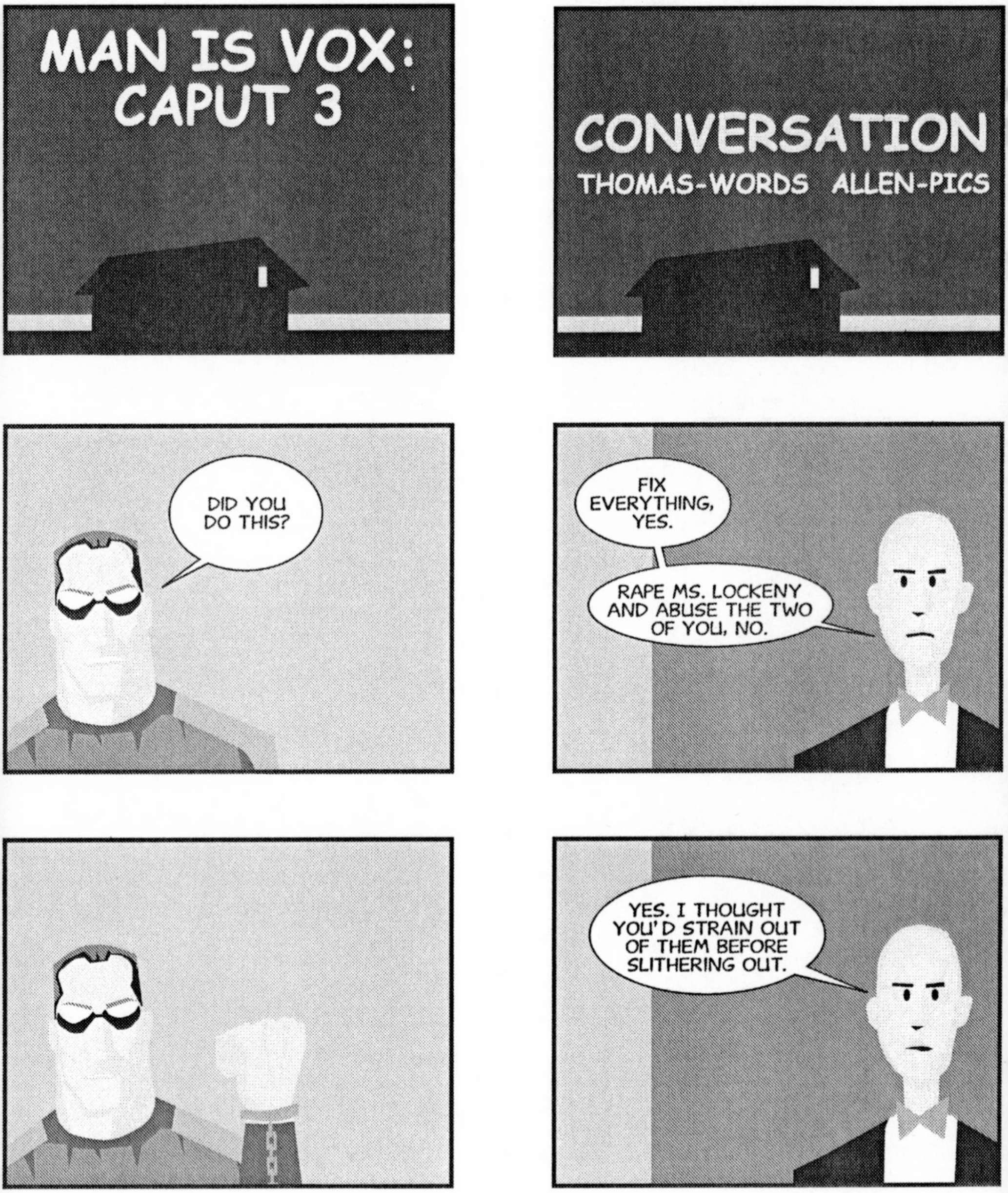
MAN IS VOX:
CAPUT 3
CONVERSATION
THOMAS-WORDS ALLEN-PICS
DID YOU DO THIS?
FIX EVERYTHING, YES.
RAPE MS. LOCKENY AND ABUSE THE TWO OF YOU, NO.
YES. I THOUGHT YOU'D STRAIN OUT OF THEM BEFORE SLITHERING OUT.

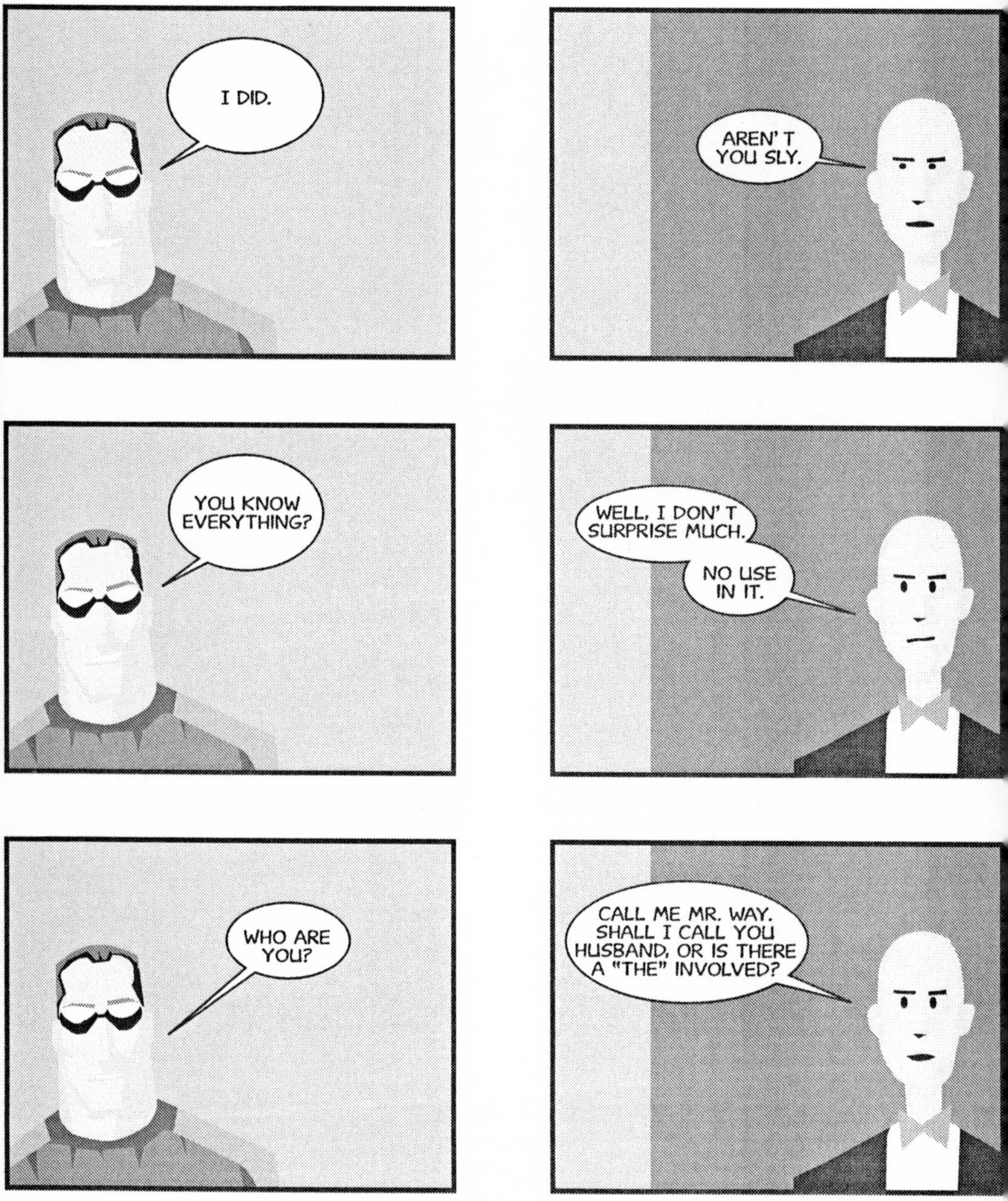
I DID.
AREN' T YOU SLY.
YOU KNOW EVERYTHING?
WELL, I DON' T SURPRISE MUCH.
NO USE IN IT.
WHO ARE YOU?
CALL ME MR. WAY. SHALL I CALL YOU HUSBAND, OR IS THERE A "THE" INVOLVED?

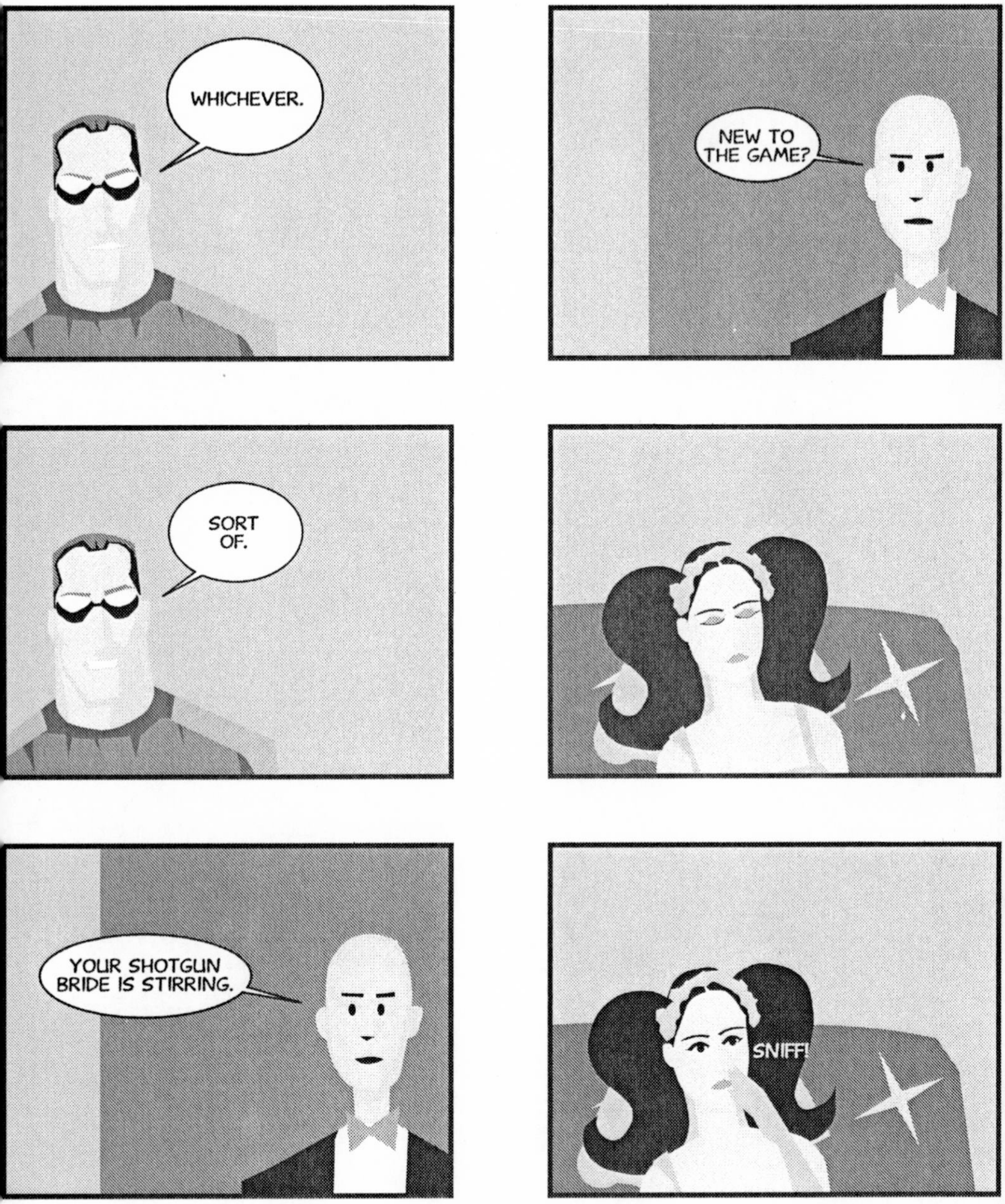
WHICHEVER.
NEW TO THE GAME?
SORT OF.
YOUR SHOTGUN BRIDE IS STIRRING.
SNIFF!

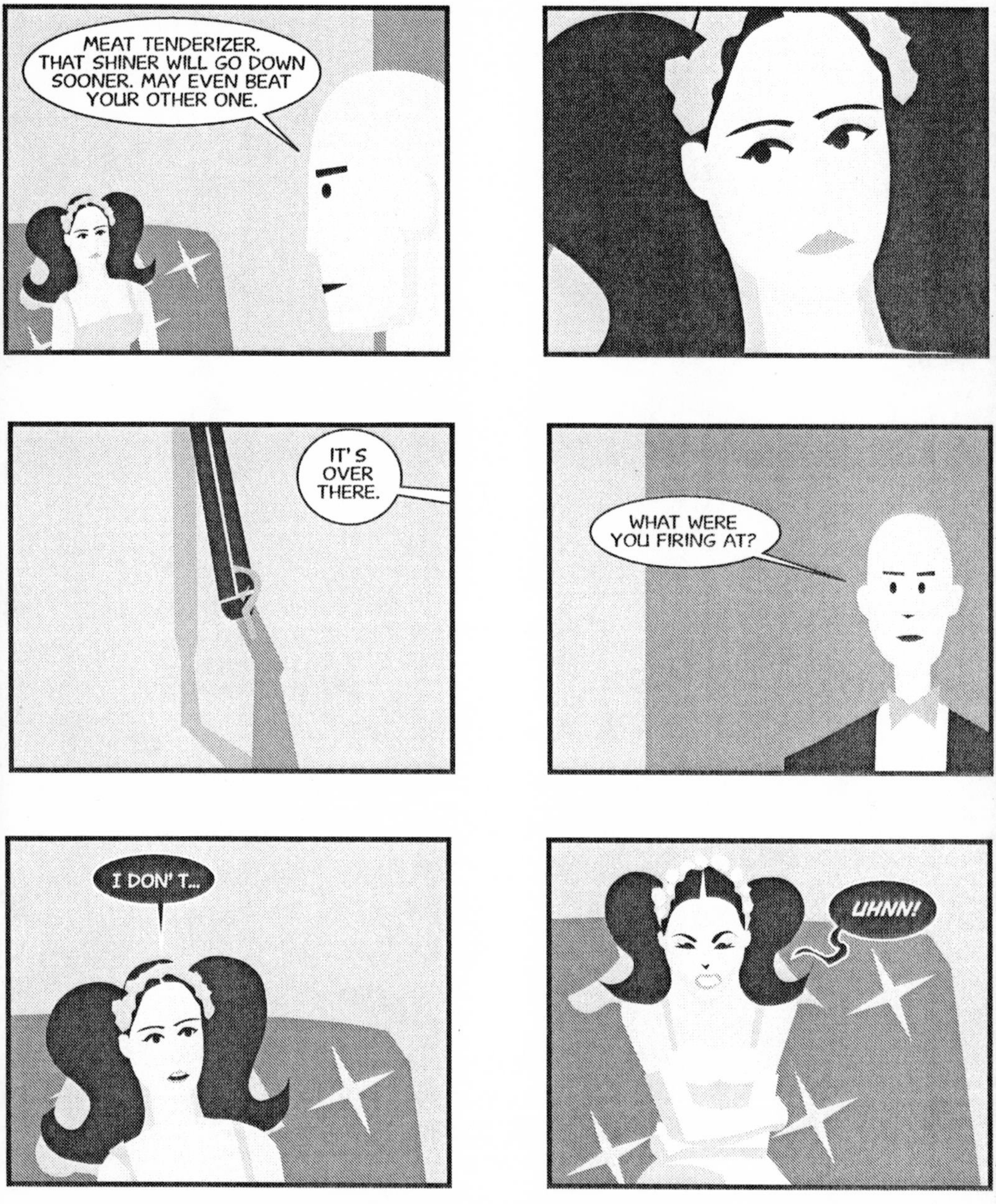
MEAT TENDERIZER. THAT SHINER WILL GO DOWN SOONER. MAY EVEN BEAT YOUR OTHER ONE.
IT'S OVER THERE.
WHAT WERE YOU FIRING AT?
I DON'T...
UHNN!

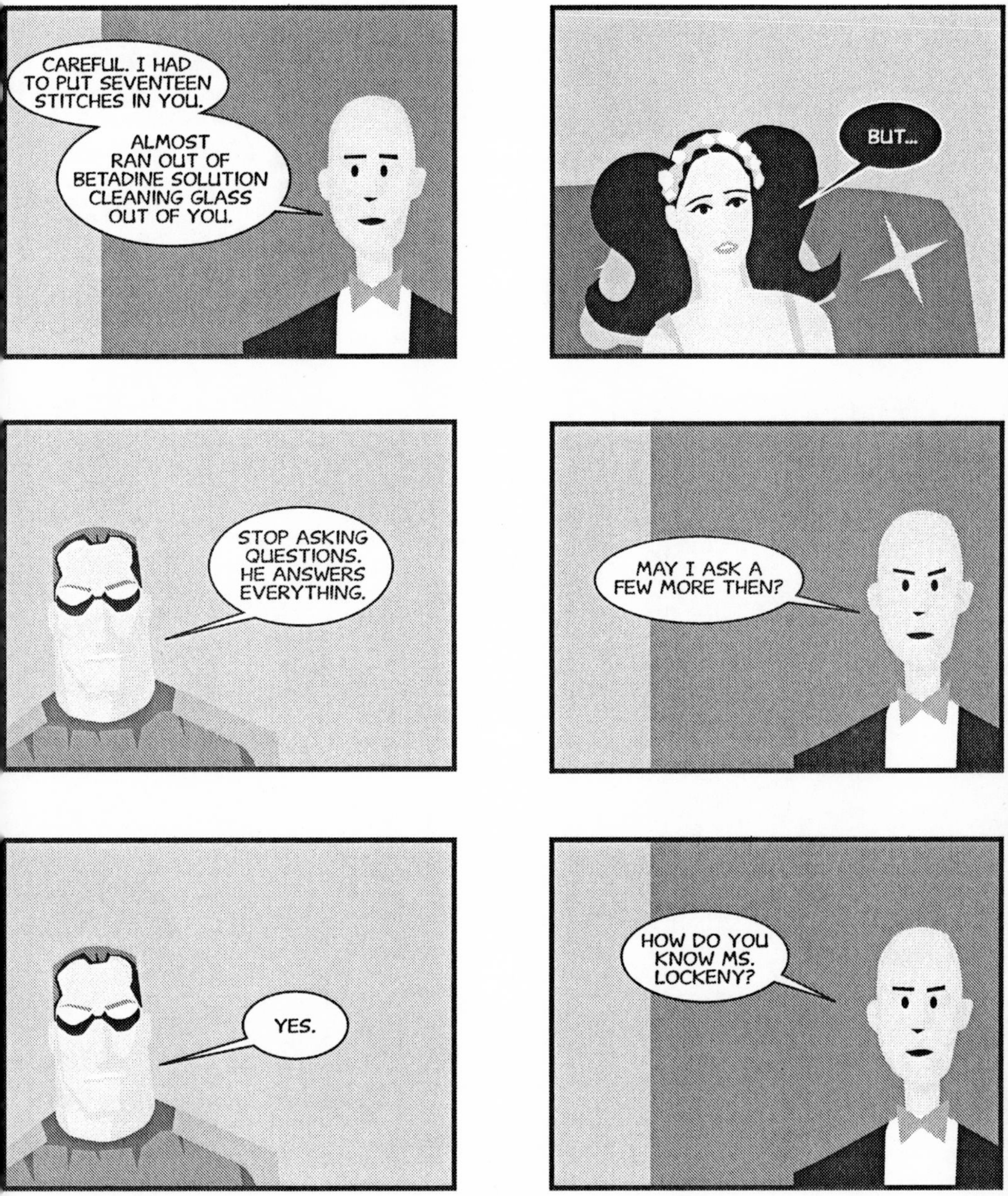
CAREFUL. I HAD TO PUT SEVENTEEN STITCHES IN YOU.
ALMOST RAN OUT OF BETADINE SOLUTION CLEANING GLASS OUT OF YOU.
BUT...
STOP ASKING QUESTIONS. HE ANSWERS EVERYTHING.
MAY I ASK A FEW MORE THEN?
YES.
HOW DO YOU KNOW MS. LOCKENY?

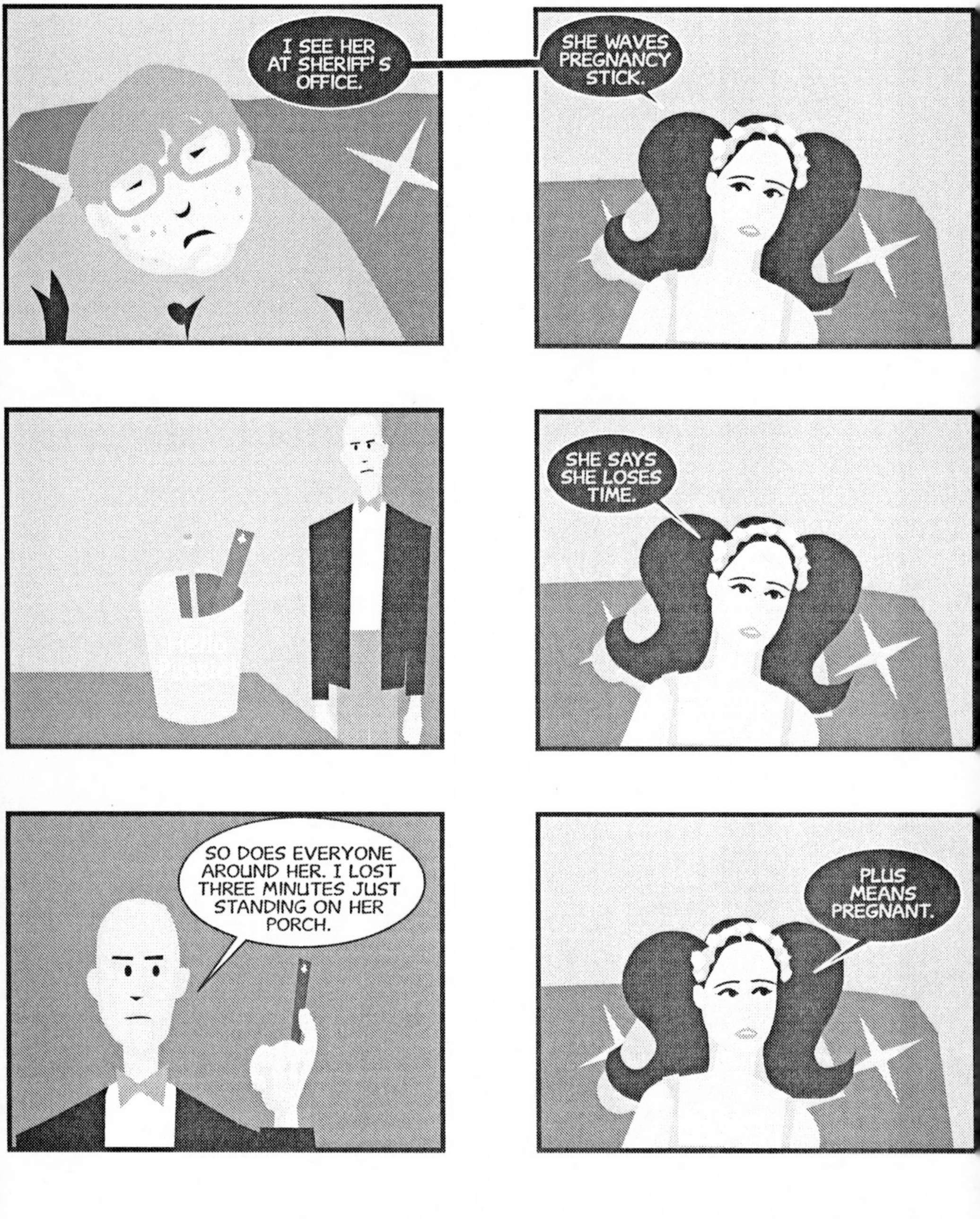
I SEE HER AT SHERIFF'S OFFICE.
SHE WAVES PREGNANCY STICK.
SHE SAYS SHE LOSES TIME.
SO DOES EVERYONE AROUND HER. I LOST THREE MINUTES JUST STANDING ON HER PORCH.
PLUS MEANS PREGNANT.

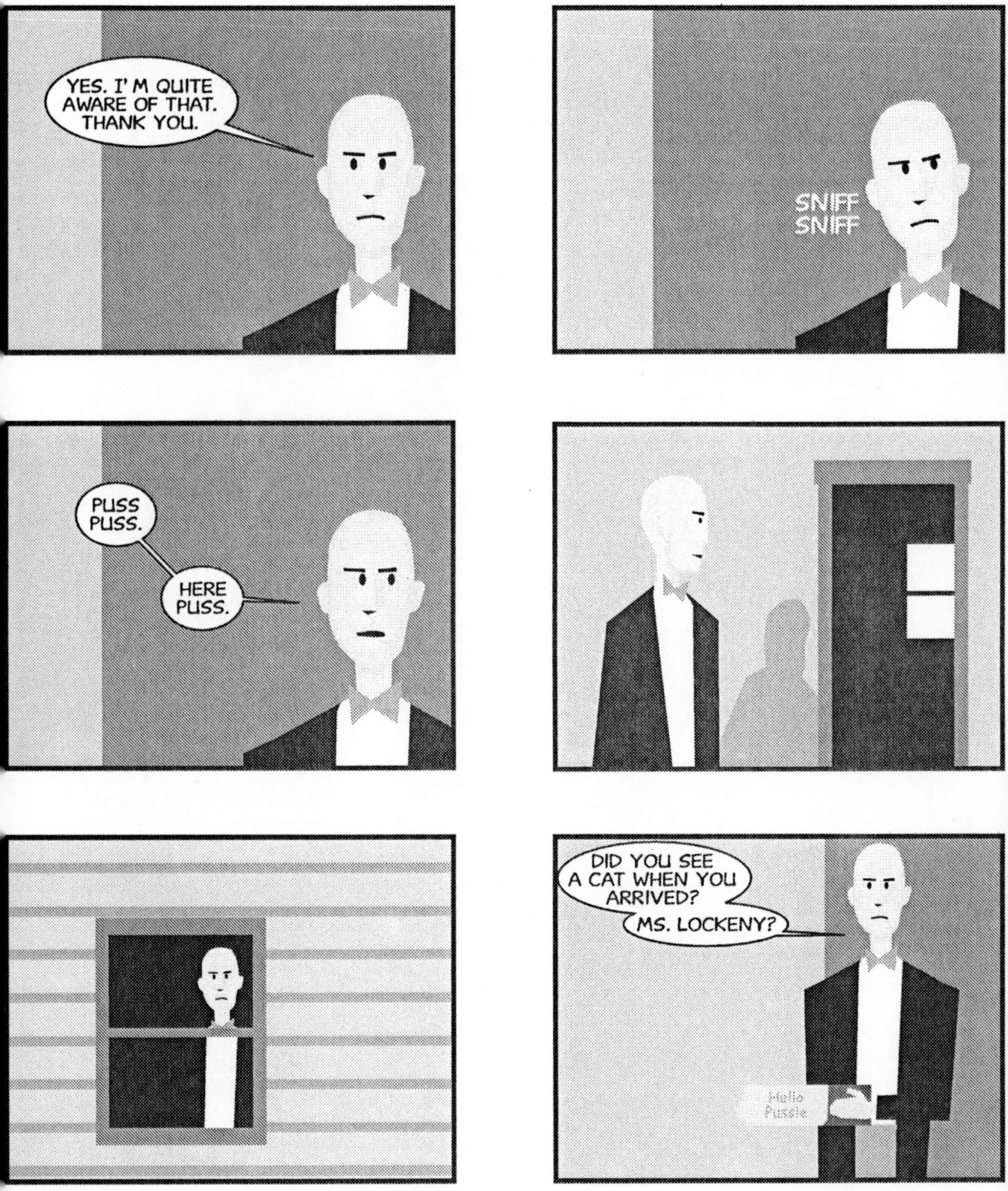
YES. I'M QUITE AWARE OF THAT. THANK YOU.
SNIFF SNIFF
PUSS PUSS.
HERE PUSS.
DID YOU SEE A CAT WHEN YOU ARRIVED?
MS. LOCKENY?
Hello Pussie

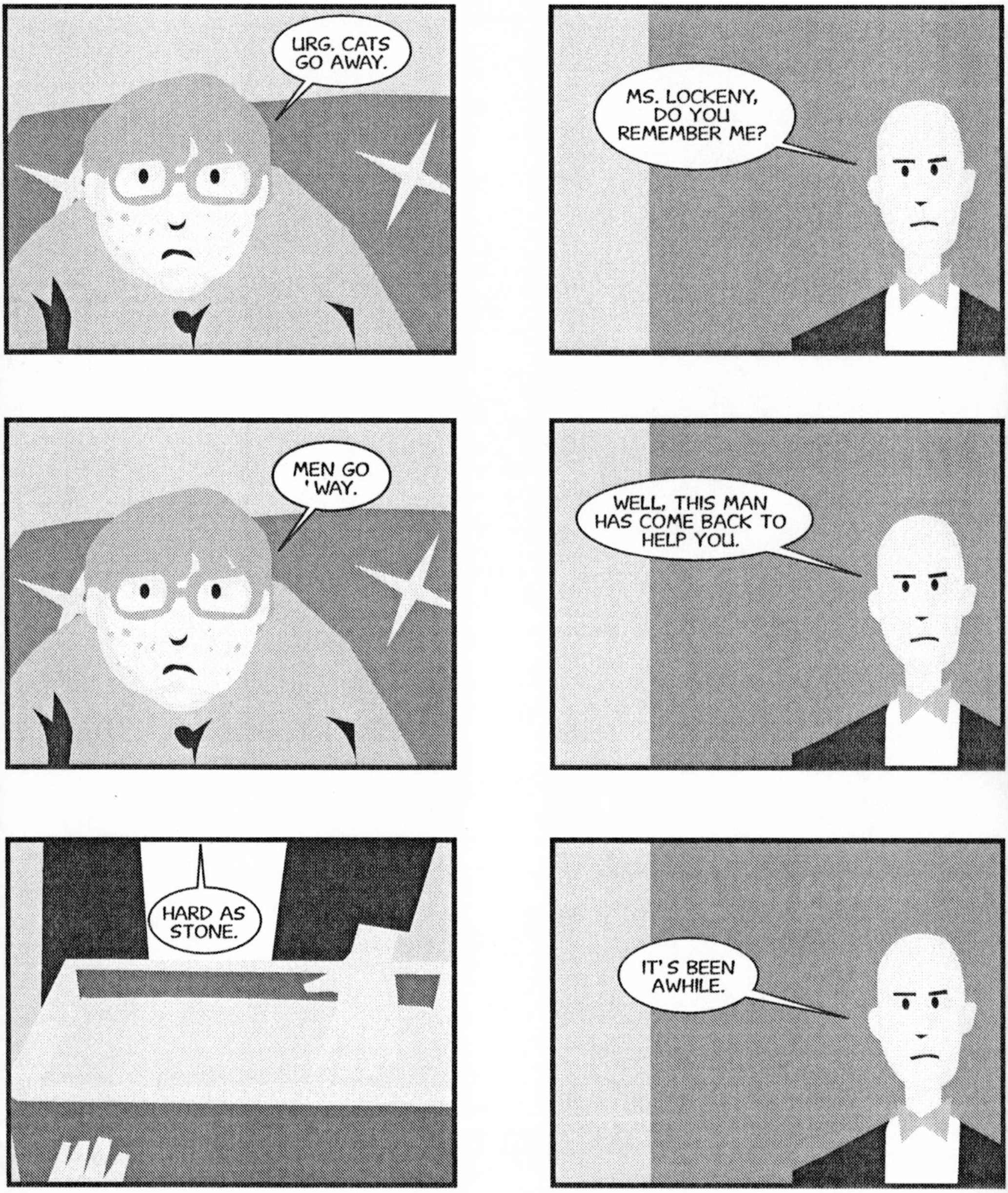
URG. CATS GO AWAY.
MS. LOCKENY, DO YOU REMEMBER ME?
MEN GO 'WAY.
WELL, THIS MAN HAS COME BACK TO HELP YOU.
HARD AS STONE.
IT'S BEEN AWHILE.

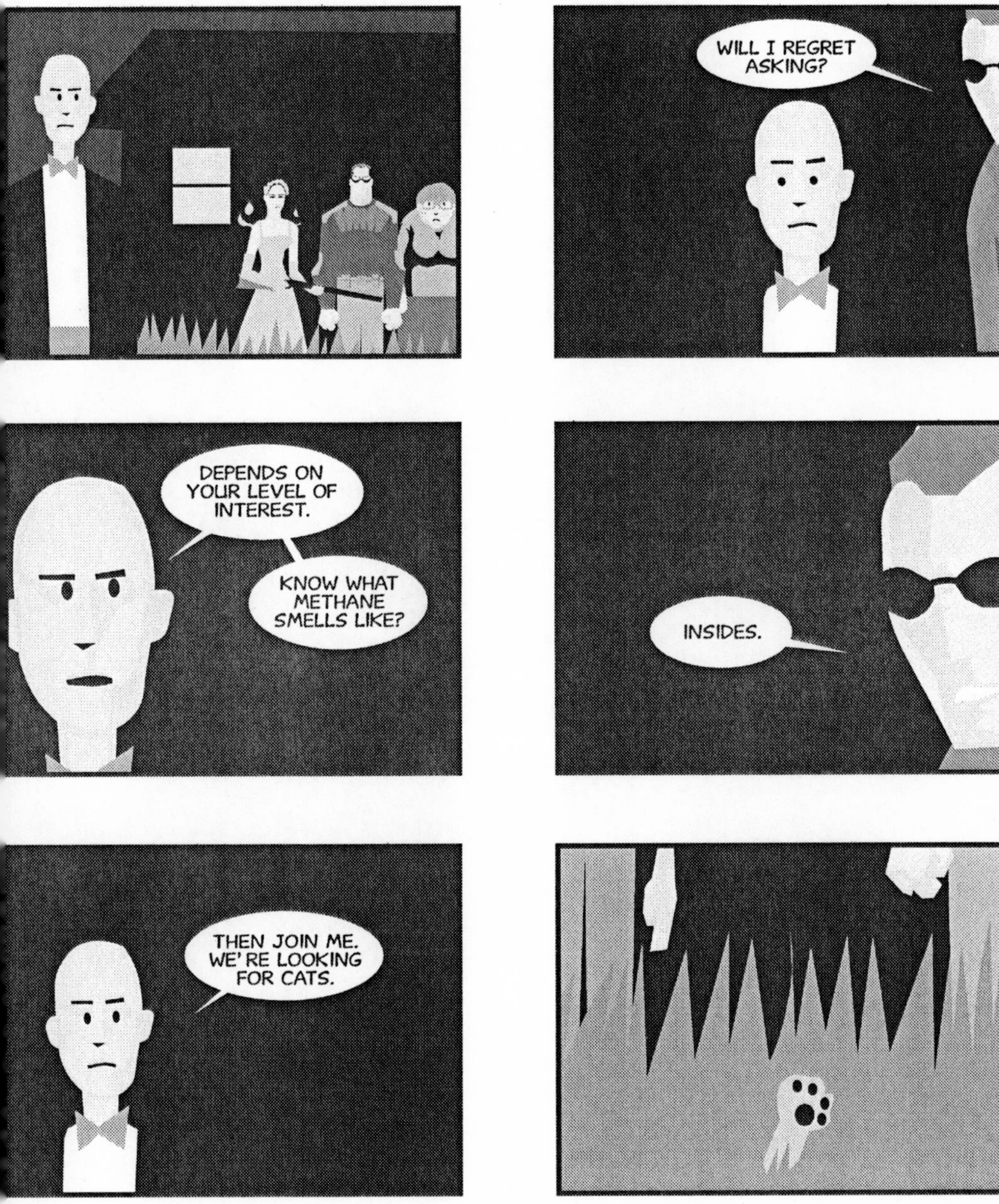
WILL I REGRET ASKING?
DEPENDS ON YOUR LEVEL OF INTEREST.
KNOW WHAT METHANE SMELLS LIKE?
INSIDES.
THEN JOIN ME. WE'RE LOOKING FOR CATS.

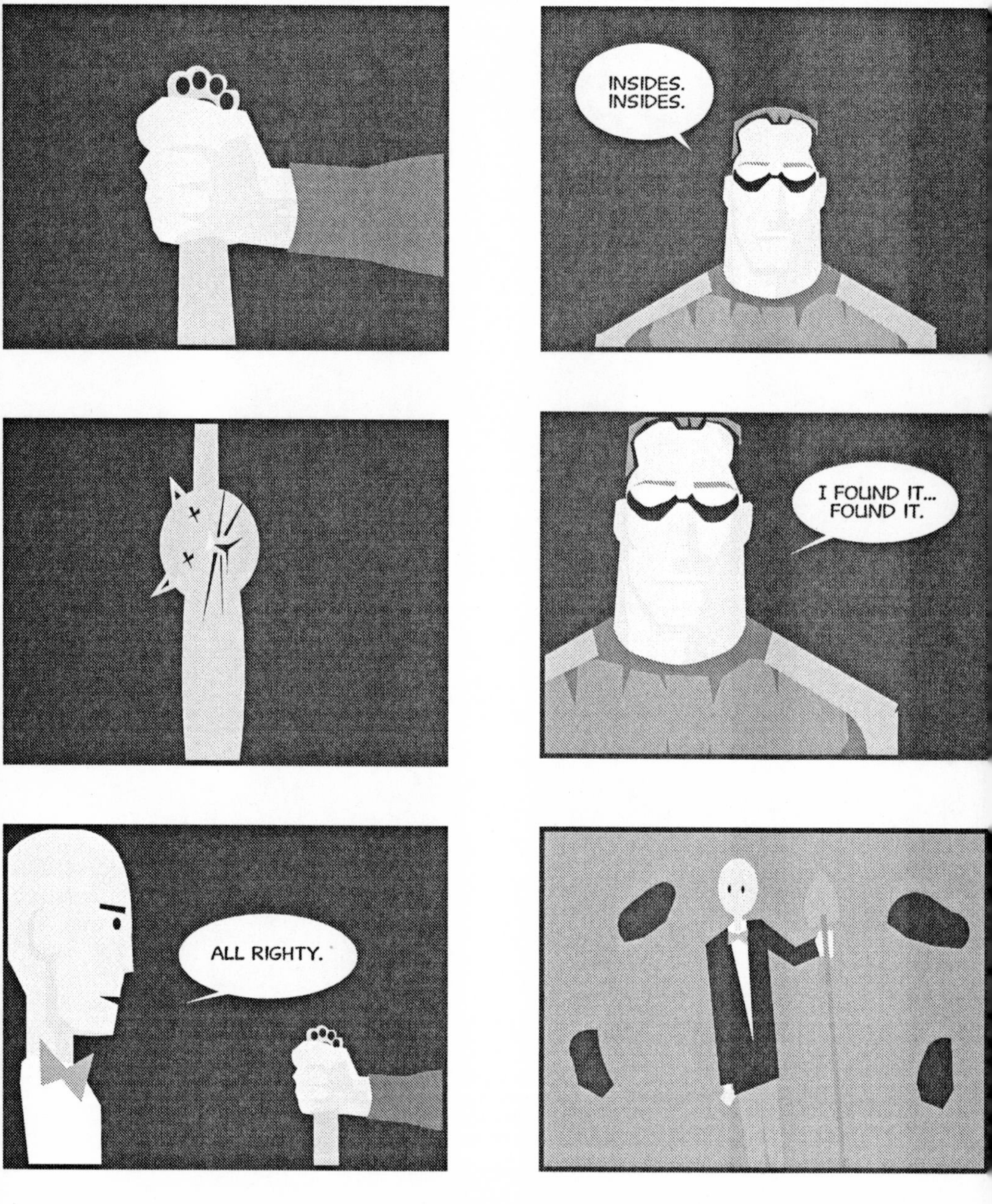
INSIDES. INSIDES.
I FOUND IT... FOUND IT.
ALL RIGHTY.

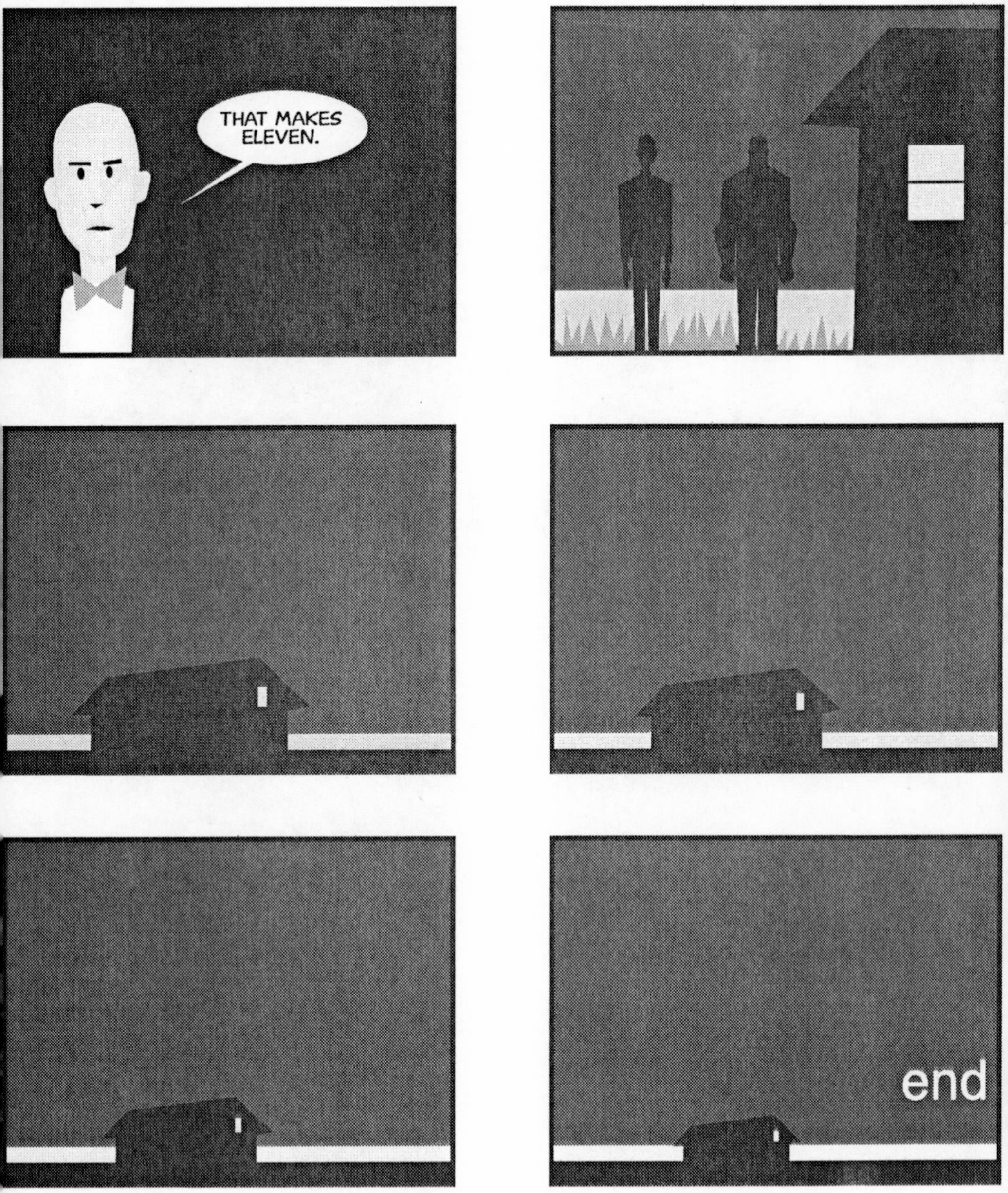
THAT MAKES ELEVEN.
end

CANDLE LIGHT PRESS™

man is vox: caput 4

MEAT

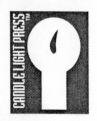

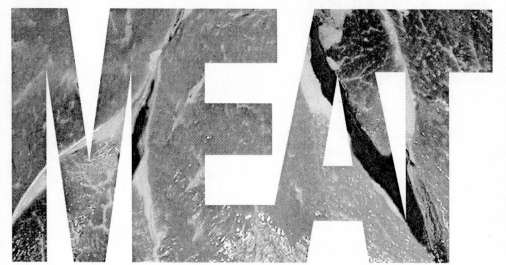

john ira thomas & carter allen

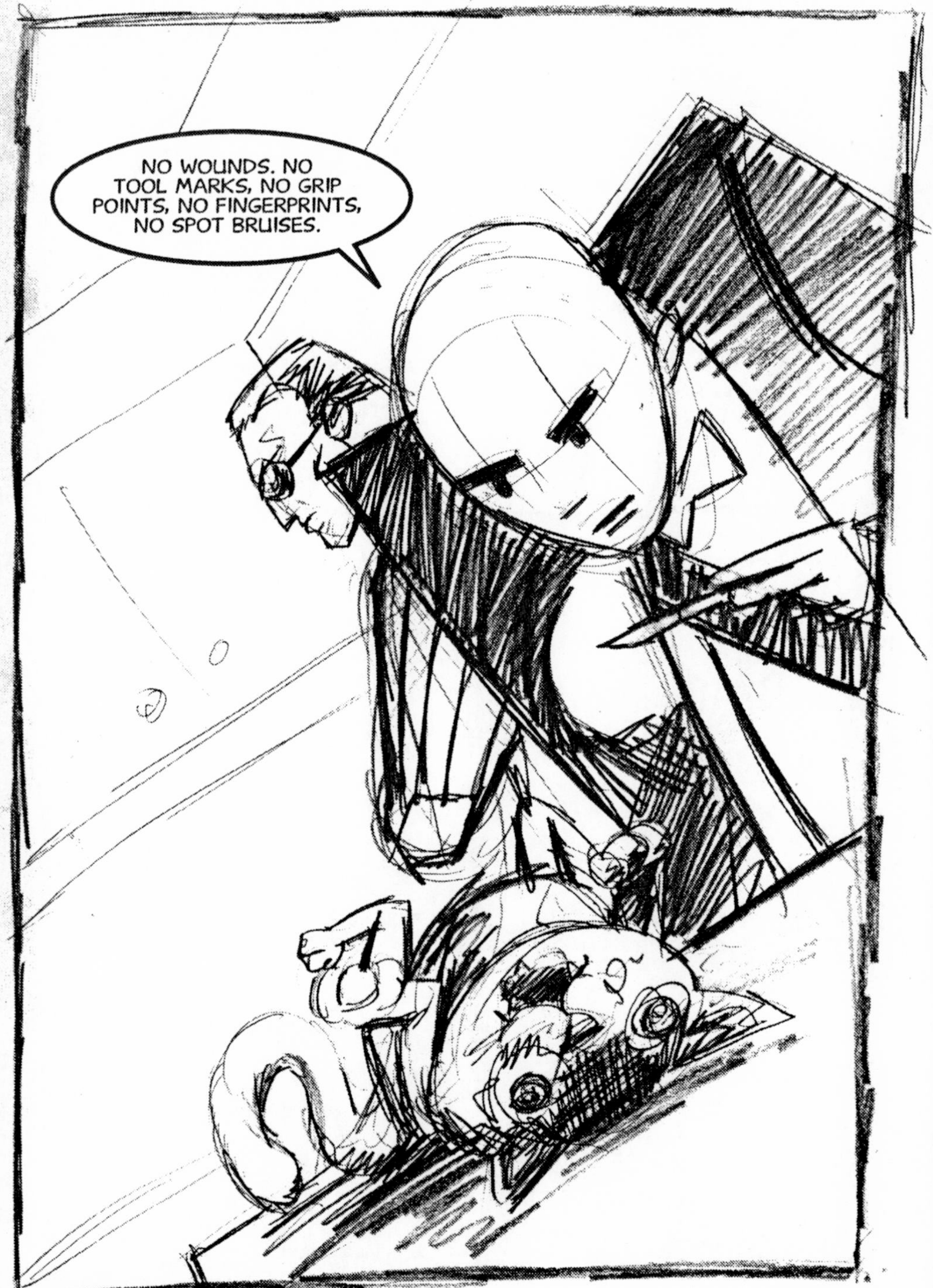
NO WOUNDS. NO TOOL MARKS, NO GRIP POINTS, NO FINGERPRINTS, NO SPOT BRUISES.

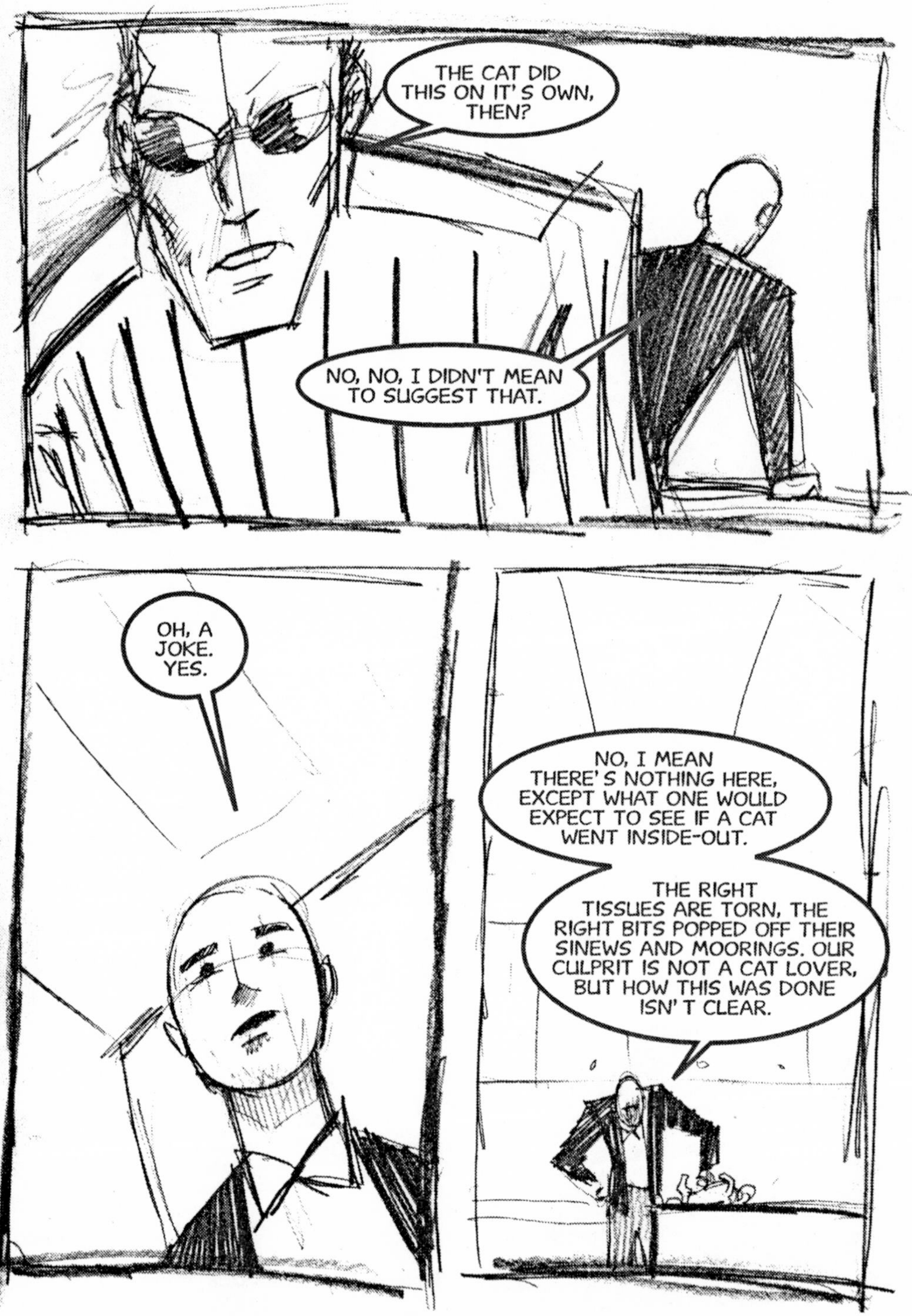
THE CAT DID THIS ON IT'S OWN, THEN?
NO, NO, I DIDN'T MEAN TO SUGGEST THAT.
OH, A JOKE. YES.
NO, I MEAN THERE'S NOTHING HERE, EXCEPT WHAT ONE WOULD EXPECT TO SEE IF A CAT WENT INSIDE-OUT.
THE RIGHT TISSUES ARE TORN, THE RIGHT BITS POPPED OFF THEIR SINEWS AND MOORINGS. OUR CULPRIT IS NOT A CAT LOVER, BUT HOW THIS WAS DONE ISN'T CLEAR.

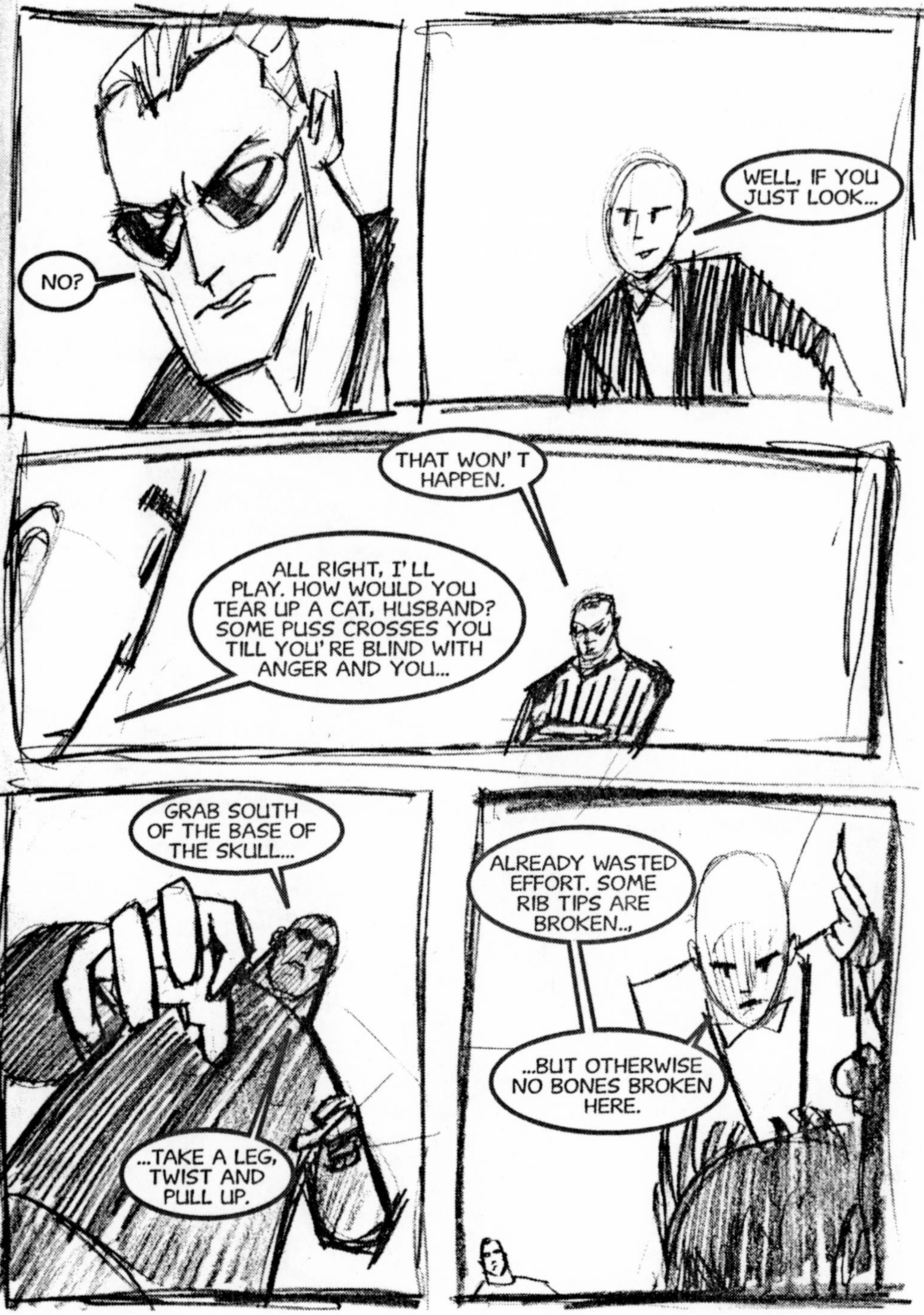
NO?
WELL, IF YOU JUST LOOK...
THAT WON'T HAPPEN.
ALL RIGHT, I'LL PLAY. HOW WOULD YOU TEAR UP A CAT, HUSBAND? SOME PUSS CROSSES YOU TILL YOU'RE BLIND WITH ANGER AND YOU...
GRAB SOUTH OF THE BASE OF THE SKULL...
...TAKE A LEG, TWIST AND PULL UP.
ALREADY WASTED EFFORT. SOME RIB TIPS ARE BROKEN..,
...BUT OTHERWISE NO BONES BROKEN HERE.

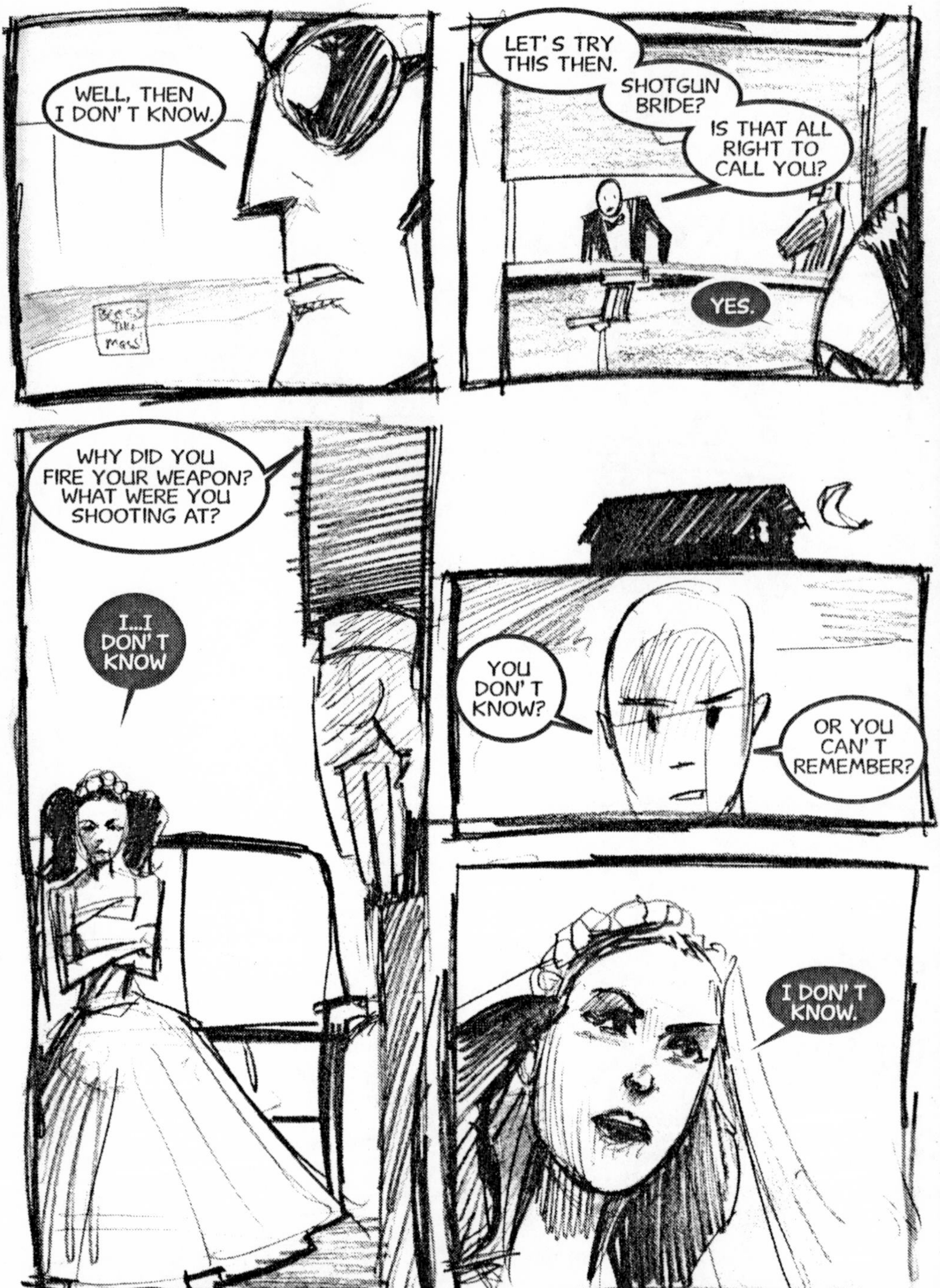
WELL, THEN I DON'T KNOW.
LET'S TRY THIS THEN.
SHOTGUN BRIDE?
IS THAT ALL RIGHT TO CALL YOU?
YES.
WHY DID YOU FIRE YOUR WEAPON? WHAT WERE YOU SHOOTING AT?
I...I DON'T KNOW
YOU DON'T KNOW?
OR YOU CAN'T REMEMBER?
I DON'T KNOW.

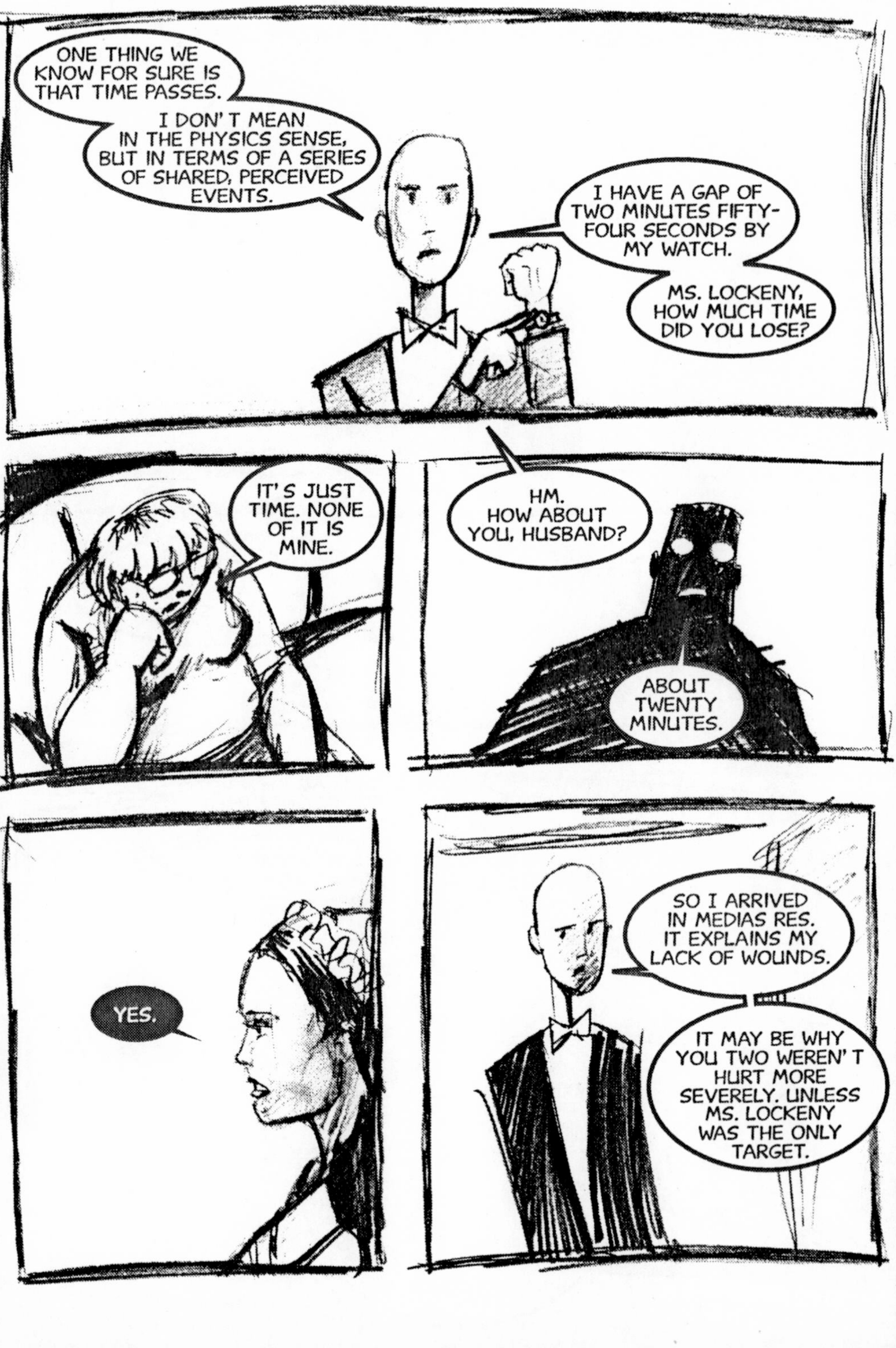
ONE THING WE KNOW FOR SURE IS THAT TIME PASSES.
I DON'T MEAN IN THE PHYSICS SENSE, BUT IN TERMS OF A SERIES OF SHARED, PERCEIVED EVENTS.
I HAVE A GAP OF TWO MINUTES FIFTY-FOUR SECONDS BY MY WATCH.
MS. LOCKENY, HOW MUCH TIME DID YOU LOSE?
IT'S JUST TIME. NONE OF IT IS MINE.
HM. HOW ABOUT YOU, HUSBAND?
ABOUT TWENTY MINUTES.
YES.
SO I ARRIVED IN MEDIAS RES. IT EXPLAINS MY LACK OF WOUNDS.
IT MAY BE WHY YOU TWO WEREN'T HURT MORE SEVERELY. UNLESS MS. LOCKENY WAS THE ONLY TARGET.

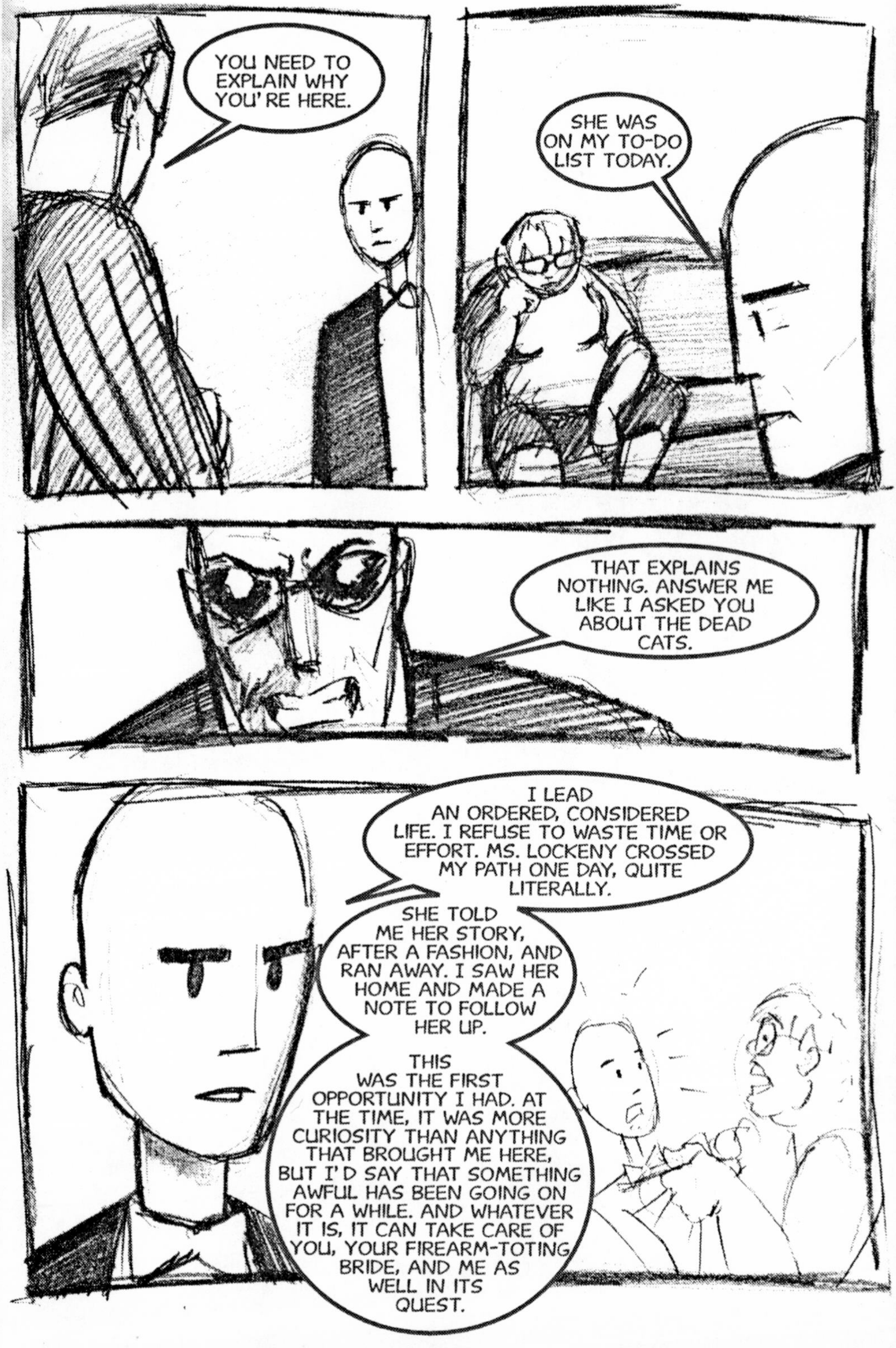
YOU NEED TO EXPLAIN WHY YOU'RE HERE.
SHE WAS ON MY TO-DO LIST TODAY.
THAT EXPLAINS NOTHING. ANSWER ME LIKE I ASKED YOU ABOUT THE DEAD CATS.
I LEAD AN ORDERED, CONSIDERED LIFE. I REFUSE TO WASTE TIME OR EFFORT. MS. LOCKENY CROSSED MY PATH ONE DAY, QUITE LITERALLY.
SHE TOLD ME HER STORY, AFTER A FASHION, AND RAN AWAY. I SAW HER HOME AND MADE A NOTE TO FOLLOW HER UP.
THIS WAS THE FIRST OPPORTUNITY I HAD. AT THE TIME, IT WAS MORE CURIOSITY THAN ANYTHING THAT BROUGHT ME HERE, BUT I'D SAY THAT SOMETHING AWFUL HAS BEEN GOING ON FOR A WHILE. AND WHATEVER IT IS, IT CAN TAKE CARE OF YOU, YOUR FIREARM-TOTING BRIDE, AND ME AS WELL IN ITS QUEST.

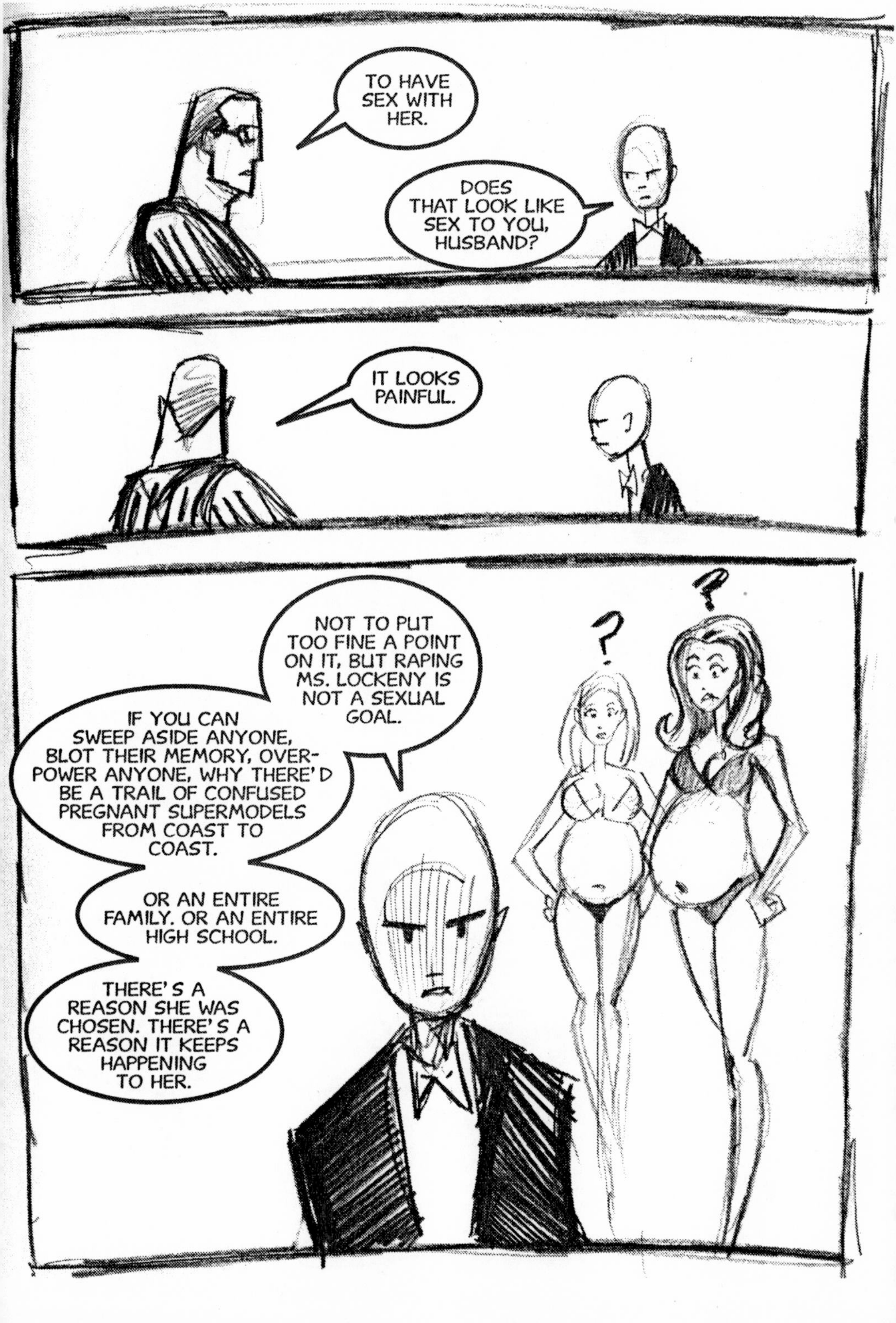
TO HAVE SEX WITH HER.
DOES THAT LOOK LIKE SEX TO YOU, HUSBAND?
IT LOOKS PAINFUL.
NOT TO PUT TOO FINE A POINT ON IT, BUT RAPING MS. LOCKENY IS NOT A SEXUAL GOAL.
IF YOU CAN SWEEP ASIDE ANYONE, BLOT THEIR MEMORY, OVER-POWER ANYONE, WHY THERE'D BE A TRAIL OF CONFUSED PREGNANT SUPERMODELS FROM COAST TO COAST.
OR AN ENTIRE FAMILY. OR AN ENTIRE HIGH SCHOOL.
THERE'S A REASON SHE WAS CHOSEN. THERE'S A REASON IT KEEPS HAPPENING TO HER.
?
?

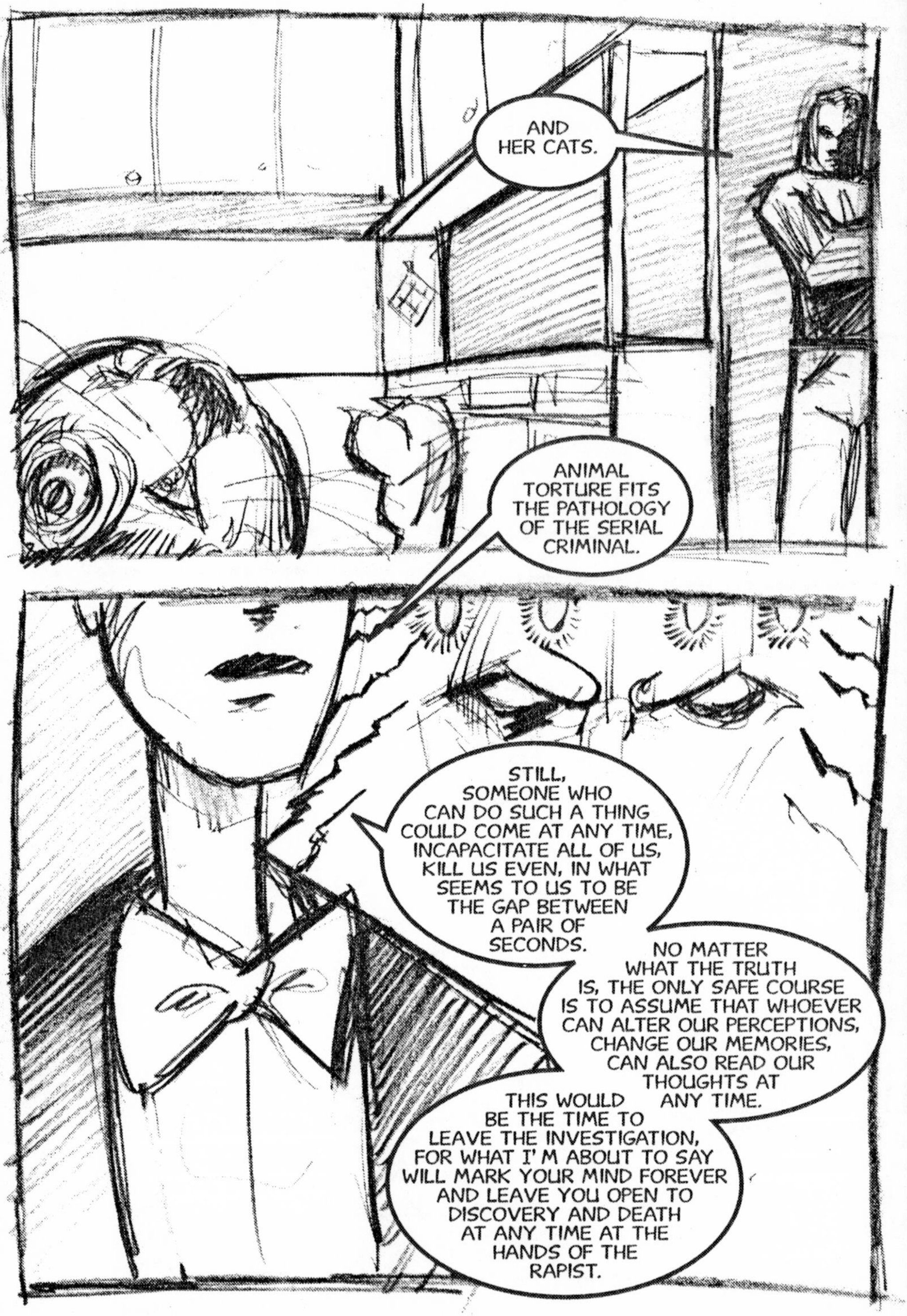
AND HER CATS.
ANIMAL TORTURE FITS THE PATHOLOGY OF THE SERIAL CRIMINAL.
STILL, SOMEONE WHO CAN DO SUCH A THING COULD COME AT ANY TIME, INCAPACITATE ALL OF US, KILL US EVEN, IN WHAT SEEMS TO US TO BE THE GAP BETWEEN A PAIR OF SECONDS.
NO MATTER WHAT THE TRUTH IS, THE ONLY SAFE COURSE IS TO ASSUME THAT WHOEVER CAN ALTER OUR PERCEPTIONS, CHANGE OUR MEMORIES, CAN ALSO READ OUR THOUGHTS AT ANY TIME.
THIS WOULD BE THE TIME TO LEAVE THE INVESTIGATION, FOR WHAT I'M ABOUT TO SAY WILL MARK YOUR MIND FOREVER AND LEAVE YOU OPEN TO DISCOVERY AND DEATH AT ANY TIME AT THE HANDS OF THE RAPIST.

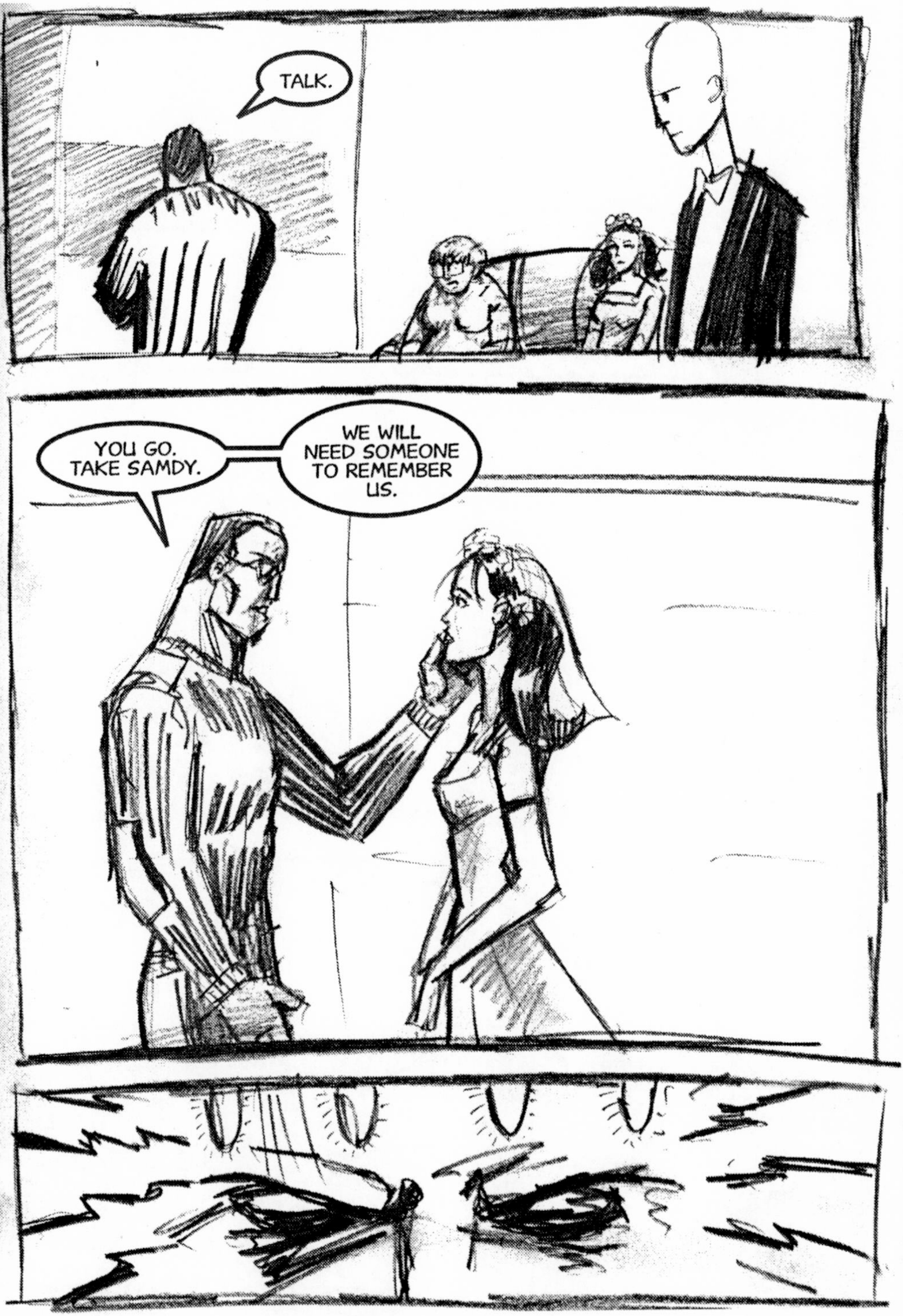
TALK.
YOU GO. TAKE SAMDY.
WE WILL NEED SOMEONE TO REMEMBER US.

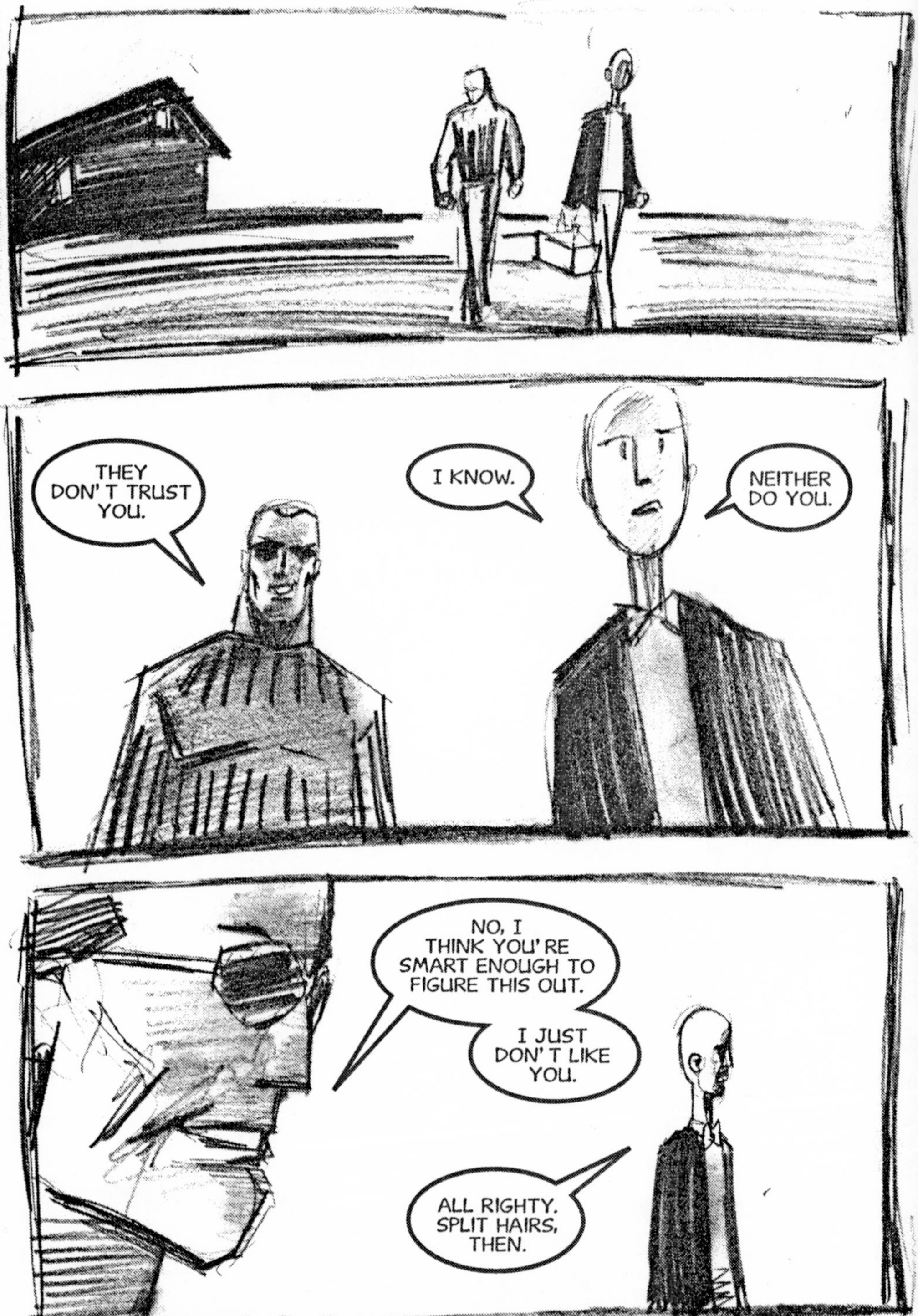
THEY DON'T TRUST YOU.
I KNOW.
NEITHER DO YOU.
NO, I THINK YOU'RE SMART ENOUGH TO FIGURE THIS OUT.
I JUST DON'T LIKE YOU.
ALL RIGHTY. SPLIT HAIRS, THEN.

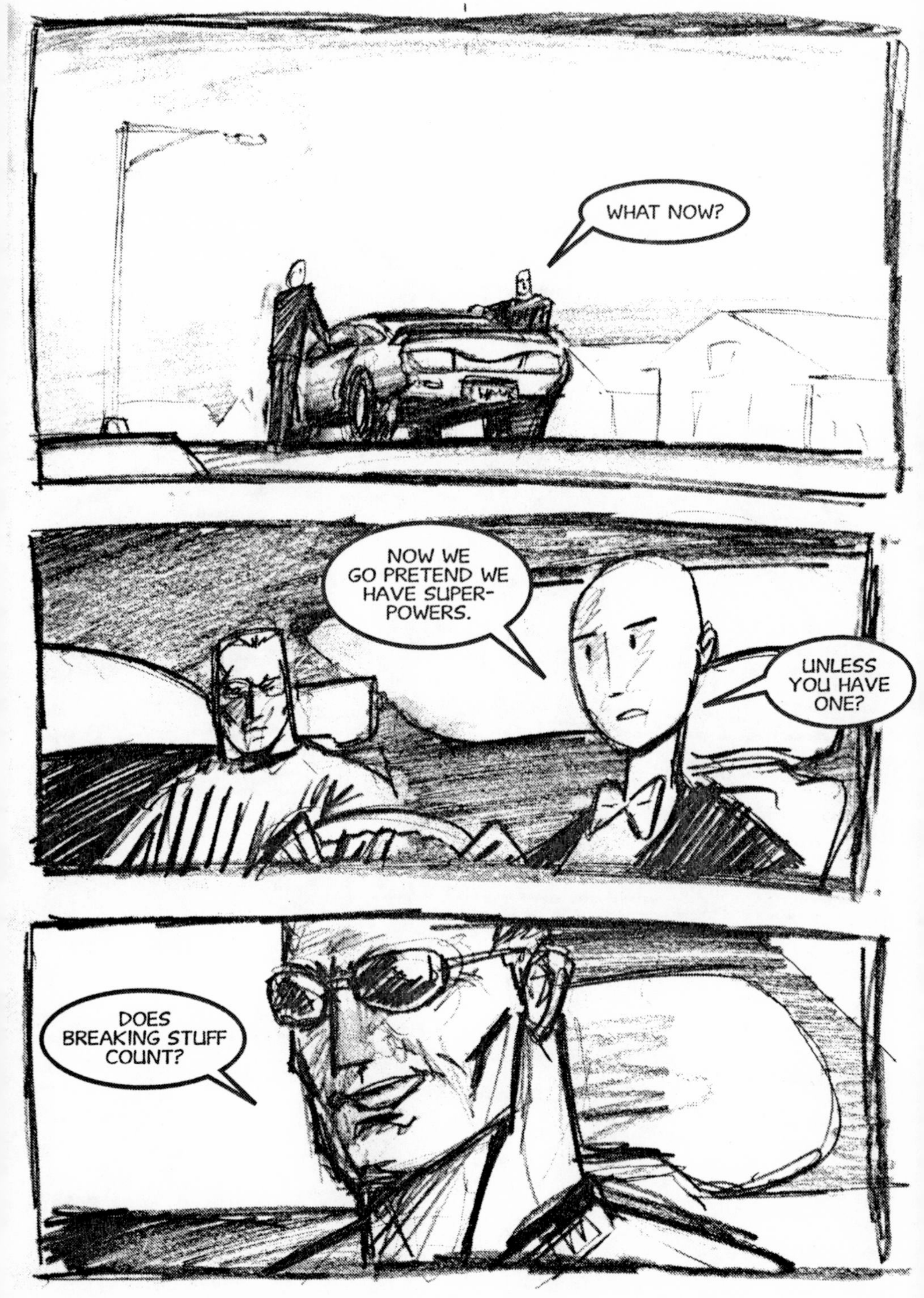
WHAT NOW?
NOW WE GO PRETEND WE HAVE SUPER-POWERS.
UNLESS YOU HAVE ONE?
DOES BREAKING STUFF COUNT?

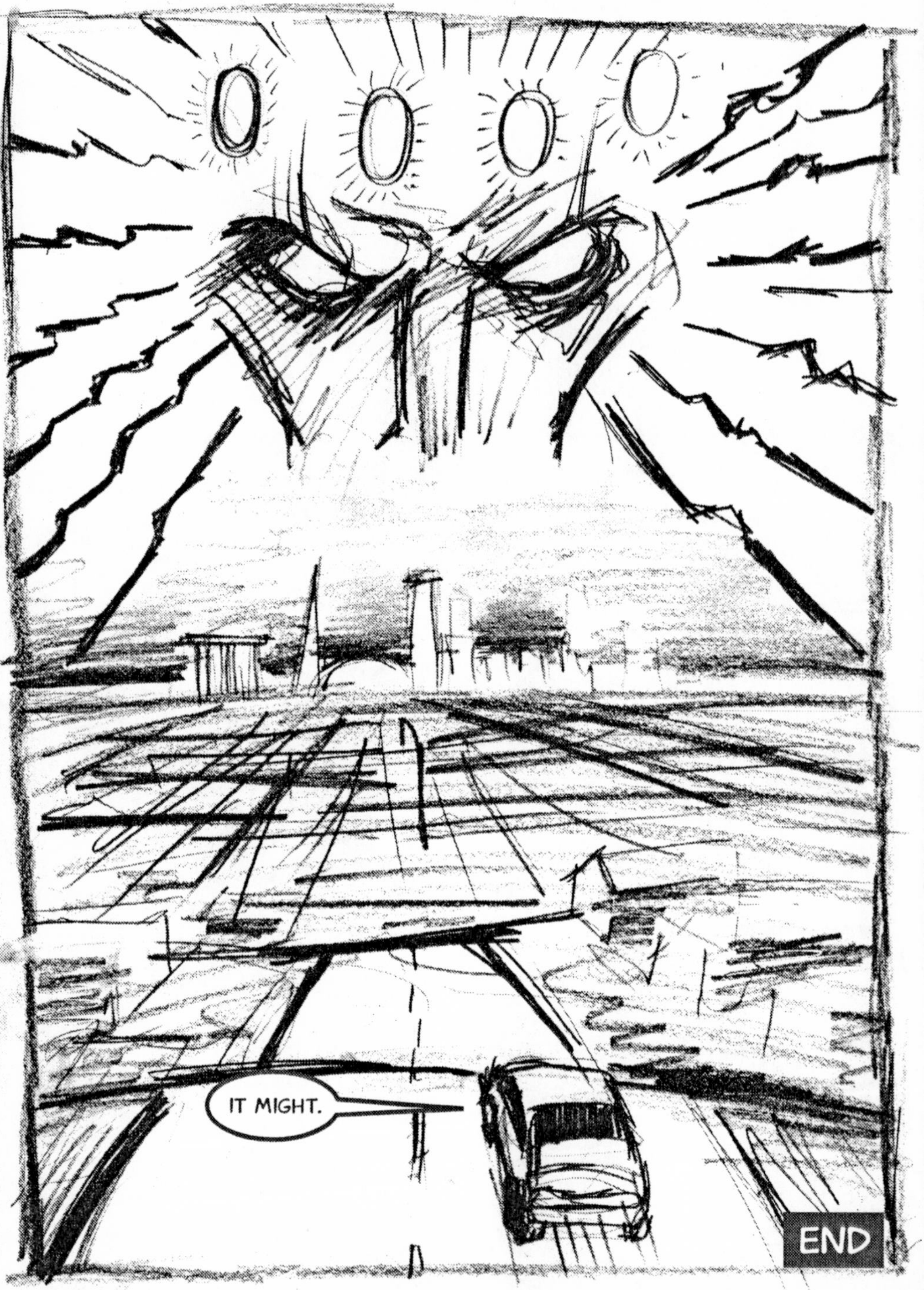
IT MIGHT.
END

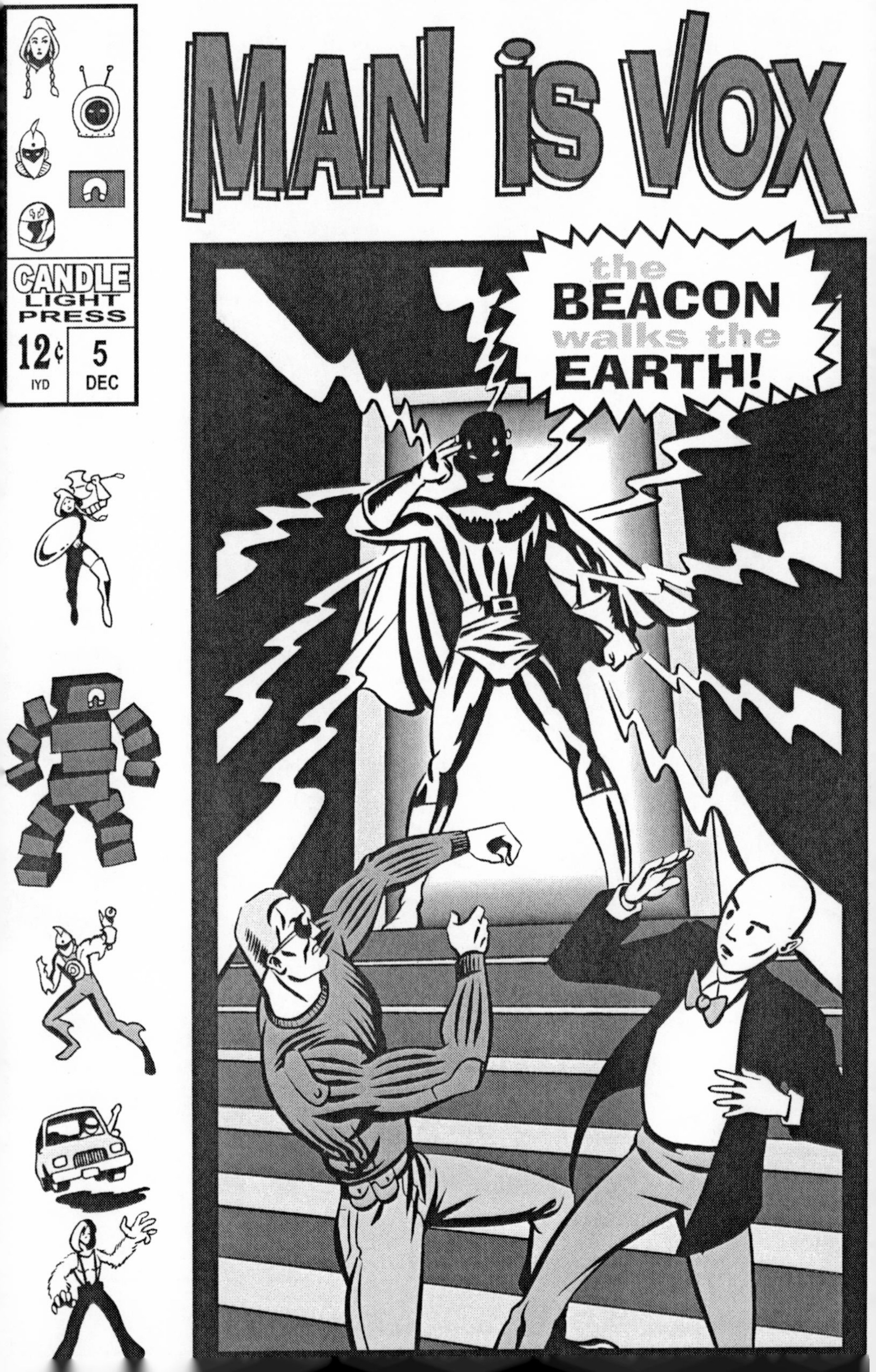
MAN IS VOX
CANDLE LIGHT PRESS
12¢
IYD
5
DEC
the BEACON walks the EARTH!

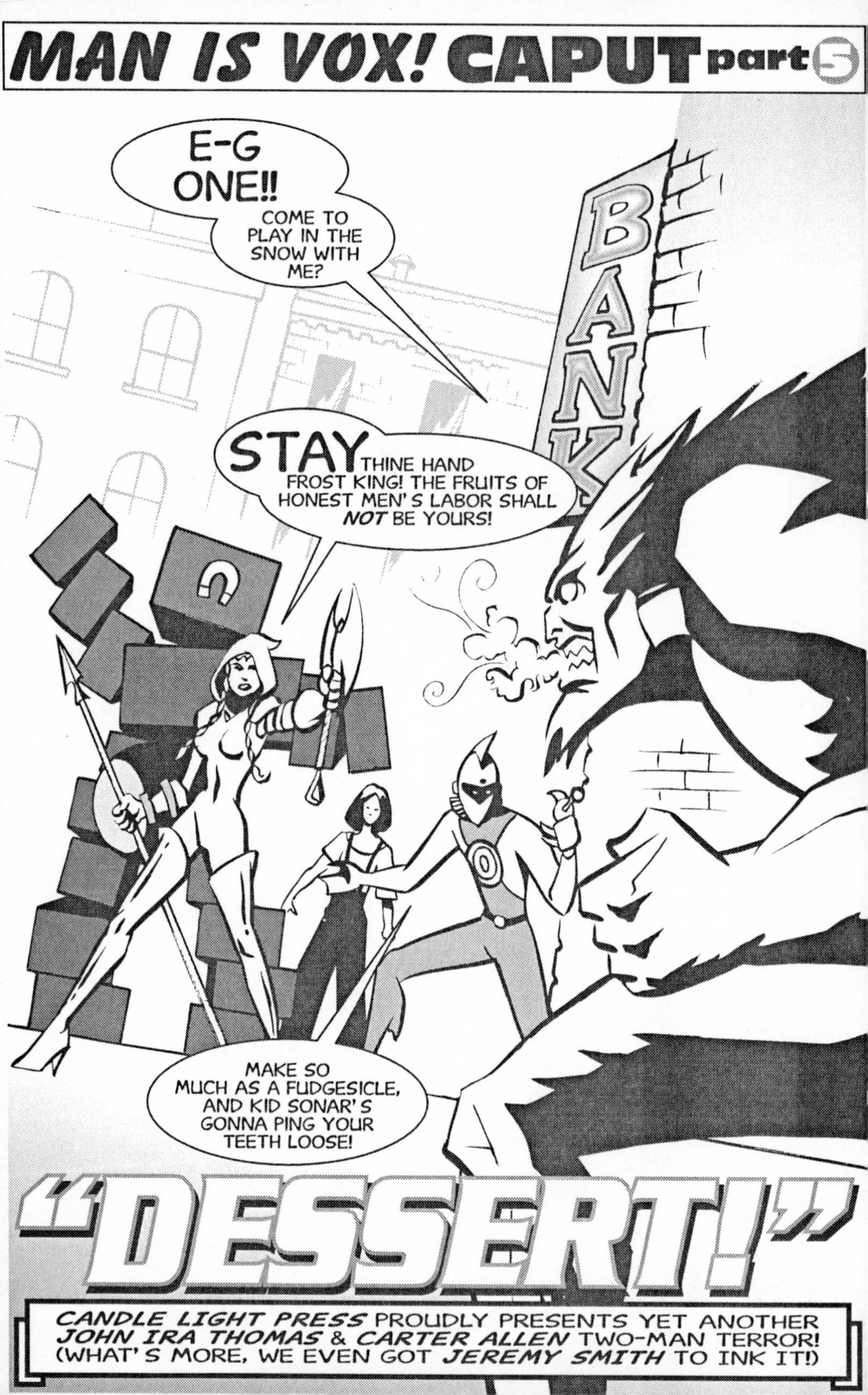
MAN IS VOX! CAPUT part 5
E-G ONE!! COME TO PLAY IN THE SNOW WITH ME?
BANK
STAY THINE HAND FROST KING! THE FRUITS OF HONEST MEN'S LABOR SHALL *NOT* BE YOURS!
MAKE SO MUCH AS A FUDGESICLE, AND KID SONAR'S GONNA PING YOUR TEETH LOOSE!
"DESSERT!"
CANDLE LIGHT PRESS PROUDLY PRESENTS YET ANOTHER *JOHN IRA THOMAS* & *CARTER ALLEN* TWO-MAN TERROR! (WHAT'S MORE, WE EVEN GOT *JEREMY SMITH* TO INK IT!)

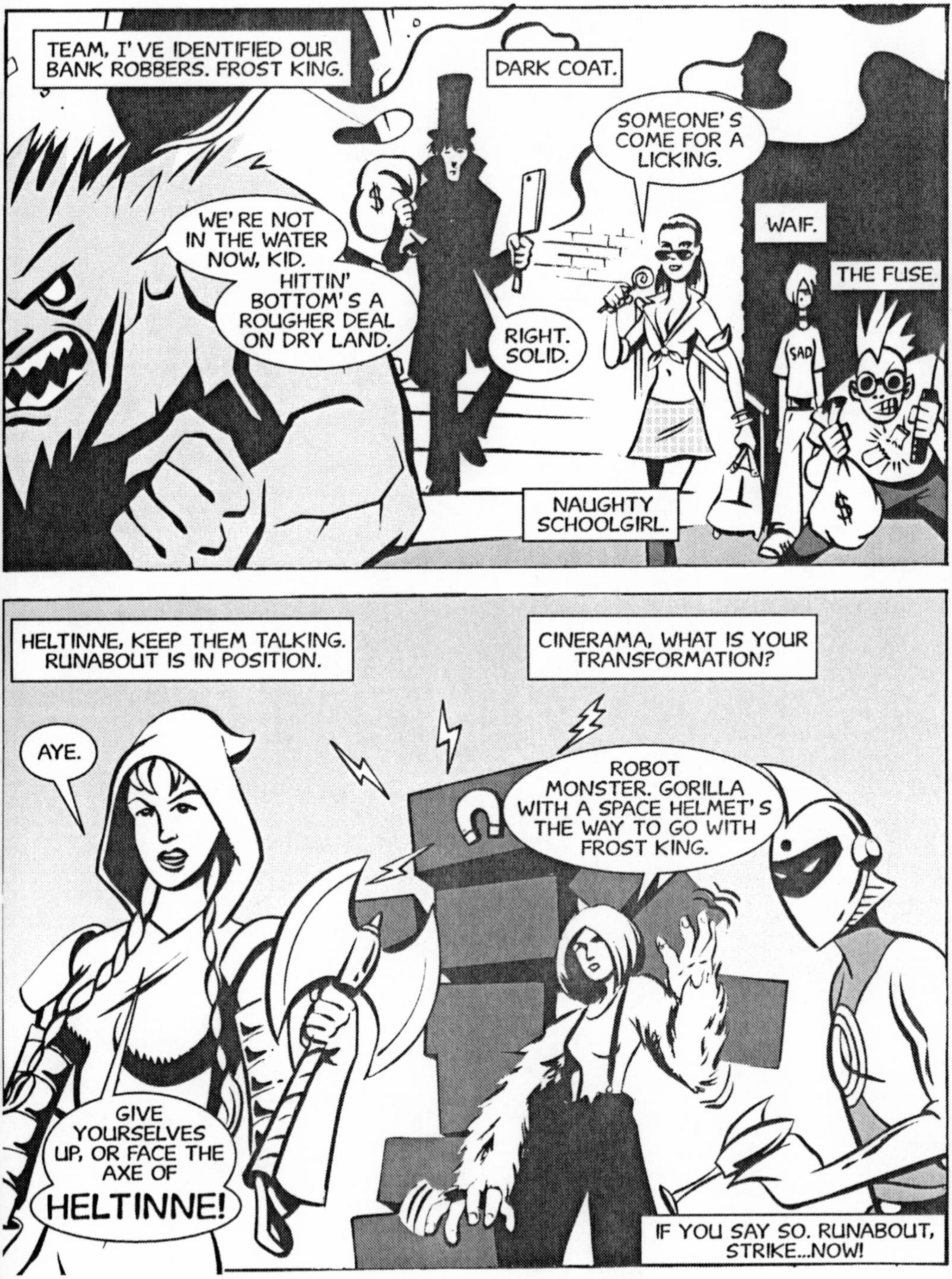
TEAM, I'VE IDENTIFIED OUR BANK ROBBERS. FROST KING.
WE'RE NOT IN THE WATER NOW, KID.
HITTIN' BOTTOM'S A ROUGHER DEAL ON DRY LAND.
DARK COAT.
RIGHT. SOLID.
SOMEONE'S COME FOR A LICKING.
NAUGHTY SCHOOLGIRL.
WAIF.
SAD
THE FUSE.
HELTINNE, KEEP THEM TALKING. RUNABOUT IS IN POSITION.
AYE.
GIVE YOURSELVES UP, OR FACE THE AXE OF HELTINNE!
CINERAMA, WHAT IS YOUR TRANSFORMATION?
ROBOT MONSTER. GORILLA WITH A SPACE HELMET'S THE WAY TO GO WITH FROST KING.
IF YOU SAY SO. RUNABOUT, STRIKE...NOW!

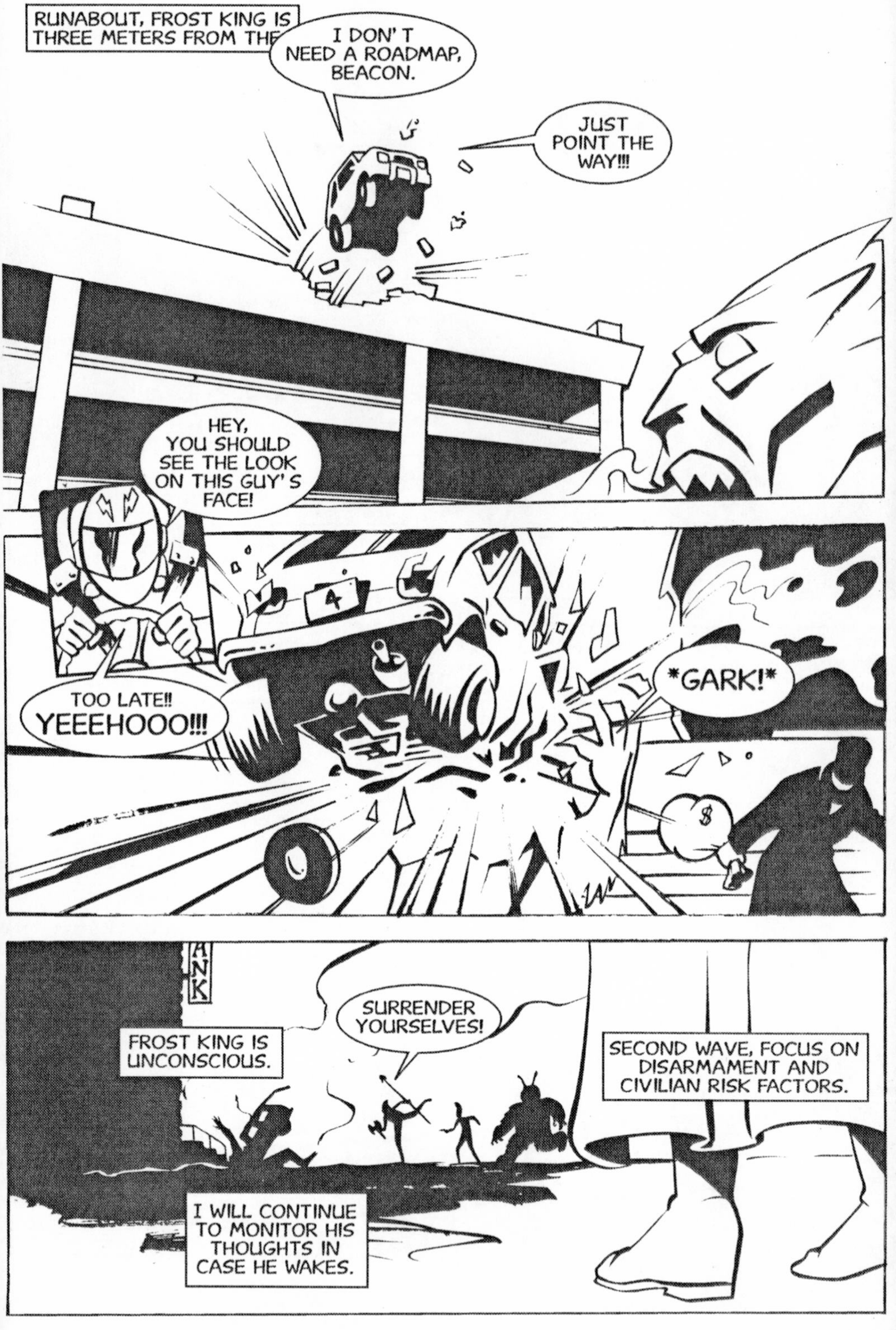
RUNABOUT, FROST KING IS THREE METERS FROM THE
I DON'T NEED A ROADMAP, BEACON.
JUST POINT THE WAY!!!
HEY, YOU SHOULD SEE THE LOOK ON THIS GUY'S FACE!
TOO LATE!! YEEEHOOO!!!
GARK!
4
FROST KING IS UNCONSCIOUS.
SURRENDER YOURSELVES!
SECOND WAVE, FOCUS ON DISARMAMENT AND CIVILIAN RISK FACTORS.
I WILL CONTINUE TO MONITOR HIS THOUGHTS IN CASE HE WAKES.

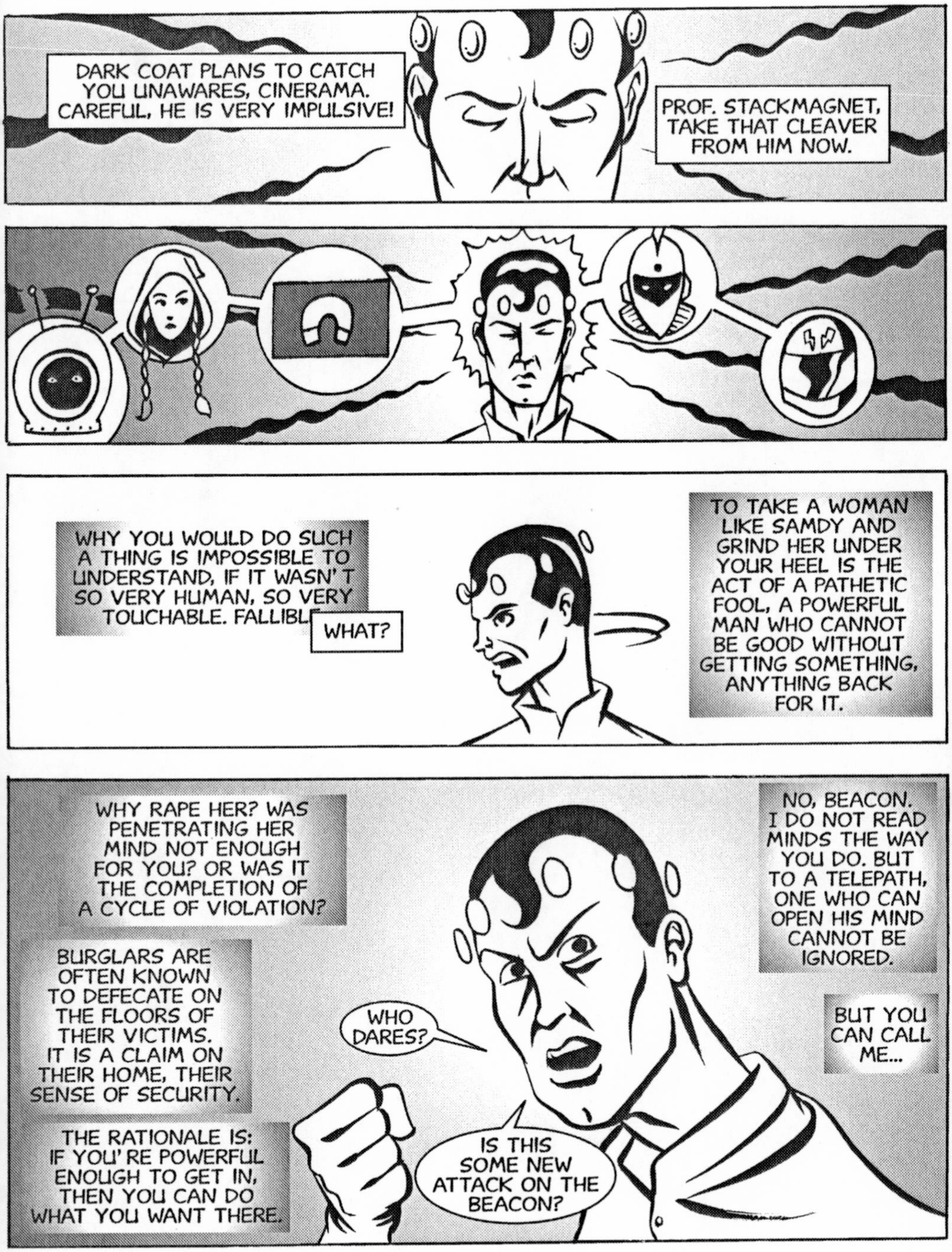
DARK COAT PLANS TO CATCH YOU UNAWARES, CINERAMA. CAREFUL, HE IS VERY IMPULSIVE!
PROF. STACKMAGNET, TAKE THAT CLEAVER FROM HIM NOW.
WHY YOU WOULD DO SUCH A THING IS IMPOSSIBLE TO UNDERSTAND, IF IT WASN'T SO VERY HUMAN, SO VERY TOUCHABLE. FALLIBLE.
WHAT?
TO TAKE A WOMAN LIKE SAMDY AND GRIND HER UNDER YOUR HEEL IS THE ACT OF A PATHETIC FOOL, A POWERFUL MAN WHO CANNOT BE GOOD WITHOUT GETTING SOMETHING, ANYTHING BACK FOR IT.
WHY RAPE HER? WAS PENETRATING HER MIND NOT ENOUGH FOR YOU? OR WAS IT THE COMPLETION OF A CYCLE OF VIOLATION?
BURGLARS ARE OFTEN KNOWN TO DEFECATE ON THE FLOORS OF THEIR VICTIMS. IT IS A CLAIM ON THEIR HOME, THEIR SENSE OF SECURITY.
THE RATIONALE IS: IF YOU'RE POWERFUL ENOUGH TO GET IN, THEN YOU CAN DO WHAT YOU WANT THERE.
WHO DARES?
IS THIS SOME NEW ATTACK ON THE BEACON?
NO, BEACON. I DO NOT READ MINDS THE WAY YOU DO. BUT TO A TELEPATH, ONE WHO CAN OPEN HIS MIND CANNOT BE IGNORED.
BUT YOU CAN CALL ME...

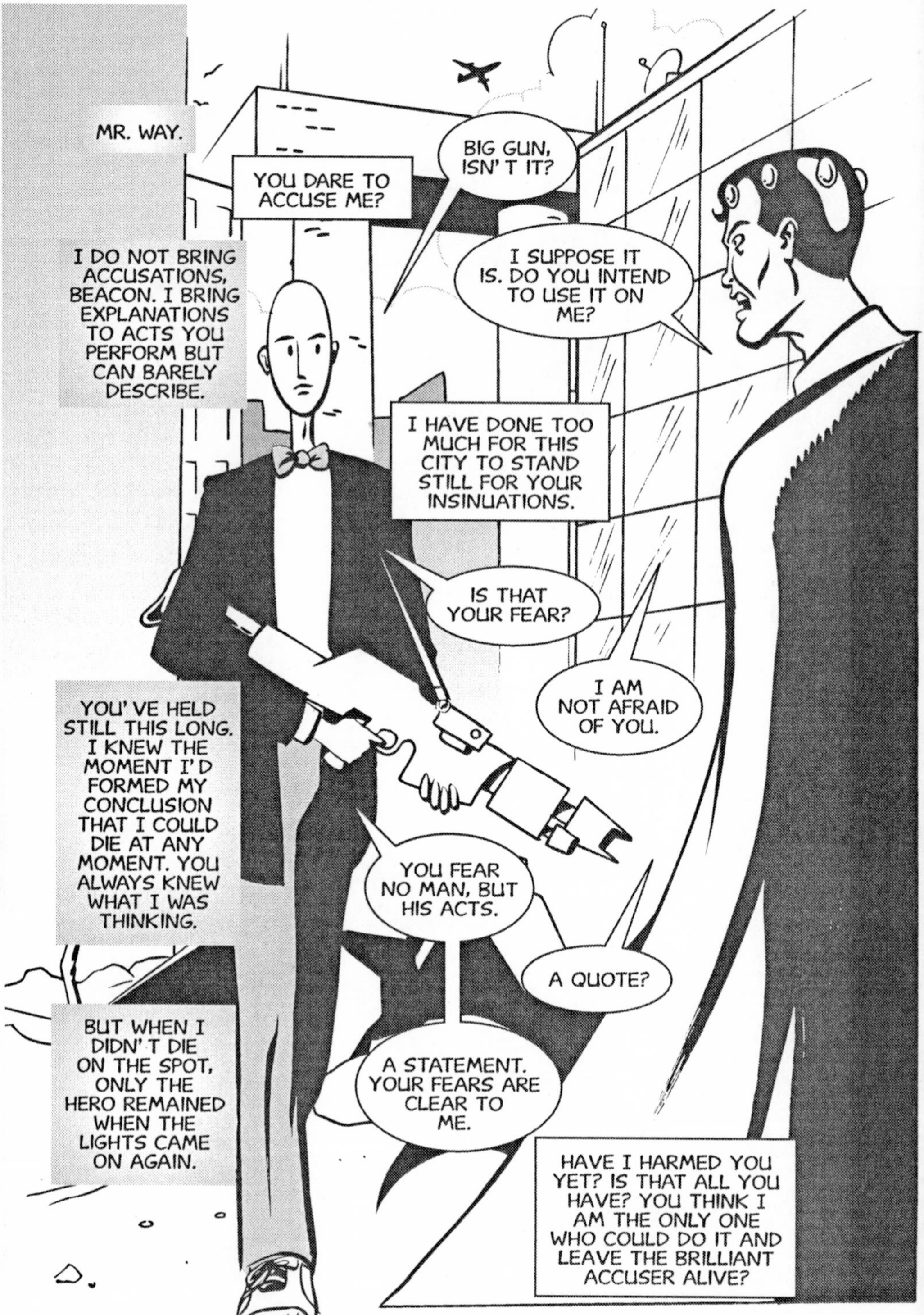
MR. WAY.
YOU DARE TO ACCUSE ME?
BIG GUN, ISN'T IT?
I DO NOT BRING ACCUSATIONS, BEACON. I BRING EXPLANATIONS TO ACTS YOU PERFORM BUT CAN BARELY DESCRIBE.
I SUPPOSE IT IS. DO YOU INTEND TO USE IT ON ME?
I HAVE DONE TOO MUCH FOR THIS CITY TO STAND STILL FOR YOUR INSINUATIONS.
IS THAT YOUR FEAR?
I AM NOT AFRAID OF YOU.
YOU'VE HELD STILL THIS LONG. I KNEW THE MOMENT I'D FORMED MY CONCLUSION THAT I COULD DIE AT ANY MOMENT. YOU ALWAYS KNEW WHAT I WAS THINKING.
YOU FEAR NO MAN, BUT HIS ACTS.
A QUOTE?
BUT WHEN I DIDN'T DIE ON THE SPOT, ONLY THE HERO REMAINED WHEN THE LIGHTS CAME ON AGAIN.
A STATEMENT. YOUR FEARS ARE CLEAR TO ME.
HAVE I HARMED YOU YET? IS THAT ALL YOU HAVE? YOU THINK I AM THE ONLY ONE WHO COULD DO IT AND LEAVE THE BRILLIANT ACCUSER ALIVE?

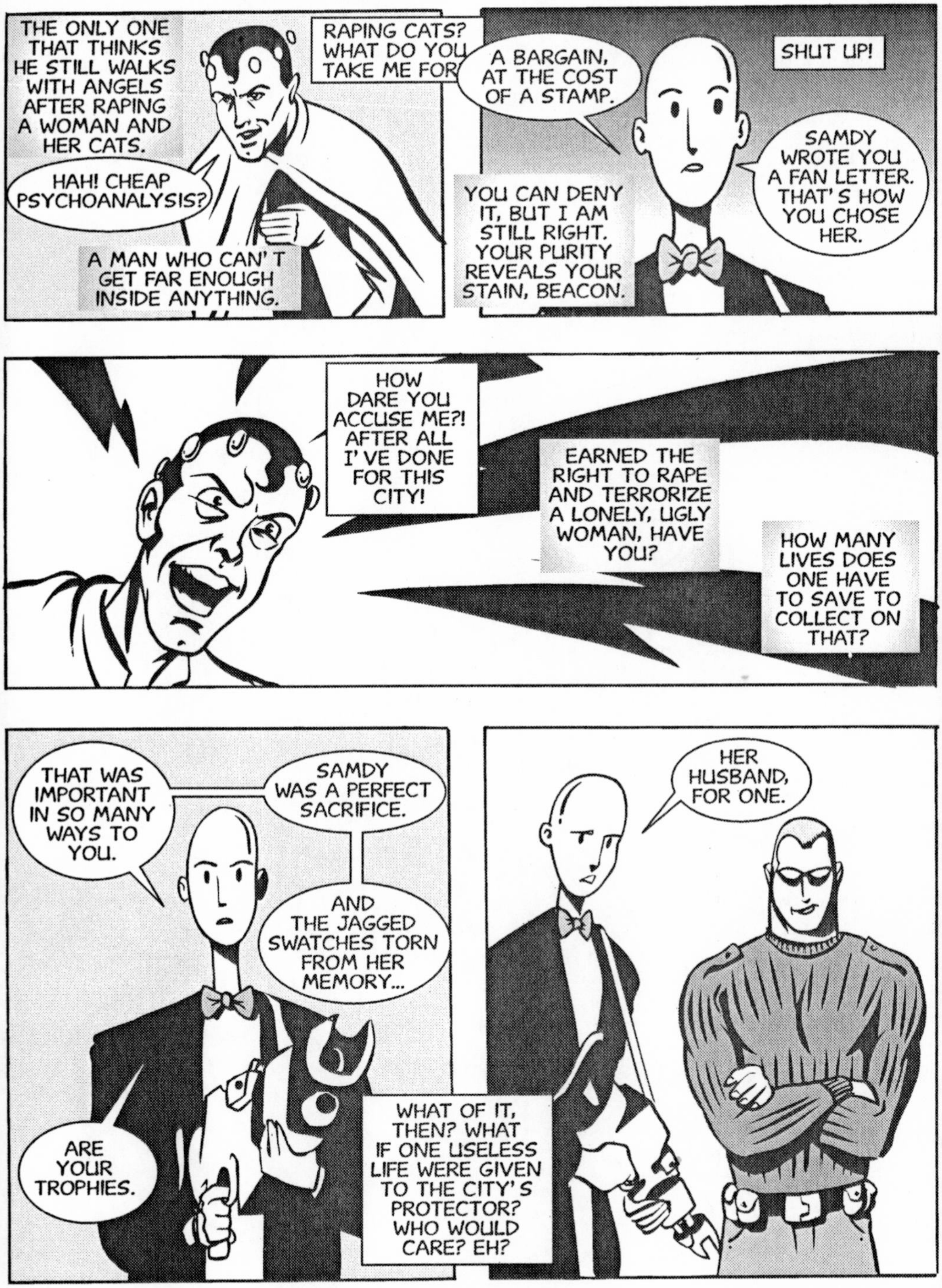

THE ONLY ONE THAT THINKS HE STILL WALKS WITH ANGELS AFTER RAPING A WOMAN AND HER CATS.
HAH! CHEAP PSYCHOANALYSIS?
A MAN WHO CAN'T GET FAR ENOUGH INSIDE ANYTHING.
RAPING CATS? WHAT DO YOU TAKE ME FOR
A BARGAIN, AT THE COST OF A STAMP.
SHUT UP!
YOU CAN DENY IT, BUT I AM STILL RIGHT. YOUR PURITY REVEALS YOUR STAIN, BEACON.
SAMDY WROTE YOU A FAN LETTER. THAT'S HOW YOU CHOSE HER.
HOW DARE YOU ACCUSE ME?! AFTER ALL I'VE DONE FOR THIS CITY!
EARNED THE RIGHT TO RAPE AND TERRORIZE A LONELY, UGLY WOMAN, HAVE YOU?
HOW MANY LIVES DOES ONE HAVE TO SAVE TO COLLECT ON THAT?
THAT WAS IMPORTANT IN SO MANY WAYS TO YOU.
SAMDY WAS A PERFECT SACRIFICE.
AND THE JAGGED SWATCHES TORN FROM HER MEMORY...
ARE YOUR TROPHIES.
WHAT OF IT, THEN? WHAT IF ONE USELESS LIFE WERE GIVEN TO THE CITY'S PROTECTOR? WHO WOULD CARE? EH?
HER HUSBAND, FOR ONE.

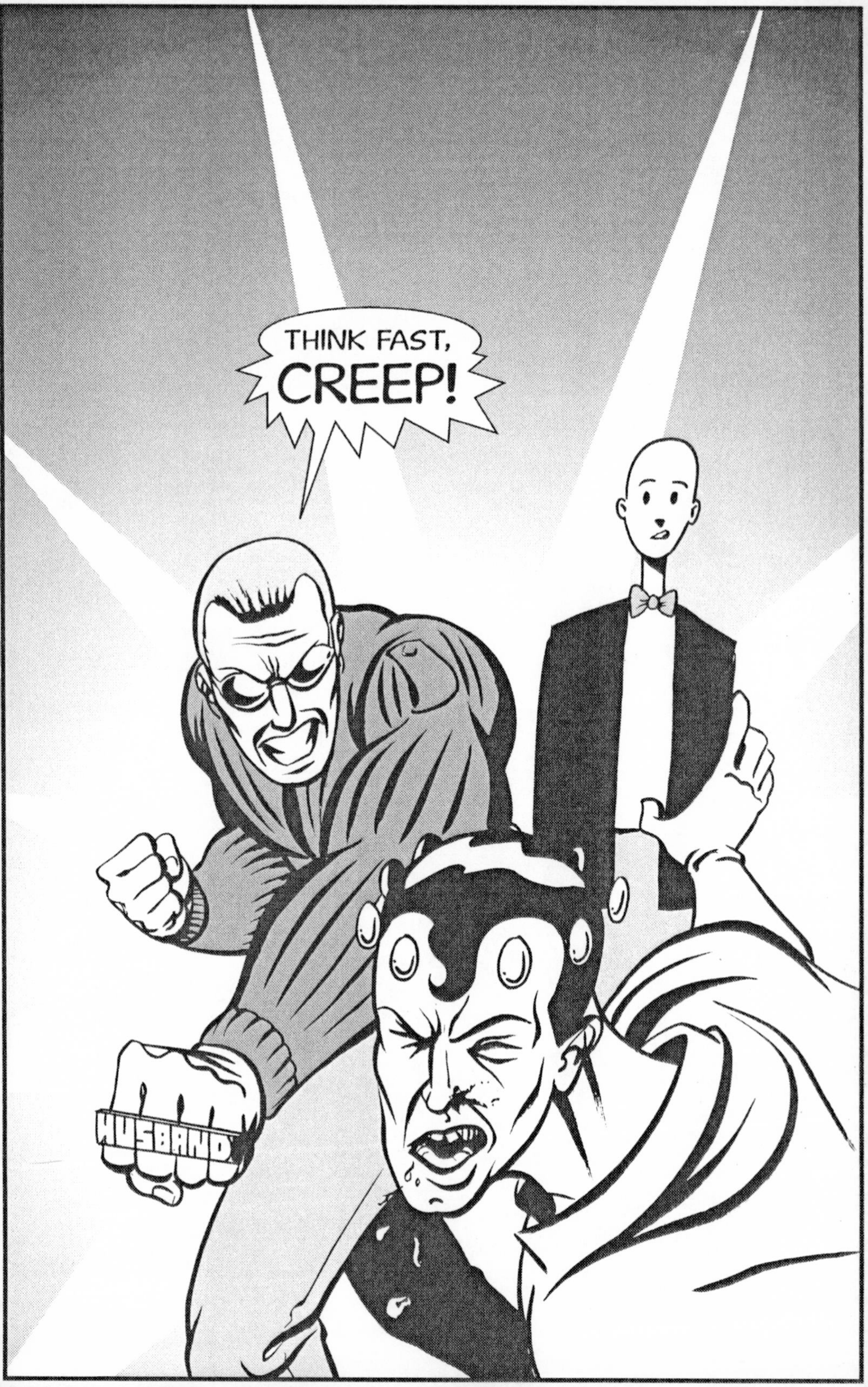
THINK FAST, CREEP!
HUSBAND

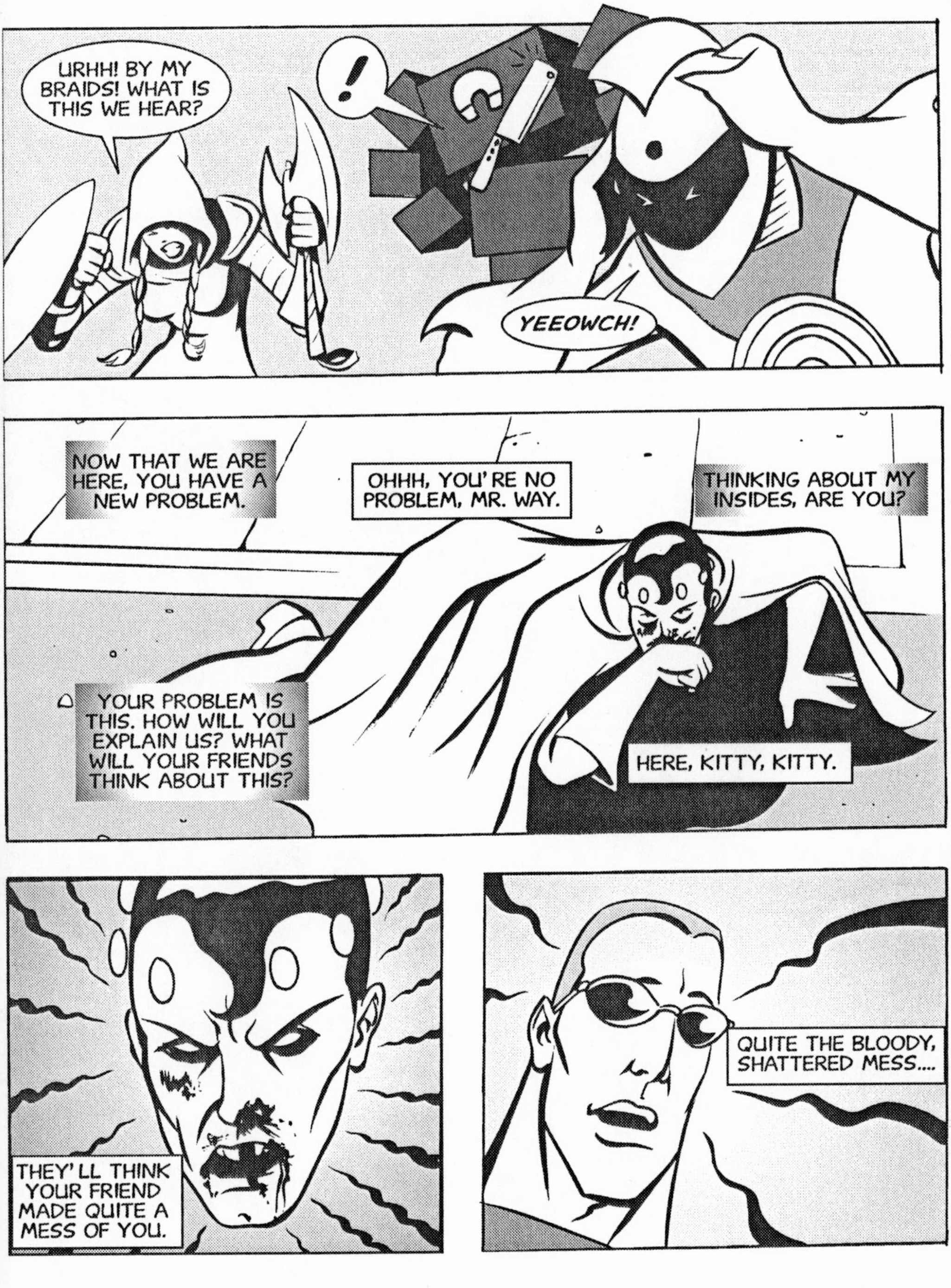
URHH! BY MY BRAIDS! WHAT IS THIS WE HEAR?
!
YEEOWCH!
NOW THAT WE ARE HERE, YOU HAVE A NEW PROBLEM.
OHHH, YOU'RE NO PROBLEM, MR. WAY.
THINKING ABOUT MY INSIDES, ARE YOU?
YOUR PROBLEM IS THIS. HOW WILL YOU EXPLAIN US? WHAT WILL YOUR FRIENDS THINK ABOUT THIS?
HERE, KITTY, KITTY.
THEY'LL THINK YOUR FRIEND MADE QUITE A MESS OF YOU.
QUITE THE BLOODY, SHATTERED MESS....

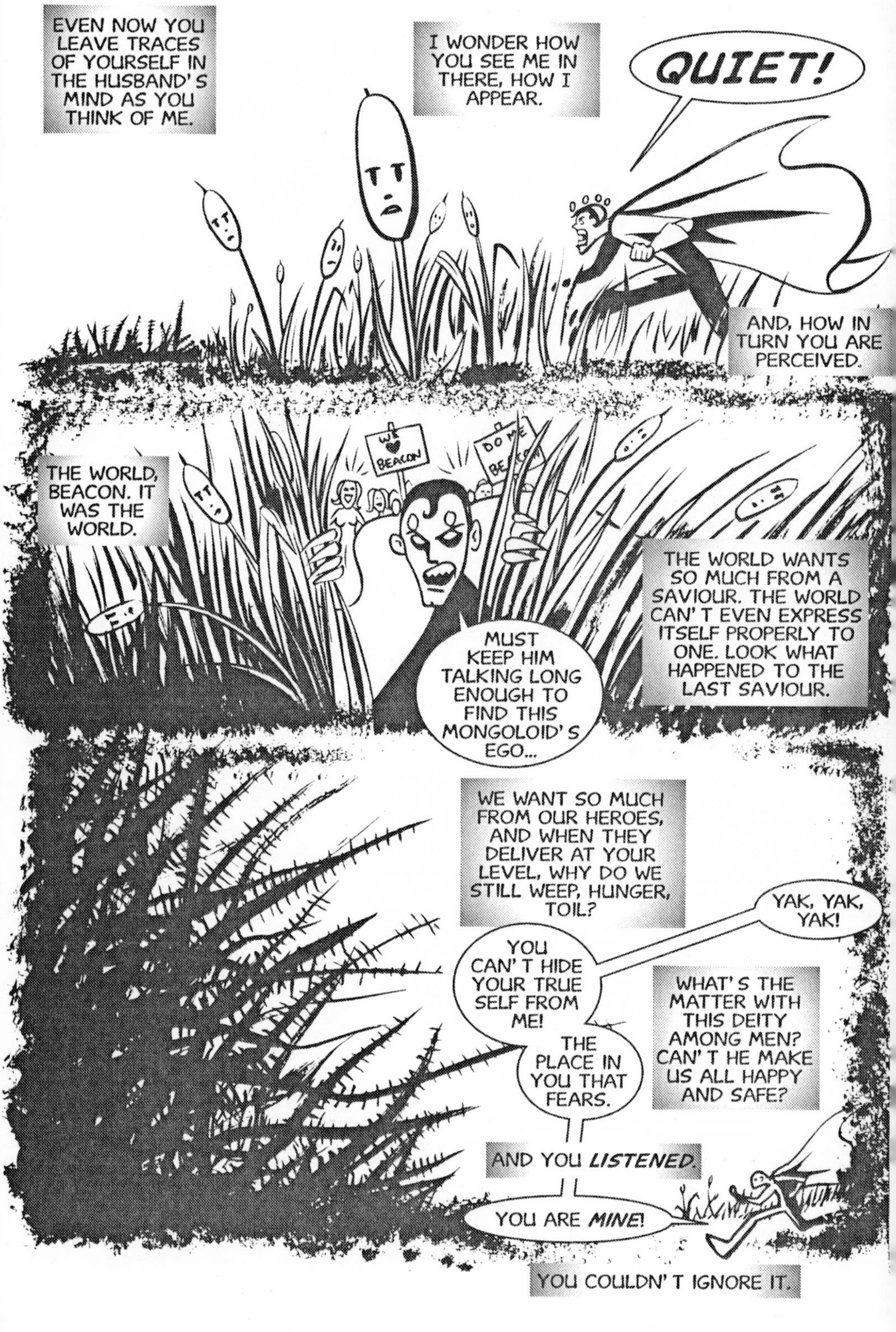
EVEN NOW YOU LEAVE TRACES OF YOURSELF IN THE HUSBAND'S MIND AS YOU THINK OF ME.
I WONDER HOW YOU SEE ME IN THERE, HOW I APPEAR.
QUIET!
AND, HOW IN TURN YOU ARE PERCEIVED.
WE ♥ BEACON
DO ME BEACON
THE WORLD, BEACON. IT WAS THE WORLD.
THE WORLD WANTS SO MUCH FROM A SAVIOUR. THE WORLD CAN'T EVEN EXPRESS ITSELF PROPERLY TO ONE. LOOK WHAT HAPPENED TO THE LAST SAVIOUR.
MUST KEEP HIM TALKING LONG ENOUGH TO FIND THIS MONGOLOID'S EGO...
WE WANT SO MUCH FROM OUR HEROES, AND WHEN THEY DELIVER AT YOUR LEVEL, WHY DO WE STILL WEEP, HUNGER, TOIL?
YAK, YAK, YAK!
YOU CAN'T HIDE YOUR TRUE SELF FROM ME!
THE PLACE IN YOU THAT FEARS.
WHAT'S THE MATTER WITH THIS DEITY AMONG MEN? CAN'T HE MAKE US ALL HAPPY AND SAFE?
AND YOU LISTENED.
YOU ARE MINE!
YOU COULDN'T IGNORE IT.

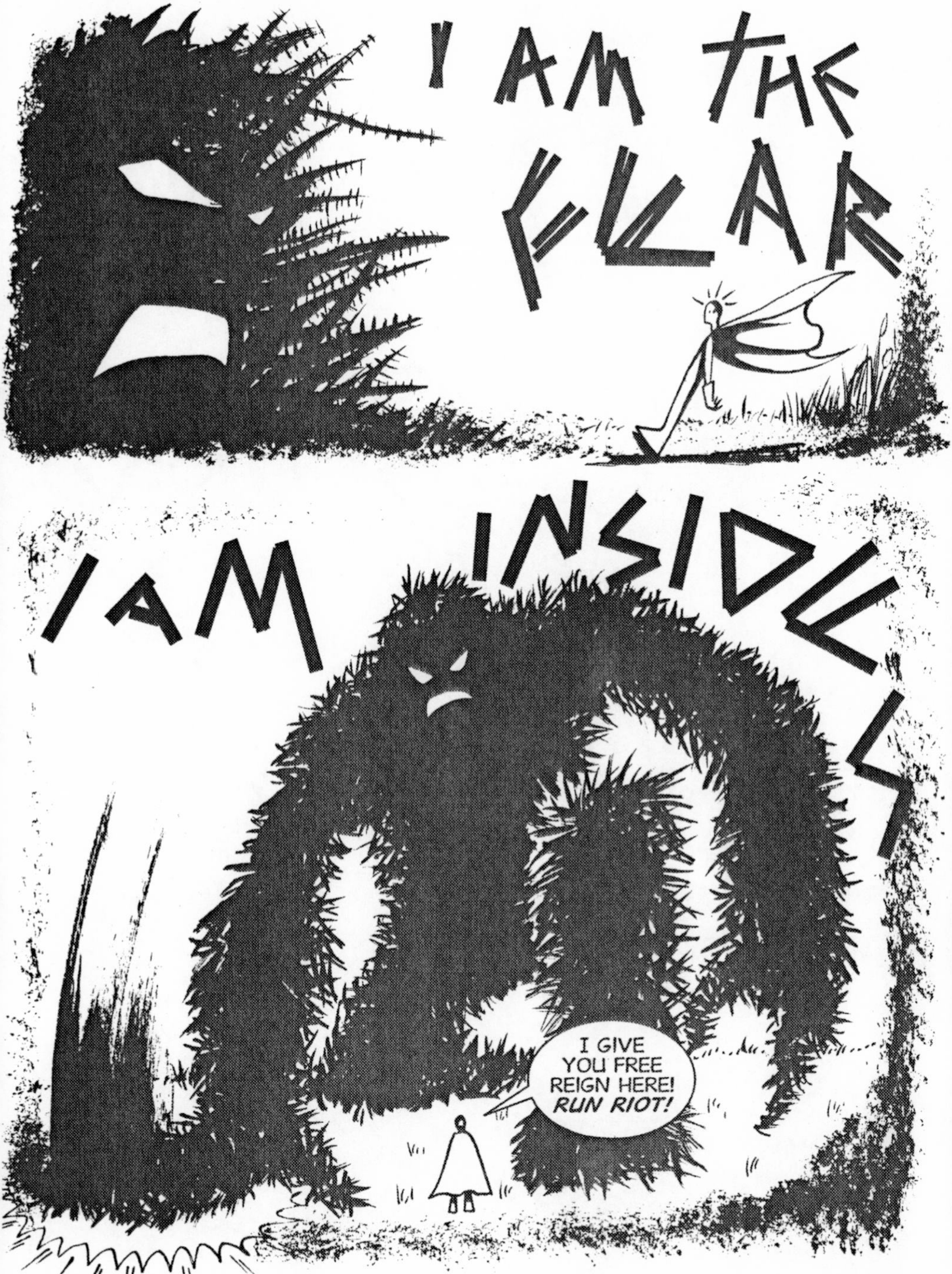
I AM THE FEAR
I AM INSIDIOUS
I GIVE YOU FREE REIGN HERE! *RUN RIOT!*

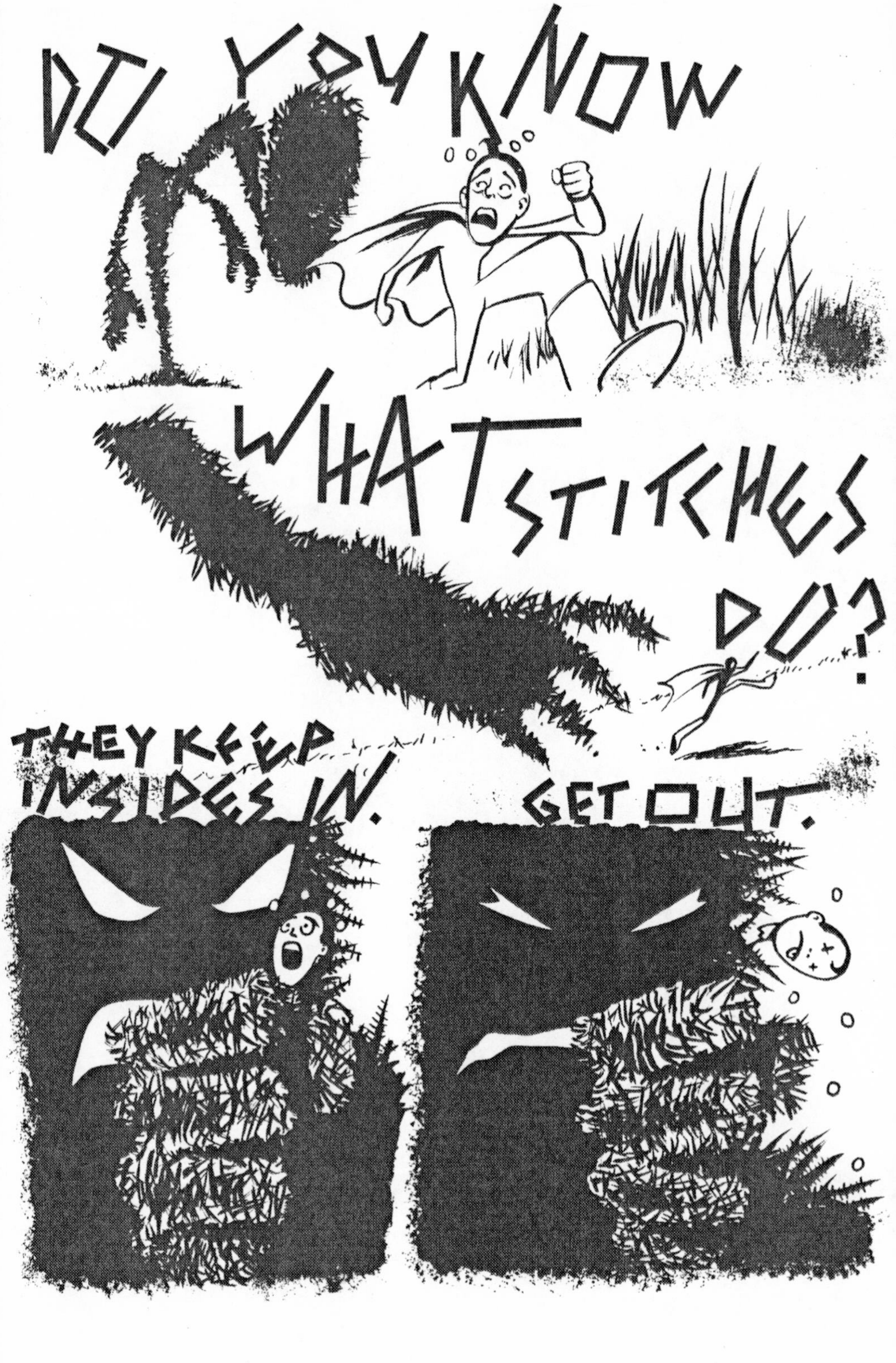
DO YOU KNOW
WHAT STITCHES DO?
THEY KEEP INSIDES IN.
GET OUT.

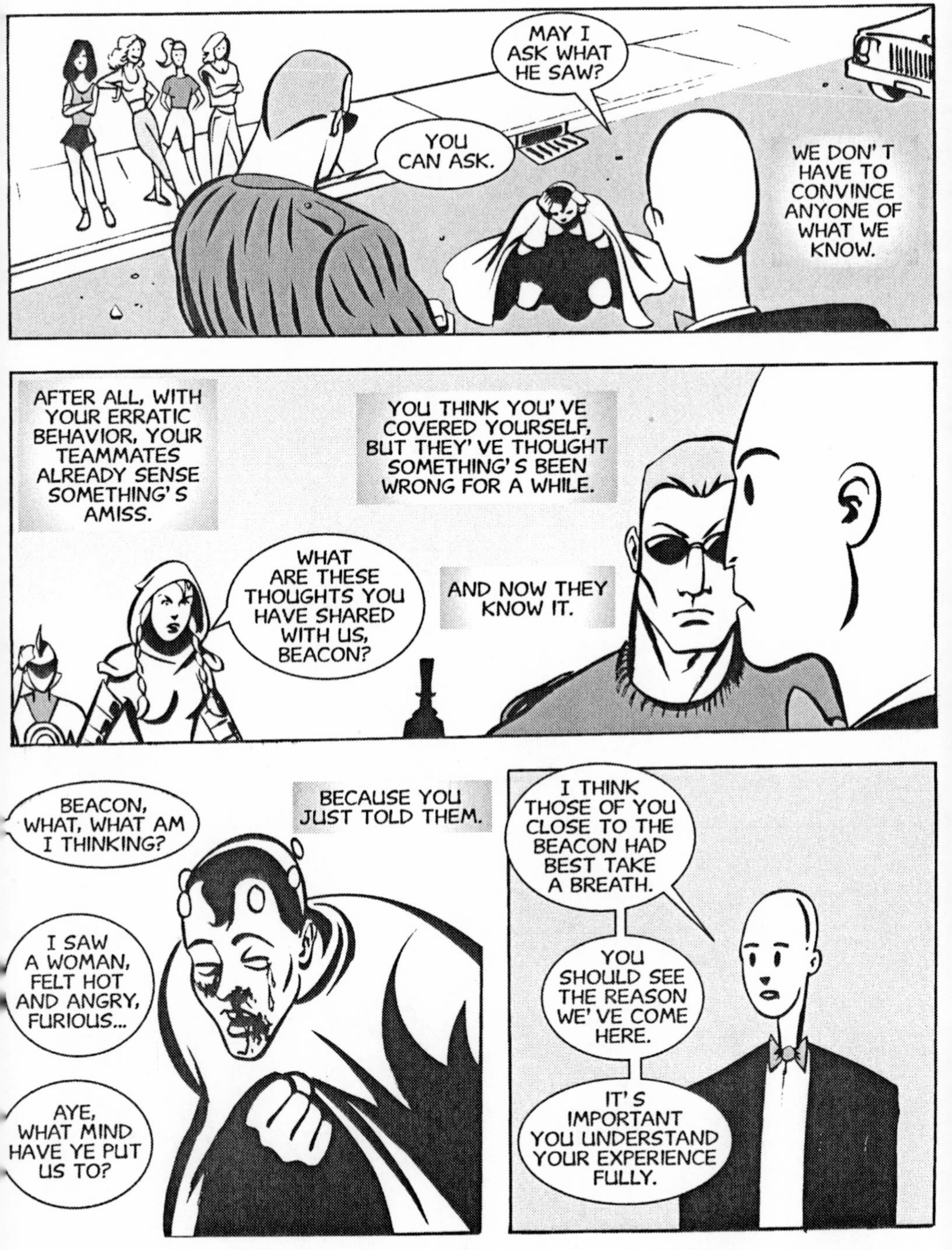

MAY I ASK WHAT HE SAW?
YOU CAN ASK.
WE DON'T HAVE TO CONVINCE ANYONE OF WHAT WE KNOW.
AFTER ALL, WITH YOUR ERRATIC BEHAVIOR, YOUR TEAMMATES ALREADY SENSE SOMETHING'S AMISS.
YOU THINK YOU'VE COVERED YOURSELF, BUT THEY'VE THOUGHT SOMETHING'S BEEN WRONG FOR A WHILE.
WHAT ARE THESE THOUGHTS YOU HAVE SHARED WITH US, BEACON?
AND NOW THEY KNOW IT.
BEACON, WHAT, WHAT AM I THINKING?
BECAUSE YOU JUST TOLD THEM.
I SAW A WOMAN, FELT HOT AND ANGRY, FURIOUS...
AYE, WHAT MIND HAVE YE PUT US TO?
I THINK THOSE OF YOU CLOSE TO THE BEACON HAD BEST TAKE A BREATH.
YOU SHOULD SEE THE REASON WE'VE COME HERE.
IT'S IMPORTANT YOU UNDERSTAND YOUR EXPERIENCE FULLY.

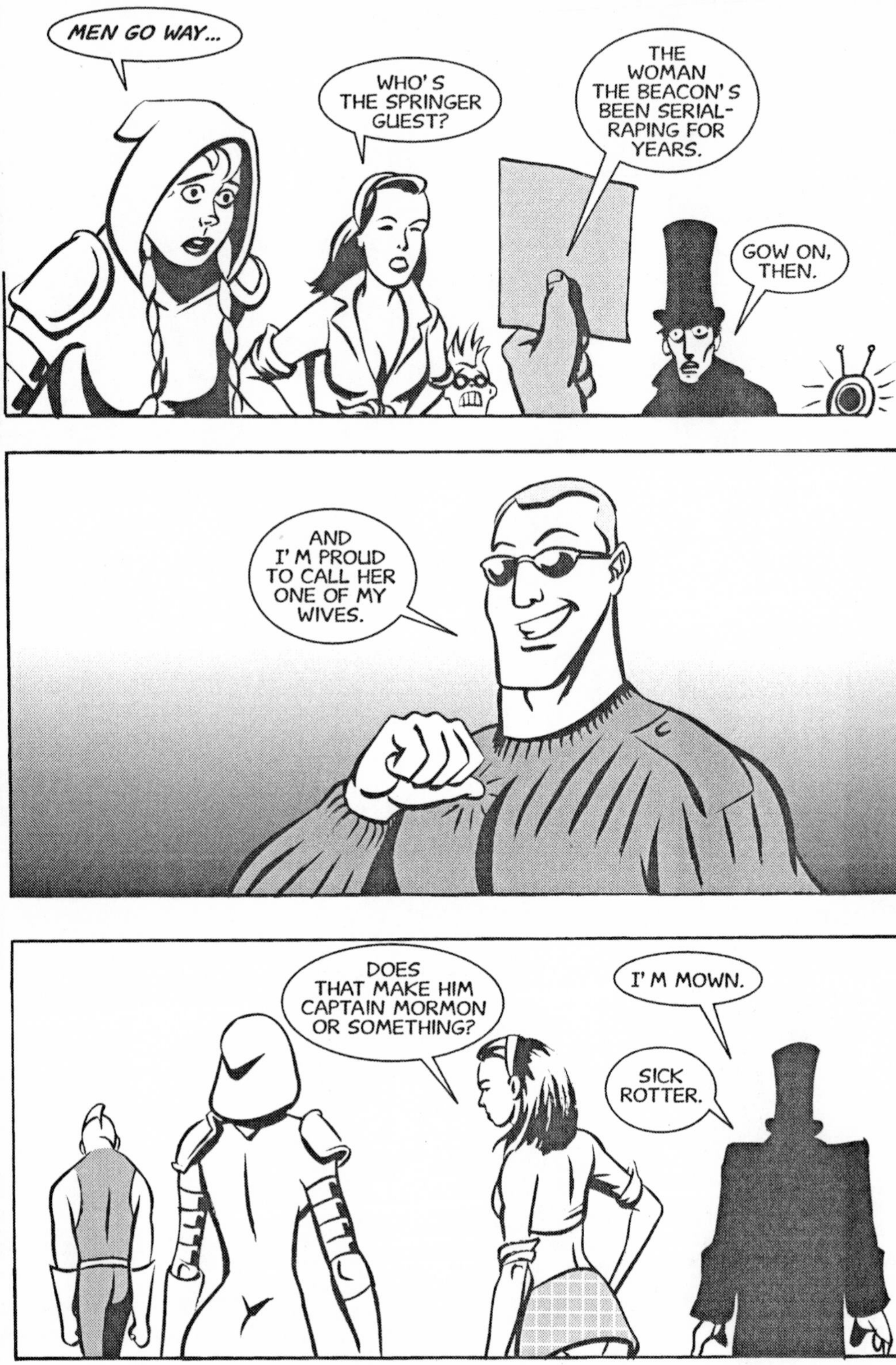
MEN GO WAY...
WHO'S THE SPRINGER GUEST?
THE WOMAN THE BEACON'S BEEN SERIAL-RAPING FOR YEARS.
GOW ON, THEN.
AND I'M PROUD TO CALL HER ONE OF MY WIVES.
DOES THAT MAKE HIM CAPTAIN MORMON OR SOMETHING?
I'M MOWN.
SICK ROTTER.

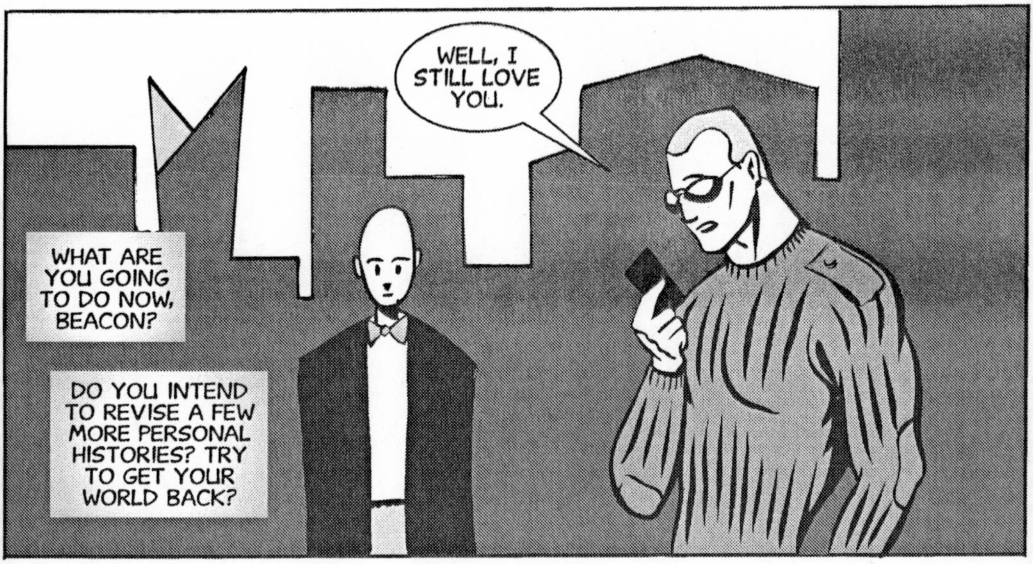
WHAT ARE YOU GOING TO DO NOW, BEACON?
DO YOU INTEND TO REVISE A FEW MORE PERSONAL HISTORIES? TRY TO GET YOUR WORLD BACK?
WELL, I STILL LOVE YOU.

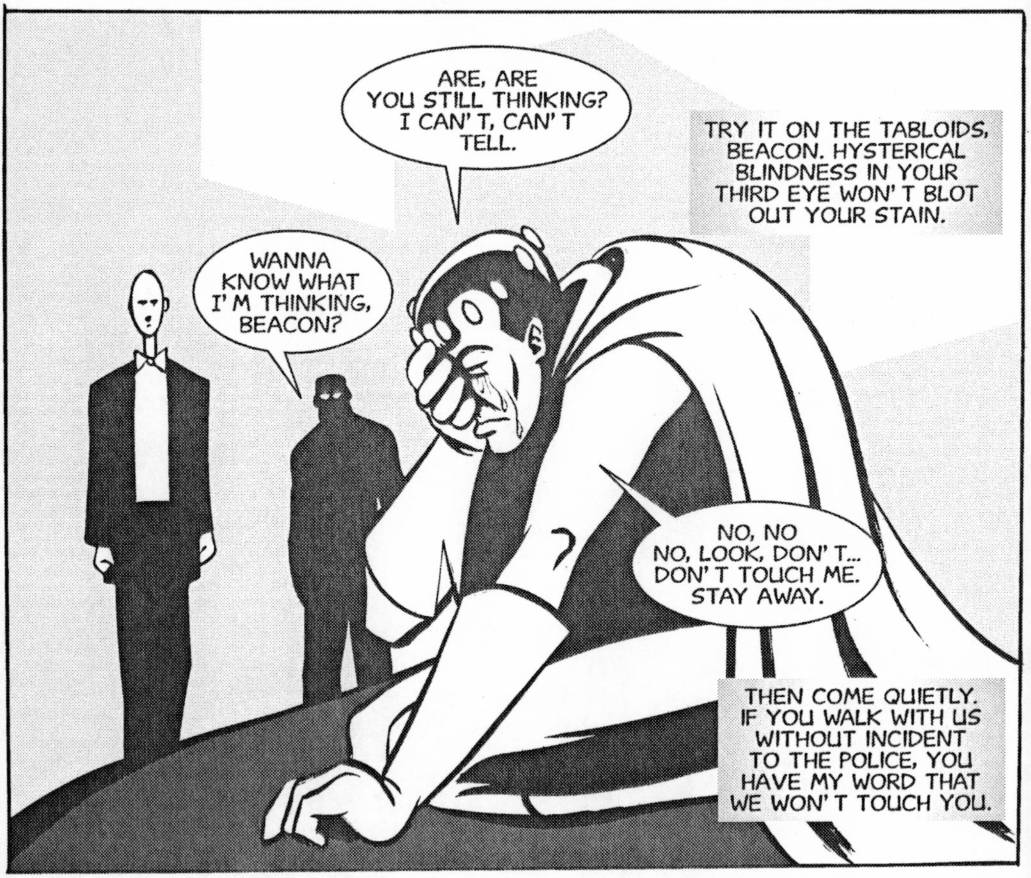
ARE, ARE YOU STILL THINKING? I CAN'T, CAN'T TELL.
TRY IT ON THE TABLOIDS, BEACON. HYSTERICAL BLINDNESS IN YOUR THIRD EYE WON'T BLOT OUT YOUR STAIN.
WANNA KNOW WHAT I'M THINKING, BEACON?
NO, NO NO, LOOK, DON'T... DON'T TOUCH ME. STAY AWAY.
THEN COME QUIETLY. IF YOU WALK WITH US WITHOUT INCIDENT TO THE POLICE, YOU HAVE MY WORD THAT WE WON'T TOUCH YOU.

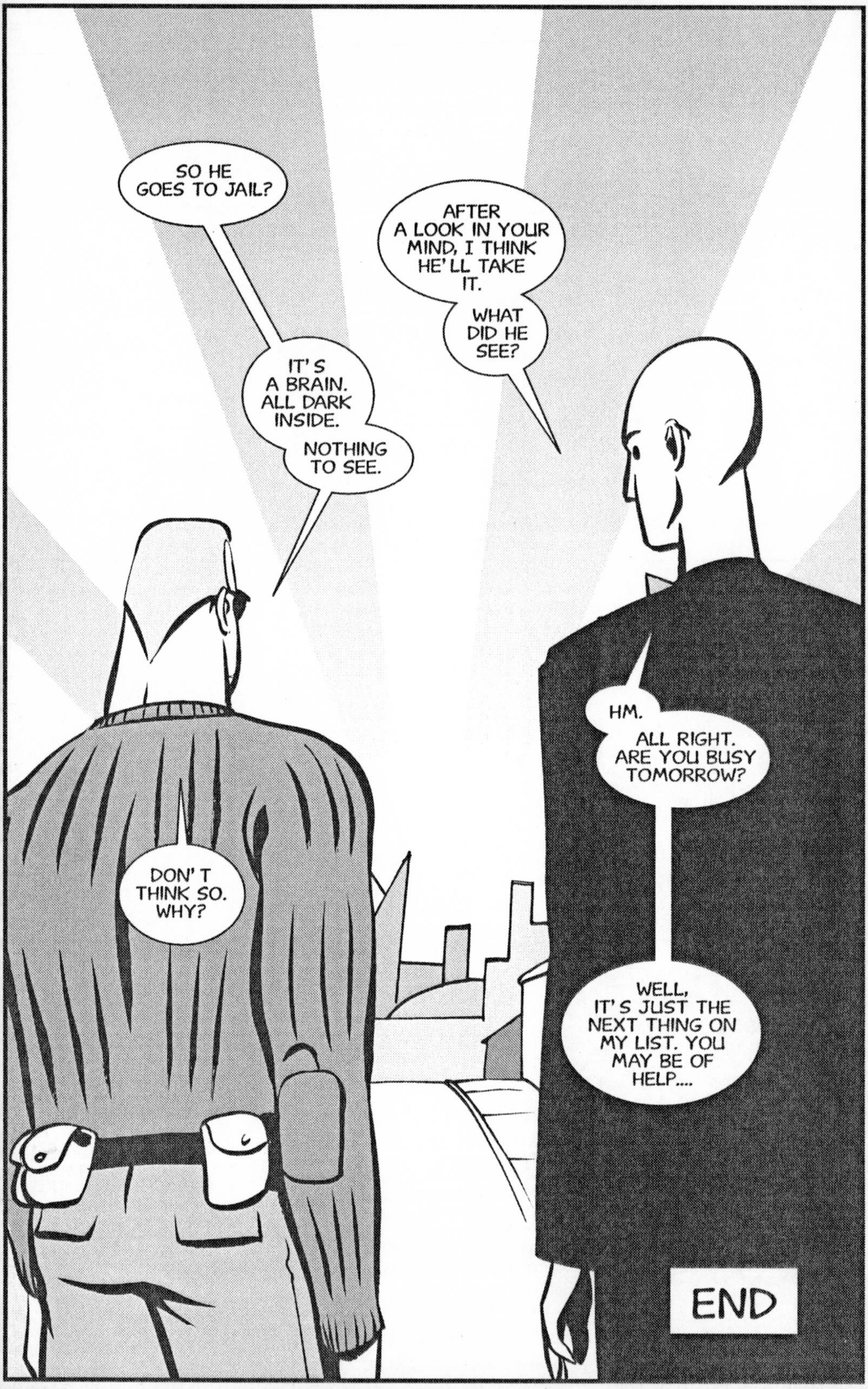
SO HE GOES TO JAIL?
AFTER A LOOK IN YOUR MIND, I THINK HE'LL TAKE IT.
WHAT DID HE SEE?
IT'S A BRAIN. ALL DARK INSIDE.
NOTHING TO SEE.
HM.
ALL RIGHT. ARE YOU BUSY TOMORROW?
DON'T THINK SO. WHY?
WELL, IT'S JUST THE NEXT THING ON MY LIST. YOU MAY BE OF HELP....
END

MAN IS VOX: BARRACUDAE

a candle light press production

"barracudae"
John Ira Thomas-writer
Carter Allen-vectorist

"salad"
John Ira Thomas-director
Carter Allen-puppeteer

"pasta"
John Ira Thomas-writer
Carter Allen-pasta wrangler

"conversation"
John Ira Thomas-writer
Carter Allen-vectorist

"meat"
John Ira Thomas-writer
Carter Allen-pencils

"dessert"
written by John Ira Thomas
and Carter Allen
pencils-Carter Allen
inks-Jeremy Smith

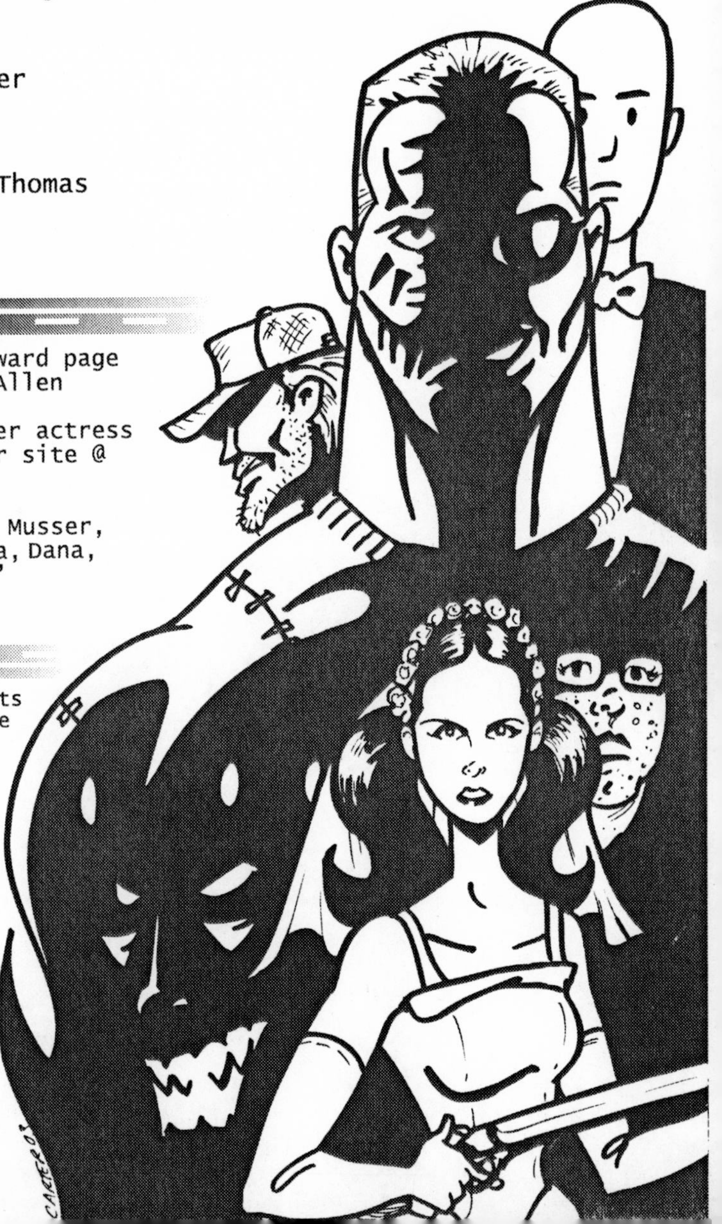

Cover, credits and forward page illustrations: Carter Allen

Cover model is character actress Rachel Grant. Visit her site @ www.rachelgrant.com

Special thanks to: Jim Musser, Karin, Rachel & Camilla, Dana, Lisa Martincik, the ol' Hawk-I Truck Stop and Joe's

Country of first publication United States of America.

Website:
www.candlelightpress.com

Feedback:
miv@candlelightpress.com

Printed in the United States
1187700001B/432-510